T0382902

Global Capitalism and National Decline

First published in 1990, *Global Capitalism and National Decline* is a major contribution to the study of British political and economic decline. The author concentrates on the global nature of capitalism as the context for the development of national capitalism, and on the relationship between internal and external factors. A long-term view of British politics enables him to demonstrate that competing popular explanations of Britain's crisis and the rise of Thatcherism in response to it, are in fact interconnected. The long decline of Britain originating in the 19th century, the inherent weakness of the post-1945 settlement, and the critical events of 1970s, acquire their fullest meaning when seen as different 'layers' of one and the same historical process. Henk Overbeek takes the story of Britain's decline through to Margaret Thatcher's tenth anniversary in office. His book will be invaluable to scholars and students of economics, politics, and history. it offers a clear perspective on the problems of national decline within a global context, and on Britain's position in Europe and in the wider world.

Global Capitalism and National Decline

Decline

The Thatcher Decade in Perspective

Henk Overbeek

Routledge
Taylor & Francis Group

First published in 1990
By Unwin Hyman

This edition first published in 2022 by Routledge
4 Park Square, Milton Park, Abingdon, Oxon, OX14 4RN
and by Routledge
605 Third Avenue, New York, NY 10017

Routledge is an imprint of the Taylor & Francis Group, an informa business

Publisher's Note
The publisher has gone to great lengths to ensure the quality of this reprint but points out that some imperfections in the original copies may be apparent.

Disclaimer
The publisher has made every effort to trace copyright holders and welcomes correspondence from those they have been unable to contact.

A Library of Congress record exists under ISBN: 0044454139

ISBN: 978-1-032-36897-9 (hbk)
ISBN: 978-1-003-33437-8 (ebk)
ISBN: 978-1-032-36898-6 (pbk)

Book DOI 10.4324/9781003334378

Global capitalism and national decline

THE THATCHER DECADE
IN PERSPECTIVE

Henk Overbeek

London
UNWIN HYMAN
Boston   Sydney   Wellington

Published by the Academic Division of
Unwin Hyman Ltd
15/17 Broadwick Street, London W1V 1FP, UK

Unwin Hyman Inc.,
8 Winchester Place, Winchester, Mass. 01890, USA

Allen & Unwin (Australia) Ltd,
8 Napier Street, North Sydney, NSW 2060, Australia

Allen & Unwin (New Zealand) Ltd in association with the
Port Nicholson Press Ltd
Compusales Building, 75 Ghuznee Street, Wellington 1, New Zealand

First published in 1990

British Library Cataloguing in Publication Data

Overbeek, Henk
    Global capitalism and national decline : the Thatcher
    decade in perspective.
    1. Great Britain. Economic conditions, history
    I. Title
    330.941

    ISBN 0-04-445413-9
    ISBN 0-04-445639-5

Library of Congress Cataloging in Publication Data

Overbeek, Henk.
    Global capitalism and national decline : the Thatcher
    decade in perspective / Henk Overbeek.
        p.   cm.
    Includes bibliographical references.
    ISBN 0-04-445413-9
    ISBN 0-04-445639-5
    1. Great Britain—Economic conditions—20th century.
    2. Great Britain—Economic policy.   3. Capitalism—Great
    Britain—History—20th century.   4. Thatcher, Margaret. I. Title.
    HC256.094   1989
338.941—dc20
                                         89–16552
                                           CIP

Typeset in 10 on 11 point Bembo
Printed and bound in Great Britain by
Biddles Ltd, Guildford and King's Lynn

Contents

List of abbreviations   *page* xi

List of tables and figures   xiii

Preface   xvii

Introduction   1

1 Long waves of class formation   11
   Class formation in the world system   11
   The temporal dimension of class formation   17
   Class formation and the political articulation of class
   interests   23
     Capital fractions   23
     Concepts of control   25
   Generations in the bourgeoisie   29

2 The rise and fall of British hegemony   35
   The making of the British class structure   35
     The rise of British capitalism   36
     The nature of the British state   37
     The logic of priority   38
     The class structure of the *Pax Britannica*   39
     The heyday of British industrial capital   41
     The aristocratization of the bourgeoisie   44
   Britain's imperial decline   46
     British foreign investment   49
     The incorporation of the labour movement   51
     The downfall of the Liberal Party   55
     Towards the General Strike   57

3 Between New Deal and fascism: depression,
   war and transition in Britain   59
   The turn to protectionism   60
   Corporate liberalism in the 1930s   63

The strength of the state monopoly bourgeoisie   68
The structure of the British economy during the 1930s   70
    The declining industries   71
    The Fordist industries   76
    The balance of depression   80
The long decline: determination vs. contingency   81

4   **The redefinition of Britain's global position 1941–73**   84

Global Fordism   84
Postwar reconstruction of the global order and the birth
of the 'special relation'   88
Britain's relationship with Europe   93
    Early European integration projects   96
    Suez and the special relationship   97
    The move towards Europe   100
The world market and the British political economy in
the 1950s   105
    The multinationalization of the British economy   105
    The effects of City dominance for British monetary policy   106

5   **The postwar Fordist offensives**   112

The postwar Labour government   113
    Nationalization   114
    The establishment of the welfare state   119
The continued decline of Britain during the 1950s   122
    Concentration and centralization of capital   123
    Labour relations in the postwar decades   125
Modernization offensives in the 1960s   128
    The rise of the Conservative corporate liberals   128
    The Macmillan era   130
    Labour back in power   132
The failure of Fordism   137

6   **Global crisis and the rise of neo-liberalism**   141

The crisis of the 1970s   141
    Capitalism and crisis   141
    The international context   144
    Britain and the crisis   147
      Weak state, strong City   151
      The problem of union strength   152
      Three options   154
The neo-liberal revolt in the Tory Party   155
    The Heath years   155
      Europe   156

Economic modernization   157
Tackling the union problem   159
The neo-liberal revolt   161
The rise of the new realism in the Labour Party   165
The crisis of 1974   165
The 1974–9 Labour government   166
International capitalist discipline   169
The real economy   173

7   Thatcherism in power   176

The Thatcherite concept of control   176
The transatlantic context of neo-liberalism: the evolution
of British foreign policy under Thatcher   181
From Atlantic partnership to unilateralism   181
The European Community   183
The Westland Affair   185
The assault on the working class   187
The miners' strike   189
The decline of the unions   191
The neo-liberal accumulation strategy   193
Industrial policy   194
Liberalizing the City   196
Pushing back the state   197
Towards a neo-liberal power bloc   199
Capital fractions and the redistribution of surplus value   200
Business organizations and the Thatcher government   202

8   Perspectives for Thatcherism   207

The decline of Britain reversed?   207
The global context   208
Is the class war over?   211
A post-Fordist accumulation strategy   213
Restructuring the landscape of British politics   216
Conclusion   219

Notes   222

References   237

Subject Index   255

Name Index   261

Author Index   264

List of abbreviations

ABCC	Association of British Chambers of Commerce
AEI	Associated Electrical Industries
AEU	Amalgamated Engineering Union
ASI	Adam Smith Institute
AWACS	Airborne Warning And Control System
BAe	British Aerospace
BCS	British and Commonwealth Shipping
BEA	British European Airways
BEC	British Employers' Confederation
BICC	British Insulated Callendar Cables
BISF	British Iron and Steel Federation
BLMC	British Leyland Motor Company
BP	British Petroleum
BSC	British Steel Corporation
BUI	British United Industrialists
CBI	Confederation of British Industry
CIA	Central Intelligence Agency
CPS	Centre for Policy Studies
DEA	Department of Economic Affairs
ECA	Economic Co-operation Administration
ECSC	European Coal and Steel Community
EDC	European Defence Community
EEC	European Economic Community
EEF	Engineering Employers' Federation
EETPU	Electrical, Electronic, Telecommunications and Plumbing Union
EFTA	European Free Trade Association
EMS	European Monetary System
EPU	European Payments Union
FBI	Federation of British Industry
FRA	France
FRG	Federal Republic of Germany
GDP	Gross Domestic Product
GATT	General Agreement on Tariffs and Trade
GKN	Guest, Keen & Nettlefolds
GEC	General Electric Company
GMWU	General and Municipal Workers' Union

IBM	International Business Machines
ICI	Imperial Chemical Industries
ICL	International Computers Ltd.
IDAC	Import Duties Advisory Committee
IEA	Institute of Economic Affairs
IEPG	Independent European Programme Group
IISS	International Institute for Strategic Studies
IMF	International Monetary Fund
IoD	Institute of Directors
IRC	Industrial Reconstruction Corporation
ISF	Iron and Steel Federation
ITT	International Telephone and Telegraph
JAP	Japan
MoD	Ministry of Defence
MP	Member of Parliament
NABM	National Association of British Manufacturers
NATO	North Atlantic Treaty Organisation
NCCI	National Chamber of Commerce and Industry
NEB	National Enterprise Board
NEDC	National Economic Development Council
NIEO	New International Economic Order
NL	Netherlands
NUGMW	National Union of General and Municipal Workers
NUM	National Union of Mineworkers
OEEC	Organisation for European Economic Co-operation
P&O	Peninsular and Oriental
PSBR	Public Sector Borrowing Requirement
RIIA	Royal Institute of International Affairs
SDI	Strategic Defense Initiative
SDP	Social Democratic Party
SI	Socialist International
SNP	Scottish National Party
TC	Trilateral Commission
TGWU	Transport and General Workers' Union
TUC	Trades Union Congress
UCS	Upper Clyde Shipbuilders
UDI	Unilateral Declaration of Independence
UGC	University Grants Committee
UK	United Kingdom
US(A)	United States of America
WEU	West European Union

List of tables and figures

Table 5.1   Indices of industrial production, 1950–8   122
Table 5.2   Days lost through industrial disputes   125
Table 6.1   Competitive position in industry, 1975–80   173
Table 7.1   Rates of return on capital employed   204
Table 7.2   The ten top donors to the Tory Party, 1982–5   206

Figure 6.1   Interest rates in selected countries, 1952–70   148
Figure 7.1   Direct taxes as percentage of current receipts,
             UK, 1968–84   201

For Ingrid, David and Bart

Preface

The origins of this book lie in a rather distant past. In 1974, in the wake of the student revolution of the preceding years, a small group of committed students and teachers in the field of international relations at the University of Amsterdam embarked on an experiment which was to prove a source of inspiration for many years to come: a project, focused on the origins of West European integration in the 1950s, in which teaching and research were integrated.

As a student assistant, I was assigned to start up a research group which was to investigate the reasons why Great Britain did not join the European Coal and Steel Community in 1950–1. The enthusiasm which guided the work of this group firmly shaped my interest in British politics and the postwar international position of Great Britain. In 1982, a new group of students came to share my interest in British politics, which resulted in a collection of research papers dealing with aspects of the crisis during the 1970s in Britain. The scope of this project was broadened in 1983–4, when a comparative analysis was attempted of the rise of neo-liberalism in Britain, West Germany, Belgium and the Netherlands, Eventually, the plan to write my dissertation (of which this book is a revised version) on the subject of the decline of Britain and the rise of Thatcherism – which had been very vague until then – began to take on a more definite shape. I am very grateful to all the students who took part over the years in the many discussions during which my thoughts gradually took shape. Without them, I would not have persisted.

I would also like to express my gratitude to all friends and colleagues in the Political Science Department at the University of Amsterdam and elsewhere, who have always been helpful, critical, and encouraging. Because it would be sad if the names of some were forgotten here, it is better to refrain from naming anybody.

The same applies to all those friends in Britain, both in the Conference of Socialist Economists and elsewhere, with whom

I have had the privilege of discussing aspects of British politics. These meetings have been enormously inspiring, and they have given me the courage to continue in spite of occasional doubts about the project.

Two exceptions must be made. Gerd Junne, my supervisor, has been a good friend and a generous supervisor throughout the entire enterprise. Gerd always left me free to explore my own path. Finally, Kees van der Pijl has been an invaluable source of intellectual inspiration, ceaselessly challenging, but always in solidarity and comradeship. I am greatly in his debt. No one, however, is to blame for what follows: the responsibility for the text and all its faults is fully mine.

Henk Overbeek
University of Amsterdam,
January 1989

Introduction

Twenty years ago the capitalist world economy showed the first signs of recession since the Second World War. In the early 1970s this recession developed into a serious and protracted crisis: growth of output and of international trade almost came to a halt, unemployment reached levels unheard of since the 1930s, and a massive restructuring of world production occurred, resulting in a record number of company bankruptcies and an unprecedented level of capital exports. These years have likewise been characterized by a deep crisis of American hegemony over the capitalist world. The United States is still the strongest economic, political and military power in the capitalist world, but its leadership is no longer accepted as a matter of course, at times not even by its most uncritical supporters. In recent years, these developments have led to increasing anxiety in the USA over the prospect that America would share the fate of Great Britain. In this context studies dealing with the 'historical laws of decline' became quite popular (hence the bestselling success of Paul Kennedy's *The Rise and Fall of the Great Powers*). Ideologically, this anxiety found another expression in the rise of what has been labelled as the 'New Right', or the 'New Conservatism', accompanied by such economic doctrines as 'monetarism' and 'supply side economics', which promised a radical break with the past and a certain (if painful) road towards recovery.

Britain's decline started, as most people will agree, sometime in the nineteenth century. But conscious recognition of this decline only became widespread in the late 1960s. The British economy never fully recovered from the 1966–67 recession, and in the years since then Britain has known alternate periods of stagnation and of more or less acute depression, without again achieving stable growth. The 1970s also brought a massive export of capital from the country, which came on top of an already strong tradition of capital export. Sooner than in other developed economies this process resulted in steady 'deindustrialization': a relative and absolute decrease of employment in the manufacturing industry. Finally, Britain was the first country where the New Right with

1

its neo-liberal economic recipes and conservative political ideology prevailed in free parliamentary elections. In Great Britain, Margaret Thatcher was brought to power by the British electorate, which was at least willing, after five years of Labour government and after the 'Winter of Discontent' of 1978–9, to try the effectiveness of a radically different approach.

The crisis in Britain in addition appears to have much deeper roots than in many other European countries, and the difference is striking enough to merit special investigation. The serious riots in British cities in 1981 and again in 1985, and the miners' strike of 1984–5, were indications of the deep-rooted cleavages in British society which came to the surface or were exacerbated as the crisis spread.

Existing interpretations of the 'decline of Britain' can be classified according to several criteria. In the course of this study, three theoretical problems will be referred to:

(a)　the level of analysis employed: many authors employ a narrow national view of the decline of Britain, ascribing the causes of Britain's decline to the 'peculiarities of the British', while others explain the continuing historical decline of Britain as the almost 'inevitable' fate of any formerly hegemonic power;

(b)　the historical time-scale employed: three groups of studies dealing with the British crisis can be distinguished, differentiated by the historical time-scale that is employed (long-term, medium-term, or short-term);

(c)　the relationship between the structural determination and the strategic (consciously pursued) direction of action by social forces.

Let me briefly consider these criteria, and their interrelation, in order to clarify the composition of the book.

(a)　The 'level-of-analysis debate' was concerned with the interaction between world-systemic, international, and domestic factors. In the field of international relations theory this problem has been hotly debated. The first instance was the discussion of the 1950s and 1960s (cf. Singer, 1961). The study of the problems of underdevelopment which gained popularity towards the end of the 1960s resulted in a new stimulus for the study of international relations and in a sense reactivated the debate concerning levels of analysis (cf. Junne, 1982). Recent systemic approaches, such as the world system theory of Immanuel Wallerstein, have stimulated the

2

study of systemic influences on national and sub-national politics, not only in the Third World but also in Europe and
North America. The study of international relations was thus
enriched with a third important level of analysis, the level of
the world system, in addition to the two levels that were traditionally important: the national level (terrain of the analysis of domestic sources of foreign policy, pressure groups,
class conflicts, ethnic and nationality problems, and so on),
and the international level (the analysis of the interaction of
nation-states, 'traditional' international relations theory). In
contrast with these two more established approaches, the
world system approach starts from the holistic premise that
the whole (world system) is more than the sum of the parts
and that consequently the parts (the nation-states that are
part of the world system) can only be understood properly
if studied in the context of their place and role in the whole
and of the way in which this place influences and possibly
even determines domestic relations (cf. Bach, 1982).

However, this does not entail an either–or choice: it is one and
the other at the same time. There is one integral historical process
in which sub-national, international and systemic factors operate
simultaneously and in dialectical interrelation. In other words, we
might speak of spatial co-ordinates, which refer to the dialectic
unity of external and internal factors. Capitalism is not a social
formation located within the confines of a particular portion of
the available global space (be it a nation-state or, as in Britain, a
'multinational state'), but it is a global social formation, with the
historical evolution of social forces tendentially also becoming
global in character.

(b) Several authors, primarily historians, have dealt with the
     interrelation of historical processes with different durations.
     Especially in the analysis of crisis, which is also the primary
     concern of this book, this 'conjuncture' of processes of dif-
     ferent duration has explanatory power (cf. Wallerstein, 1974,
     passim).

To be more specific, the analysis can be divided into three
'perspectives':

(1) the 'long-term perspective', tracing the present situation
     back to the establishment and rise to world dominance of
     British capitalism;

(2)   the 'medium-term perspective', tracing the present situation back to the formative period of the postwar social, political and economic order which is now in crisis;

(3)   the 'short-term perspective', analysing the present crisis primarily in terms of its own, short-term, dynamic.

These 'perspectives' function primarily as an ordering principle: considered by themselves they have little value. The concrete historical process is a process of struggle, conflict and compromise between social forces, a process of class formation in the broadest sense of the word. This process of class formation, which is the real and concrete historical process, is located in a dynamic framework of constantly redefined co-ordinates of time and space. Co-ordinates of time refer to historical processes evolving with distinct 'durations', and to the implications of this insight for an understanding of the overall historical process.

(c)   The analysis of time–space co-ordinates forms the framework for the analysis of the process of class formation and the political articulation of class interests. The relation between the structural underpinnings of capitalist development (that is, the 'laws of motion' of capital and of capitalist society) and the strategic action undertaken by concretely identifiable social and political actors is analysed with the help of the notion of 'comprehensive concepts of control' (cf. Van der Pijl, 1984), based on a study of the fragmentation, or fractionation, of the bourgeoisie. Most of the structural divisions within the ruling class, which are the focus of analysis here, concern the relationship between the ruling class and the dominated classes, and the problem of class domination is at the very heart of the notion of a 'concept of control'. In this sense, the contradictory capital–labour relation is the central point of departure, even if the main focus is on the ways in which the bourgeoisie manages to organize and control this contradictory relationship. Historically, four comprehensive concepts of control have become hegemonic: classical liberalism during the nineteenth century, the state monopoly tendency during the early decades of the twentieth century, corporate liberalism during the years 1940–70, and neo-liberalism during the 1980s.

This book attempts to combine existing interpretations and theoretical orientations to produce a new interpretation which integrates the three elements outlined here and elaborated in

Chapter 1. An analysis of Britain's decline in these terms results in a more comprehensive view of the factors and processes that are involved, and particularly of how they are interrelated.

In short, the view to be elaborated in this book is as follows.

During the first months of 1979 Britain experienced a 'conjuncture' of crises which reactivated the longstanding crisis of hegemony which the Labour government had temporarily tempered in 1974–5. In fact, this conjuncture involved three levels, or dimensions, of history.

At the level of the short cycle, the events culminating in the beginning of 1979 were a wave of serious labour unrest resulting from the government's attempt to limit wage increases; the loss of the majority in Parliament of the partners in the Lib–Lab pact of 1977; and, finally, the provisional culmination of Scottish nationalism in the ambiguous outcome of the referendum on Scottish devolution.

At the level of the long cycle, of the prevailing regime of accumulation, the three crises of 1979 can be restated: they consisted in the final breakdown of the class compromise underpinning Fordism, the collapse of the party which had been the representative of corporate liberalism *par excellence*, and internationally the decline of American hegemony also implying the further decline of Britain's position in the interstate system.

At the level of the long-term development of the capitalist system, the Winter of Discontent was the conjunctural manifestation of the crisis of the archaic capital–labour relationship in Britain corresponding to the pre-industrial stage of capitalist development; the acute crisis of the political system reflecting the 'unfinished bourgeois revolution' in Britain; and the imminent crisis of the form of the 'multinational' British state reflecting the incomplete 'nationalization' of state formation in the British Isles and the constantly reproduced denationalization of the British bourgeoisie.

The long-term decline of Great Britain

In Chapter 2 I reconsider those explanations of the British crisis which locate the origins of the present crisis in processes of long duration, such as the early, but incomplete, bourgeois revolution in Britain, the early industrialization in Britain eventually resulting in Britain's 'hegemony' in the world system, and the onset of imperial decline from about 1870. I examine the structure of social classes in Britain resulting from the early (pre-)hegemonic era, and its influence on the ideological and political outlook and fractionation of both the ruling and the working classes. To what degree did Britain's specific place in the nineteenth century world economy make the British ruling class receptive to specific concepts of control rather than others? In what manner can an understanding of Britain's place in the international division of labour prior to the era of classical imperialism contribute to an explanation of the specificities of the British working class, its strengths and weaknesses, its partly archaic, partly radical and militant character? These are some of the questions to which Chapter 2 attempts to give answers.

The transitional interwar years (Chapter 3), and especially the period after the General Strike of 1926, signify the definitive failure of radical working-class action in the period after the First World War. The effects of the Ottawa system of imperial preferences on the structure of the British economy and its differential effects on distinct classes and class fractions are examined. As we will see, dominant interests successfully resisted modernization of important branches of industry, such as iron and steel, thus prejudging developments after the Second World War.

The failure of Fordism

Chapters 4 and 5 deal with those approaches that explain the renewed decline of Britain after the Second World War by reference to medium-term historical processes and to specific stages or phases of capitalist development. The central argument here is that in Britain the introduction of the 'intensive regime of accumulation' (Aglietta) – also called 'Fordism' and/or referred to as the Keynesian welfare state (Jessop) – has been incomplete. Fordism in Britain failed to achieve fully what it achieved in the United States after the 1930s, and in Western Europe after the 1950s: the introduction of mass production techniques in the automobile and related industries resulting in an enormous increase in labour productivity, a restructuring of the working class along corporatist lines, and a concomitant restructuring of the ruling class along the same lines, oriented basically to developing the domestic market for consumer durables by coupling rising productivity to rising real wages.

The renewed decline of Britain after the 1950s was due to the articulation of the structures of postwar British capitalism (permeated, if not determined, by the *Pax Americana* as the mode of organization of the world economy and the international state system after 1945) with the century-old class structure which resulted from Britain's rise to world hegemony, and which was 'frozen' by the advent of the era of the 'New Imperialism' after 1870.

Three epochs in postwar British history, which was in some ways a history of the failure of Fordism, were crucial in this respect:

The first was the period of the postwar Labour government, and the wartime prelude to most of its relevant actions. How was it possible that a government could come to power by a landslide electoral victory and with a clear mandate for radical change, but still fail to achieve its central goals such as the rationalization and modernization of British industry? The relations of force between different fractions of capital, resulting in a power bloc which rested primarily on the coalition of colonial and financial interests, played an important role, successfully preventing the full-scale introduction of those conditions of production essential to modern industry. The influence of outside powers, first and foremost the United States, and the domestic reflection of Britain's role in international capitalism were also essential.

The second period is the period 1956–63. The Suez fiasco led to a realignment of interests in which the colonial fraction of the bourgeoisie was left in disarray, and new forces came to the fore, finding political expression in Macmillan's premiership. Eventually this led to the application for British membership of the EEC, a step which might have led to a full 'Fordization' of the British social economy. Which outside and inside forces prevented this from happening? Was there a 'systemic coalition' between Gaullist France on the one hand and traditional imperialist forces within Britain on the other, confronting the Macmillan/Kennedy axis supported by industrial capital and the corporatist majority in the Labour Party leadership?

Finally, there is the period of the Labour government of 1964–70. The Wilson government was quite outspoken in its intention to deepen the Fordist accumulation regime in Britain, and its failure set the stage for the developments of the 1970s.

This postwar period will be dealt with in two chapters. Chapter 4 deals with the global context of the years 1945–70, and with the redefinition of Britain's place in that context. In Chapter 5 the modernization offensives of the three periods outlined above will be discussed.

The rise of neo-liberalism

In the final chapters the analysis turns to the period of the 1970s and 1980s. During the 1970s, the effects of the world economic crisis were superimposed upon the ongoing process of imperial decline, and were aggravated by the structural imbalances in the postwar British economy. The severity of the impact of the world crisis upon Britain when compared to developments in other European countries is remarkable, and can only be understood properly when the conjuncture of these three 'crises' is grasped. Towards the end of the 1960s the Conservative Party shifted to a position close to what would later come to be known as 'Thatcherism': it favoured an attempt to break the resistance of the working class and of corporatist industry to deal with the increased international competition that would (and did) result from entry into the Common Market.

When it became clear, however, that the project was ill-prepared, Edward Heath returned to the established policies of the 1960s after having effected British entry to the European Community. Nevertheless, the Heath government did not succeed in placating the trade unions, and was eventually toppled by the combination of a miners' strike and an international energy crisis. The years 1973–75 were decisive: in these years neo-liberalism triumphed in the Conservative Party, and Margaret Thatcher became the new party leader.

At the same time, the Labour Party was also caught up in a process of transition. The replacement of Wilson by Callaghan and the demotion of Tony Benn marked the rise of the new realism. The acceptance of the terms of the IMF loan in 1976 marked the introduction of monetarist policies in Whitehall. This shift in ideological and politico-economic thinking in both major parties, which was also expressed in the emergence of the SDP, was related to trends in the real economic sphere. The deepening crisis of accumulation gave a sudden credibility to doctrines and ideologies which had been expressed throughout the 1950s and 1960s but which during those years appeared to most serious politicians, economists and so on to be out of date and out of tune with reality.

Although the Labour government of James Callaghan introduced monetarism, it did not possess any clear political and ideological programme to complement the 'technical' monetarism of its economic policies. It therefore put the economic burden of its austerity policies on the wage-earning classes without compensating these groups in the political and ideological fields. The corporate-liberal concept of control as a result lost its hegemony in Britain, which became clearly evident in the Winter of Discontent of 1978–9.

In the Conservative Party, the corporate-liberal fraction had been losing the key positions since 1975, and the Thatcherite fraction had entrenched itself firmly and used the stay of execution provided to Callaghan by the Liberal Party to prepare for power (Chapter 6).

The election of 1979 eventually brought Thatcher to Whitehall, followed a year later by the inauguration of President Reagan in the United States. This triumph of neo-liberalism on both sides of the Atlantic ushered in a new era of radically transformed transatlantic relations, eventually also making itself felt on the European continent with the establishment of neo-liberal regimes in the Netherlands (Lubbers), Belgium (Martens), West Germany (Kohl), and France (Chirac).

Domestically, the Thatcher government was not very successful initially in terms of its own policies: inflation accelerated, anti-union legislation proved difficult to push through, government expenditure could not be lowered, and so on. It needed such 'outside' factors as the Falklands conflict and the EC budget row to regain enough popularity to survive the 1983 general election. After winning this, the Thatcher government made a serious start with tackling union power: it introduced new legislation (in 1984, and again in 1987) and engaged in a fierce battle with one of the strongest and most radical unions of all, the National Union of Mineworkers. Thatcherism in power is analysed in Chapter 7.

Finally, in Chapter 8, the perspectives for Thatcherism and for a post-Thatcherite Britain are briefly considered.

CHAPTER 1

Long waves of class formation

Class formation in the world system

The cycle of hegemony and decline is not an historical contingency, a stroke of lightning inexplicably affecting the fate of an individual nation. Hegemony and decline are structural characteristics of the world order. The recent renewed popularity of theories of decline arises from the relative decline of American power since the second half of the 1960s and its perceived parallels with Britain's decline. The first to expound the view that hegemony and decline are ingrained in the structure of the modern world system was Immanuel Wallerstein, who defines hegemony as that 'short moment in time when a given core power can manifest simultaneously productive, commercial and financial superiority *over all other core powers*' (Wallerstein, 1980, pp. 38–9).

According to Wallerstein, there have been three instances of hegemony in the history of the capitalist world economy: the United Provinces (1620–72), England (1815–73), and the United States of America (1945–67). All these powers first achieved a relative advantage in agro-industrial production, then in commerce, and finally in finance. There is thus an analogy in the 'sequencing of achievement of advantages' in these three economic domains.

The second analogy is to be found in the ideological outlook of the hegemonial power, both in its dealings with other powers and in its domestic affairs: 'Hegemonic powers tended to be advocates of global "liberalism" ' (Wallerstein, 1984, p. 47).

Finally, in all three cases, as in fact was also the case with such earlier powers as Venice, Spain and Portugal, military power rested primarily on *naval* capabilities. (The military and strategic aspects of hegemony in the world system are given priority by Paul Kennedy (1988).)

The principal objections to Wallerstein's approach have been its almost complete neglect of the inter-state system, and its alleged economic determinism.

According to the critics, the international state system is an 'analytically autonomous level of transnational reality' (Skocpol, 1979, p. 22; see also Skocpol, 1977), and it constitutes the 'missing link' in Wallerstein's system (Zolberg, 1981). The allegation is not fully convincing. After all, Wallerstein considers the particular structure of interstate relations (that is, its fragmentation) in early modern Europe to have been a precondition for the consolidation of the modern world economy, and one of its defining characteristics (cf. Wallerstein, 1974, pp. 348–9). Nevertheless, it is true that Wallerstein's approach is not an international relations approach.

In his alternative world system theory, the political scientist George Modelski focused precisely on the missing link, that is, the interstate system. The fact that there is no central authority in the interstate system does not mean, he argues, that there is no international order. Rather, the reverse is true:

> The global political system is ... self-regulating within its confines, because it is closed (having boundaries that distinguish it from other systems, e.g., the economic) and because it is self-maintaining (incorporating self-correction, feedback and rhythm). (Modelski, 1981, p. 65)

The structure of this system is provided by the long cycle of world leadership. These long cycles are actually, according to Modelski, the 'central political process of the modern world system' (Modelski, 1981, p. 123). The 'capacity for global reach' is decisive in the attainment of world leadership: the aspiring power must be securely located, preferably on an ocean, it must possess ocean-going sea power (potentially more than half of all available sea power), it must have sufficient financial resources to pay for its navy, and it must have a political structure which can lend coherence to a global enterprise (Modelski, 1983, p. 117). The principal challengers, at least to Britain and the United States, have been land powers (France, Germany and the Soviet Union).[1]

One key aspect of Modelski's approach has been the emphasis on the ideological component of world leadership. Leadership does not rest on the exercise of force alone, but in part consists in 'exploiting the possibilities for common interest and minimizing the areas of conflict' (Modelski, 1983, pp. 120–1). World leadership, though gained through victory in war, is primarily exercised by presenting the world power's interest as the common interest of (a large part of) the inter-state system. Leadership is a 'legitimate form of world politics' because it accords with the 'common interest' (Modelski, 1983, p. 122). Modelski opposes this notion of leadership to the notion of hegemony, which he defines as 'rule for the benefit of the rulers alone ... arising when the power and the pretensions of the producers of order become excessive' (Modelski, 1983, p. 122). Disregarding here the normative character of the definitions of leadership and hegemony, it is clear that Wallerstein's notion of hegemony more or less coincides with Modelski's category of leadership.

'Hegemony' is preferable for our purposes because it corresponds to the use of the same notion applied to *national* political relations by Antonio Gramsci. Robert Cox has pointed out the relevance of Gramsci's notion of hegemony for international relations theory (cf. Cox, 1983). A state becomes hegemonic when it succeeds in building a world order which is *universal* in conception, and which is found by most other states to be compatible with their own interests. A hegemonic order is therefore characterized by a maximum of consent, and a minimum of coercion. Hegemony begins to falter when subordinate states no longer accept by consent the leadership of the hegemon, and must instead more often be coerced into acceptance. Gramsci's conception enables Cox to go beyond Modelski's insights: hegemony enables

> the forces of civil society to operate on the world scale ... The hegemonic concept of world order is founded not only upon the regulation of inter-state conflict, but also upon a globally-conceived civil society, i.e. a mode of production of global extent which brings about links among social classes of the countries encompassed by it. (Cox, 1983, p. 171).

In this way, Cox shows how world economy approaches and traditional international relations approaches are complementary, and must be integrated into an overall approach.

The greatest promise of the world system approach has been the recognition, which had been eclipsed in Stalinist Marxism, that capitalism and capitalist class relations were from their very inception located in a *global* context (the world economy) and not in national economies. Andre Gunder Frank was the first postwar author to formulate this essential notion: 'In fact, though there are state generated organizational discontinuities within the world capitalist system, there are in a very real and important sense no "national" economies at all' (Frank, 1963, p. 93).[2]

The fact that political power is organized within national states, and that the classes *für sich* primarily crystallize on a national level, presents us with a paradox which must be dealt with in theoretical terms. This however is something Wallerstein disappointingly

13

leaves for others to solve: the basic unit in world system analysis is not social at all: it is geographical. If Wallerstein emphasizes that the position in the international division of labour is the main determinant, it is primarily the position of geographical units that he is concerned with, not that of classes or class fractions.

The world economy is characterized, in the words of Wallerstein himself, by 'an ever greater polarization between the core and peripheral zones' through a 'transfer of part of the total profit (or surplus) being produced from one zone to another' (Wallerstein, 1983, pp. 30–1). The process of hierarchization is at one point described as 'a game of geographical musical chairs' (Wallerstein, 1984, p. 11).

Another protagonist of world system theory, Albert Bergesen, seems at first sight to have recognized the problem. In an article bearing the title 'The class structure of the world system', he argues that what is needed is to 'identify the world system's distinctive *world class relations*' (Bergesen, 1983, p. 44). But it soon becomes clear what Bergesen means:

> Most of the world's means of production have been under the control of the core, making the core–periphery relation a class relation rather than an unequal exchange relation ... ['Class' can be used for] characterizing the relationship between whole zones of the world economy. (Bergesen, 1983, pp. 50–1)

So, world class relations, or global class relations, turn out not to be class relations at all (that is, relations between *social* entities or groups) but relations between *geographical* entities, that is, 'zones' of the world economy.[3]

To locate class relations in their relevant historical setting, we have to relate the concept of class formation to the concepts of *mode of production* and *social formation*.

For Wallerstein, the world economy became capitalist with the 'discovery' of America, and it has remained capitalist ever since. The ruling class has also been capitalist ever since: the aristocracy became bourgeois, the bourgeoisie appears (in his work) as a homoogeneous class, divided by competition but not torn apart by structural separations. On the other pole of the worldwide process of class formation, an image is evoked of all human labour being exploited directly and indirectly by capitalists – both in the core and in the peripheral areas of the world economy – whether it be in the form of slavery, bonded labour, or free wage labour. In accordance with this view, Wallerstein defines capitalism in a way that abstracts from class relations or relations of production.

Capitalism for him is 'production for the market with profit maximization as the ultimate goal' (Wallerstein, 1979, p. 15), or simply
to 'the endless accumulation of capital' (Wallerstein, 1983, p. 91).
To this end, capitalists can make use of many 'modes of labour
control' (a term Wallerstein prefers over 'mode of production').[4]

The root of the problem with this view is to be found in its
specific understanding of the concept of 'mode of production'.

On the one hand, it is of paramount importance to understand
the nature of the defining characteristics of the capitalist mode
of production: in this respect Brenner's critique of what he has
called 'neo-Smithian Marxism' has been very valuable indeed
(Brenner, 1977; see also Wolf, 1982). But Brenner tends to lose
sight of the world market as the necessary external condition
for the emergence of capitalist relations. The interrelationship
of international circulation and relations of production should
be understood as a mutually conditioning one: production relations are decisive for shaping dominant as well as dominated
modes of production and the structure of exchange relations.
International circulation relations however serve to accelerate
the development of capitalism where its internal conditions of
existence have already emerged, while they block the development of capitalist relations where these internal conditions are
absent.

The concept of 'mode of production' in Marx's work is an
abstraction, an 'ideal type' in the Weberian sense, which does
not as such exist in real history. Historical capitalism (that is, the
'capitalist world system') is not a mode of production at all. It is a
social formation (for an elaboration of this distinction, see Amin,
1976, pp. 13–22). The real thesis of the world system approach,
reformulated in these terms, would then be that, since the rise of
capitalism, the world economy as a whole must be considered to
constitute a capitalist social formation – that is to say, the capitalist
mode of production is dominant.

> In fact, in every social formation, we find the dominance of
> one mode of production, which produces complex effects of
> dissolution and conservation on the other modes of production
> and which gives these societies their overall character (feudal,
> capitalist, etc.) (Poulantzas, 1975, p. 22).

These points are important if we want to understand why
capitalist penetration in peripheral areas had such diverse
consequences. In the Caribbean, the plantation system with
its widespread use of slave labour was introduced on the basis
of the almost complete annihilation of pre-existing society;

15

South America was colonized by the pre-capitalist or at best proto-capitalist Spanish and Portuguese, who were forced to leave at least part of the pre-existing social order intact, and who installed a ruling bloc (made up of semi-feudal landowners, merchants and usurers) which precluded the rise of industrial capitalism just as much as did the disadvantageous trade relations of South America with Europe; in most of Asia, European colonialism was unable to destroy indigenous social relations and structures and for a long time could do nothing else but position themselves at the top of the pre-existing tributary hierarchy (hence the value of some notion of the 'Asiatic mode of production', as argued in Overbeek and Silva, 1986); in Africa, finally, capitalist penetration did not result in the wholesale establishment of capitalist production relations either, let alone in the rise of an African industrial bourgeoisie.

Nevertheless, the notion that capitalist expansion from Europe partly took place through the subordination (not displacement or destruction) of non-capitalist economies to the needs of capital accumulation in the core in no way contradicts 'orthodox' Marxism, as is often maintained.[5] On the contrary, Marx himself recognized the fact that, from the very beginning, the introduction of slavery and of the plantation system in the New World played a central role in the development of industrial capitalism in England: 'Liverpool grew fat on the basis of the slave trade. This was its method of primitive accumulation' (Marx, [1867] 1979, vol. 1, p. 924; also see the classic study by Eric Williams, 1944).

Not only was the rise of industry in England predicated upon the slave trade; more fundamentally, the breakthrough of capitalism as such had been conditioned by the widening of international exchanges from the end of the fifteenth century (Marx, [1894] 1979 vol. 3, pp. 450–1).

Wallerstein is able to interpret industrial capitalism as well as late feudalism, mercantile capitalism, monopoly capitalism, and even 'really existing' socialism, as epochs or integral parts of the capitalist world economy only by employing a very superficial concept of capitalism, by abstracting both from concrete class relations and from the historical transformations that capitalism went through in the course of its development.

In contrast to this view, the international division of labour can more fruitfully be conceived as the 'vehicle' through which production relations spread and class formation is 'nationalized', that is, as the process through which global class formation is articulated with the processes of nation-building and state formation.

It is precisely this dialectical view of the relation between 'external' and 'internal' factors which is also essential for a better understanding of the nature of hegemony in international relations.[6] In the words of Cox, world hegemony is

> an outward expansion of the internal (national) hegemony established by a dominant social class ... [it] is not merely an order among states. It is an order within a world economy with a dominant mode of production which penetrates into all countries and links into other subordinate modes of production. It is also a complex of international social relationships which connect the social classes of the different countries. World hegemony is describable as a social structure, an economic structure, and a political structure; and it cannot be simply one of these things but must be all three. (Cox, 1983, pp. 171–2)

The temporal dimension of class formation

In the world system approach, class formation is essentially reduced to circulation relations. From this results a tendency to overemphasize the spatial dimension of capitalism. This tendency can be traced back to the French historians of the Annales school such as Labrousse, Bloch and Braudel.

A second major element in the approach of Annales historiography, the temporal dimension of the 'multilayered' historical process, has also been incorporated into the world system approach. In his monumental study, *The Mediterranean*, Fernand Braudel organized his material around three histories:

- *structural history*, primarily situated in the extremely slow-moving field of geography and nature, and therefore with a very long duration (the famous *longue durée*);
- *conjunctural history*, situated in the (socio-)economic field, with a medium-length duration;
- *narrative history* (histoire événementielle), situated in the political field (that is, traditional history, made by great personalities and made up of events), with a short duration.

The book, as Braudel writes, represents

> an attempt to write a new kind of history, total history, written in three different levels, perhaps best described as three different conceptions of time, the writer's aim being to bring together in all their multiplicity the different

17

measures of time past, to acquaint the reader with their coexistence, their conflicts and contradictions, and the richness of experience they hold. (Braudel, 1973, p. 1,238).

Roughly the same theoretical constructions have been employed by other authors, social scientists as well as historians.

Thus, in analysing the 'crisis of feudalism' leading to the emergence of the capitalist world economy, Immanuel Wallerstein argues that the crisis in fact represented the 'conjuncture' of three crises, each with its own specific dynamic and duration (Wallerstein, 1974, pp. 37, 98).

Ernest Labrousse employed a comparable scheme in an analysis of the origins of the French Revolution. This revolution forms the climax of three distinct historical schedules, namely the 'long time' of the century-long expansion of the eighteenth century coming to an end, the 'medium time' of the long depression of 1774 to 1788 and the 'short time' of the seasonal depression of 1789; the French Revolution is the result of the superimposition of the effects of the three crises involved (Labrousse, quoted by Anderson, 1980, p. 74).

We need not go into the finer distinctions between these and other comparable schemes here. What we want to retain at this point is the notion that 'history' involves processes of different duration, which mutually influence each other and periodically come together in one 'conjuncture'. What exactly is the nature of these different dimensions of time or duration, or 'intersecting planes of temporality' (Giddens, 1981, p. 19)?

The first point to make is that in a chronological sense there is only one 'time', in which all these temporalities are measured and to which they can in the final instance be reduced.[7]

To avoid misunderstanding, it is perhaps best to speak of 'time' only in relation to chronological time, and of 'duration' when speaking of the 'length' of historical periods. Every historical or social process, then, has its own 'pattern of duration' (Anderson, 1980, p. 74).

How are these different temporalities interrelated, and how can an understanding of this interrelation enhance our understanding of concrete historical class structures and processes of class formation?[8]

In one sense we are dealing here with the relation between the 'history' of the parts, and the 'history' of the whole. The analysis of the political economy of a particular country must take into account, indeed must take as its point of departure, the stage of development of the capitalist world economy as a whole. In other words, analyses of historical processes in parts of a larger system (such as the 'world system') 'must first establish "where" the system is during the period of time being considered' (Thompson, 1983a, p. 36). In this context Thompson uses the term 'world system time'. In the same vein, Perry Anderson speaks of 'the need to integrate the times of each particular social formation into the much more complex general history of the mode of production dominant in them' (Anderson, 1980, p. 76).

A second aspect of the question concerns the fact that historical processes of long duration 'comprise' processes of shorter duration. The *longue durée* is characterized by 'laws' and regularities which are valid for all times; yet these regularities acquire their fullest meaning only in a historically specific setting, which is defined by historical processes of shorter duration.

In sum we can say that every particular historical conjuncture is the composite outcome of several 'histories', of several different historical processes with their own pattern of duration, and for every 'history' the bounds within which it can conceivably develop (or could have developed) are determined by the stage of development (the 'time') of historical processes with a longer duration.

The attempts that have been made so far to employ the idea of multilayered historical time have been most successful or inspiring when the notion was applied to the analysis of crises or revolutions (Anderson, 1980, p. 76).[9] In the case of Britain, Tom Nairn has remarked that

> there are two levels of 'crisis' built into Britain's recent history (by which I mean the history of the last century), the enduring or chronic disorder of imperial decline and the temporary eruptions or fevers to which that disorder has made Britain susceptible.

What we need, adds Nairn, is a 'historical and specific model, one which takes in the longue durée of British capitalist development' (Nairn, 1979, pp. 44, 53).

Crisis – by which term we mean structural disruptions of the regularities or phenomena under consideration, and not superficial fluctuations – perhaps provides the best opportunity to gain insight into the way in which processes of different duration intersect, reinforce or counteract each other, or reactivate tendencies which had been subdued.

The contradictions inherent in the historical processes of longer duration (temporarily overcome by the specific constellation of social forces resulting from the previous crisis) are, as it were, reactivated by the onset of crisis in a shorter term dimension. As

19

a result there then develops a conjuncture of crises of the different historical processes, and the depth and severity of the crisis are magnified to an extent that would be incomprehensible if looked at from the perspective of a single time-dimension.

In other words, when processes with different 'durations' at the same time lapse into crisis, the dialectical unity of the overarching total historical process is re-established with force, and the ostensible 'autonomy' of these different 'instances' is resolved.

The interim conclusion at this point can be that the present world crisis, and with it the specific position of Great Britain, should in principle be analysed from different temporal perspectives which are not chosen arbitrarily but rather correspond to structural layers of the total historical process. For our purposes it is sufficient to distinguish three dimensions in time, three patterns of duration in history.[10]

We speak of the *long-term perspective* when considering the history of a specific mode of production, and here in particular of the capitalist mode of production,[11] and the historical process of the formation of the main social classes of capitalism. The emerging new paradigm of world system analysis tends to present a strongly ahistorical picture of the capitalist world system. This may seem a peculiar statement about work that deals with so much history. But historical analysis involves more than using empirical material from the past.

Global capitalism is certainly characterized by regularities and cycles which have remained much the same since the sixteenth century. But in the history of capitalism there have also been certain structural transformations, qualitative breaks in patterns of production and extraction of surplus value (which is what capitalism is all about). The world economy of the twentieth century is not the same world economy that existed in the sixteenth century with only the core having shifted from Holland via England to North America. The difference is that between commercial capitalism and late capitalism, or mercantilism and monopoly capitalism: these represent separate stages of development of the world economy, sharing certain common characteristics, but also distinguishable by other, equally structural, characteristics. The study of history, especially of the history of the highly dynamic capitalist mode of production, requires that change and transformation are acknowledged at a methodological level. *Transhistorical straitjackets* (C.Wright Mills, 1970), on the contrary, will produce inexplicable paradoxes.

In this long-term perspective, the present crisis is seen as a moment (perhaps not decisive, but at least heralding that decisive moment in the future) in the transitional period in which the world system is transformed from a capitalist world economy into a socialist world economy. According to this view, the world is now in a 'long twentieth century' (analogous to the long sixteenth century marking the transition from feudalism to capitalism), the beginning of which was signalled by the October Revolution of 1917. Thus, the long-term temporal approach and the world system 'spatial' approach combine to yield a historical but rather abstract view of crisis. This abstract quality is brought out very clearly in the analysis of the structural regularities perceived to operate in the capitalist world economy: the long-term approach appears to tend towards an ahistorical position, and towards a position in which the social character of the historical process is neglected or even denied.

Which processes underlie the regularity, the cyclical movement, in the world system of states, according to the world system theorists? The most elaborate attempt to establish the nature of the relation between economic cycles and political cycles was made by Nicole Bousquet, who expected 'to find a clear temporal coincidence between a given pattern at the core and a given phase of a known cycle within the world economy' (Bousquet, 1980, pp. 46–7). However, she stumbled over the discontinuity of historical evidence: 'In general, historians agree on the existence of secular trends for the sixteenth through the eighteenth centuries but not afterwards, and on the incidence of Kondratieff waves since the beginning of the nineteenth century but not before' (Bousquet, 1980, p. 47).[12]

However, these long waves – precisely because of the characteristics with respect to technological development Kondratieff ascribed to them – could only arise when industrial capitalism had reached a certain maturity, and not before. One must take into account the historical specificity of the structures and regularities involved here, and not just the more abstract characteristics one phase of capitalism shares with others. Some of the contributions to the 'long-wave controversy' can illustrate this.

Long waves are characterized, in their expansive (the so-called A–) phase, by the rapid diffusion of basic innovations in key sectors of the economy, or of 'new technological webs' (Roobeek, 1987), particularly in the field of energy and transportation (Schumpeter, 1942; Mandel, 1975, 1980; see also the very useful collection edited by Freeman, 1983).

The expansive phase of the long wave comes to an end when the basic innovations concerned have been generally introduced throughout the economy and no longer provide any economic dynamism, and there are no more extra profits to be realized from introducing them. The growth of productivity declines, profits begin to fall, and investments decrease and are reserved for 'improvement innovations'.

However, as Mandel remarks, although it is possible to explain 'the cumulative nature of each long wave, once it is initiated', and it is possible to explain 'the transition from an expansionist long wave to a stagnating long wave', it is far more difficult to explain the turn from a stagnating phase to an expansionist one (Mandel, 1980, p. 21). In this context Mandel criticizes the technological determinism inherent in long-wave analysis. The history of technology is full of examples of technological breakthroughs which were introduced in the production process only years or sometimes decades after their original invention. A new upswing, involving the massive dispersion of new technologies throughout the core economies of the world, must be explained by extra-economic radical changes in the overall environment in which the capitalist mode of production operates.

We are particularly interested here in the *social* context in which technological development takes place: the massive introduction of new technologies requires a fundamental restructuring of the labour process in key industrial sectors which not only applies to the technical labour process, but just as much to the social, indeed political, dimensions of the labour process.[13] Therefore, the innovation of the technological foundation of production, which is exactly what is involved in a new 'upswing', can take place only in an appropriate social environment, and to a certain extent an appropriate political structure is required as well.

Rather than speaking of long waves or cycles (a concept which stresses the essential continuity of the development of global capitalism) we should, in order to emphasize the structural discontinuities, speak of *stages of development*, a notion which takes us into the realm of the *medium-term perspective*.

Stages of development are distinguished by specific configurations of social and political institutions, each with their own characteristics.[14] More precisely, stages of capitalist development are defined by reference to a historically specific combination of relations between social classes and class fractions, forms of state power and ideological hegemony, and of the organization of the capitalist world economy and the inter-state system.

The prototype of the view according to which capitalism develops in stages can be found in Lenin's views on the rise of monopoly and the role of finance capital. Lenin, however, was too preoccupied with the vision of the final collapse of capitalism to work out a more refined theory of the development of capitalism through different stages.

In their elaboration of this notion of developmental stages, some French theorists, inspired by the work of Michel Aglietta in particular, have proposed the notion of *regimes of accumulation* by which term is meant the socio-economic and political structure in which accumulation is embedded. The stage of development of world capitalism which originated in the 1920s and 1930s in the United States and in the 1940s and 1950s in Western Europe is in this approach usually designated with a term borrowed from Antonio Gramsci – *Fordism*.

In the *short-term perspective*, the third layer of history, we are concerned with the short cycle, with the conjunctural dynamic of crisis, not just in a strict economic sense but rather in a wider social, political, indeed historical, sense. Following Gramsci and Poulantzas, we speak of a structural crisis in capitalism, or a crisis of capitalist hegemony, when existing social relations must be radically restructured to ensure the renewed domination of the bourgeoisie over the working classes and over the greatest possible part of the globe.

The question of the restoration of bourgeois hegemony brings us to the question of the relation between structural and strategic determination of the action of class forces. This problematic is here approached from the point of view of the fractioning of capital and the consequent fractionation of the ruling class. It constitutes the third major thrust of our theoretical argument, and gives the other two theoretical departure points (the *global* character of the process of class formation, and the *multilayered* character of this process) their full historical meaning.

Class formation and the political articulation of class interests

Capital fractions

Capital fractions are portions of the total social capital, distinguished from each other by some structural characteristic referring to distinct positions in the process of capital (re-) production and circulation. Bode (1979, p. 18) considers five major criteria on the basis of which fractions of capital can be distinguished:

(a) the functional-institutional forms of capital (commercial capital, landed capital, banking capital, and industrial capital):

23

we should keep the underlying distinction between fixed and circulating capital in mind here;

(b)   the use value of the products: means of production, wage goods, services, and so forth;
(c)   the 'productivity conditions' in different branches (emphasis on absolute vs. relative surplus value for example);
(d)   the specific relation of the capitals in question to labour and to the working class;
(e)   the geographical orientation of the different capitals (producing for home market or for export, colonial vs. European-or Atlantic-oriented capital, and so forth).

At the highest level of abstraction, capital is fractionated, according to the functional forms it assumes in the overall process of expanded capitalist reproduction, into money capital, commodity capital, and productive capital. The first two functions belong to the sphere of circulation, the last to the sphere of production.

As a first and most elementary approximation, these functional forms distinguished by Marx (money capital, commodity capital and productive capital) still suffice. Further elaborations and subdivisions, resulting in a more complex picture of the fractionation of capital, will always have to be based upon structural characteristics describing the position of groups of individual capitals in the overall accumulation process. Groups of individual capitals arising out of some incidental concurrence of interests do not constitute fractions of capital, but are single-issue pressure groups.

It is important to stress that a distinction should be made between 'fractions' as abstractions, as expressions of the forms which social capital assumes in the total process of reproduction (that is, as *functional forms* of capital), and the *institutional forms* in which capital appears in the real world (cf. Overbeek, 1980, p. 102). The conceptual pair 'money capital/productive capital' refers to the first: it denotes the functional fractionation of capital as analysed by Marx in *Capital*, vol. 2. The concepts 'banking/industry' on the other hand usually refer to the institutional division of capital into separate firms and enterprises with distinct activities. This process is a continuous product of capitalist accumulation, whereby the circuits of money and commodity capital (subsumed under the category of circulating capital) appear to become *external* to the circuit of productive capital, resulting in independent units of social capital (banks, merchant houses, and so on). It is defined here as the process of the *fractionation of capital*.

If this process is operative continuously as capital accumulates, so is its opposite: the different circuits of capital are tendentially reintegrated and must be, because they are but moments of *one* historical process. This means that money capital and productive capital are interdependent. Capitalist circulation cannot be conceived of as existing independently of capitalist production. The dependence of circulation on production, however, is not confined by spatial limits: circulation and production can take place in quite distinct geographical locations, so much so that within specific boundaries (countries, for example) productive and circulating capital may in fact be quite independent of each other, and circulating capital, appearing to be 'independent of productive capital', may be strongly connected to productive spheres in other parts of the world economy. There is no need for money capital to maintain the capacity of domestic industry to produce a certain amount of surplus value, if it is possible at lower cost and fewer risks to turn to foreign activities and take a handsome profit out of the surplus value created by and extracted from workers elsewhere in the world economy. And this of course is exactly what British financiers have been doing since the last quarter of the nineteenth century.

Concepts of control

Capital fractions are thus groupings of capitalists with structurally comparable positions in the overall circuit of capital. Conflicts between fractions of capital tend to transcend the competition between individual capitalists, because these conflicts do not take place within the existing framework of the economic, political and ideological conditions for capital accumulation but are concerned with changing these conditions. When they do so, we can speak of fractions of the bourgeoisie (cf. Bode, 1979, p. 19). So, at any time, there are potentially several political programmes comprising fractional economic and political strategies.

However, specific fractional programmes are no more than the direct expression in political terms (that is, in terms demanding state action) of fractional interests, typically shared only by a small minority of social and political forces. More or less stable coalitions of interests can only arise around programmes formulated in such a way as to represent at least the most essential interests of at least so many other fractions and social forces as is necessary to prevail in the political arena. Such programmes transcending specific fractional interests, indeed presented as the 'general interest' or the 'national interest', comprise a coherent set of strategies in the areas of labour relations, socio-economic policies, ideological matters, and the international position of the country in question. The basis for such a programme is laid by a class compromise through which the dominated classes and class fractions are adequately compensated (economically or ideologically) for accepting the domination of the hegemonic fraction. These 'concepts of strategy' (Poulantzas, 1975, p. 24), 'class strategies' (cf. Gamble, 1981), or 'hegemonic projects' (cf. Jessop, 1983a; 1983b) are here called *comprehensive concepts of control* (cf. Bode, 1979).

A comprehensive concept of control, then, consists in a coherent formulation of the 'general interest' which transcends narrowly defined fractional interests and which combines mutually compatible strategies in the fields of labour relations, socio-economic policy and foreign policy on the basis of a class compromise entailing specific economic and/or ideological rewards for the dominated classes and class fractions involved.

Concepts of control have a structural economic foundation in the sense of clustering around two ideal typical concepts essentially reflecting the circulating and the productive capital vantage point. Two proto-concepts of control can be characterized in general terms by looking a little closer at the distinction between productive capital and circulating capital – or, as Shortall formulates it, between fixed and circulating capital (Van der Pijl, 1984; Shortall, 1986).

The *productive function* is first of all performed by industry. Industrial capital is primarily interested in continuity of production and in the sale of the commodities it produces. In both instances workers play a central and essential role: any concept developed or adhered to by industrial capital will therefore contain elements meant to neutralize the conflict of interest between the opposed classes and also elements meant to emphasize the harmony of interest between them. Of course, class relations in capitalist production are necessarily contradictory: on the one hand the possibility of higher wages is conditional upon the general profitability of the firm, while at the same time the profitability of the firm partly depends upon the minimization of wage costs and the maximization of surplus value. Harmony of interest and conflict of interest in capitalist production are but aspects of the same reality. Of course, the proportion of these two sets of elements changes over time, according to the general state of the class struggle. The most reactionary mix was the fascist corporatism of the interwar period; the modern reformist variety was the one developed in the New Deal in the US, and in Sweden, during the 1930s, which was later 'generalized' through Keynesianism and social democracy. As regards the organization of production at the level of the firm, the predominance of the productive function of capital enhances the 'rise of the manager', and of what has been called 'economic property' (cf. Poulantzas, 1975, p. 21), indeed the loss of direct control over the production process by the capitalists, represented by the board of directors. While facilitating the rapid development of the forces of production, therefore, preponderance of the productive function threatens to drive production beyond the confines of capitalist relations of production.

The *circulation function* is performed by institutions such as banks, insurance companies, trading companies (including oil companies whose activities consist largely of trading), and service sectors such as advertising agencies. Essential for circulation is the safeguarding of the free movement of capital (especially in money form) and the convertibility of currencies. The money-capital concept (linked to the classical liberal ideology) is attractive not only to bankers and financiers, but also to those class elements dependent on the largest possible freedom of manoeuvre and on the minimization of regulatory practices and institutions (petty bourgeois elements, professional people, and skilled workers in high-growth sectors of the economy). At the level of the firm, the standpoint of circulation is the standpoint of 'legal property', and is represented by the 'owners' (oriented to maintaining existing property relations) and the 'financial experts' (concerned only with the maximum rate of profit, not with the nature and quality of the product to be marketed). Preponderance of the circulation function tendentially leads to speculation and to stagnation in the development of the productive forces.

In both cases, then, we are concerned with dynamic and contradictory tendencies, not with static phenomena. Both functions are essential to the overall process of capitalist accumulation, which proceeds through the periodic resolution of these contradictions, which are not simply the *result* but the *mode of existence* of capital.

The contradictions involved here, however, are not resolved 'automatically'. Their resolution within the outer boundaries of capitalist property relations requires the active strategic intervention of social and political agents, and these interventions take place in the political and ideological arena.

Comprehensive concepts of control are therefore not simply the immediate extensions of these ideal types; rather, they represent the unity of:

- a more or less coherent set of ideas and programmes;

27

- a 'critical mass' of interests forming the socio-political basis for such a programme; and
- the constellation of (national and international) economic and class forces providing the structural context in which interests are politically articulated.

As Van der Pijl writes, when productive capital is in crisis, the money-capital concept

> 'presents itself' as the obvious, rational, solution ... It is this correspondence between the objective state of capitalist society and the particular solution proposed by a single class-fraction (in this case, the bankers and owners), which allows the rest of capitalist society a view of the whole which under other circumstances only bankers have: hence, which makes for bankers' class consciousness to crystallize and gain the upper hand. (Van der Pijl, 1984, pp. 33–4)

To give a concrete example – important for our own purposes since it relates to the rise of neo-liberalism in Britain in the 1970s – of the essence of this broader unity: both monetarist and wider 'neo-liberal' ideas and proposals were formulated since the late 1940s in the context of the Mont Pelerin Society established by Friedrich Hayek and Milton Friedman amongst others. However, these ideas remained without any concrete socio-political impact during most of the 1950s and 1960s. It was only towards the end of the 1960s that structural transformations in the world economy and a realignment of political forces within Britain transformed the neo-liberal set of ideas into a realistic (that is, feasible) political programme, into a concept of control, and eventually into the dominating concept of the 1980s.

The essential nexus involved – the fundamental unity of the ideological, the political and the economic – was expressed by Gramsci in the following way:

> Undoubtedly the fact of hegemony presupposes that account be taken of the interests and the tendencies of the groups over which hegemony is to be exercized, and that a certain compromise equilibrium should be formed – in other words, that the leading group should make sacrifices of an economic-corporate kind. But there is also no doubt that such sacrifices and such a compromise cannot touch the essential; for though hegemony is ethical-political, it must also be economic, must necessarily be based on the decisive function exercised by the

leading group in the decisive nucleus of economic activity. (Gramsci, 1971, p. 161).

For 'global conceptions of the world' (Gramsci) to become hegemonic, it is not enough that they are based in economics, although they usually are:

> An appropriate political initiative is always necessary to liberate the economic thrust from the dead weight of traditional policies – i.e. to change the political direction of certain forces which have to be absorbed if a new, homogeneous politico-economic historical bloc, without internal contradictions, is to be successfully formed. (Gramsci, 1971, p. 168)

More or less 'objectively' present ('embryonical') ideal typical concepts of control ('previously germinated ideologies' Gramsci calls them) become 'political' when they are formulated in terms of a general interest (to which a variety of groups and interests can subscribe) in a specific concrete historical context, and

> come into confrontation and conflict, until only one of them, or at least a single combination of them, tends to prevail, to gain the upper hand, to propagate itself throughout society – bringing about not only a unison of economic and political aims, but also the intellectual and moral unity, posing all the questions around which the struggle rages not on a corporate but on a 'universal' plane, and thus creating the hegemony of a fundamental social group over a series of subordinate groups ... the dominant group is coordinated with the general interests of the subordinate groups (Gramsci, 1971, pp. 181–2)

Generations in the bourgeoisie

We have argued that historical capitalism has from its inception been a global system. The history of this system has been, in the Hegelian sense, the history of the dialectical process of the realization of this global nature, the history of the process of the globalization of capitalist class relations. This process has not been an evolutionary one; rather, it has developed through stages, separated from each other by crises and each characterized by regularities and class relationships specific to that one stage of development. By viewing the history of capitalism in this way, we will be able to overcome the seeming irreconcilability between the 'long arch' of capitalism on the one hand and the historical discontinuities which lie at the heart of the conflict between Perry Anderson (1987) and Michael Barratt Brown (1988).

Each stage of development involves different geographical and historical settings in which particular classes originate and in which they are defined by their relation to other classes.

Nowhere did the capitalist class constitute a single, unified bloc. The ruling class is divided along lines of a functional nature, and moreover, these fractions by and large represent different 'generations', as it were, of the ruling class, in the sense of originating in different historical epochs of capitalist development. In the commercial stage and in the age of the export of money capital and of the 'financial oligarchies', different outlooks or perspectives developed in the ruling classes of the capitalist world, ultimately related to functional 'roles' in the overall circuit of industrial capital.[15] Particular perspectives tend to become dominant or hegemonic with the historical prominence of such roles.

The period from the creation of a capitalist world economy until around 1850–70 was the period in which capital internationalized through the circuit of commodity capital, by means of a steady expansion of the scope of international trade. In this period international trade was transformed into the international circulation of capital in commodity form, handled by a particular fraction of capital, *merchant capital*. The period between 1500 and 1750 hence saw the rise of a commercial bourgeoisie, first in the Italian city-states and the Iberian peninsula, then in Holland, and finally in England. These merchants played the leading role in the expansion of the capitalist world market and in the inclusion of large parts of the globe into the European world economy. From 1750 onwards an English/Scottish industrial bourgeoisie gradually rose to economic prominence, but it remained subordinate to powerful commercial, shipping and financial interests.

Laissez-faire liberalism became the ideology of British commercial (and industrial) capital once mercantilism had ensured its dominance in the world markets. The nineteenth century thus became the age of competitive capitalism, and at once the age of British hegemony, of the *Pax Britannica*. Britain's hegemony in the world system was founded upon its productive superiority. British industry enjoyed a near monopoly on the world markets, and the *industrial bourgeoisie* rose to unprecedented prominence. The repeal of the Corn Laws in 1846 can be considered the heyday of the industrial bourgeoisie in Britain. However, the English industrial bourgeoisie was never able to replace the aristocracy as the hegemonic class fraction in Britain. It was instead forced to enter into an alliance with the commercial and financial fraction of the British ruling class. In other parts of the world economy, particularly in peripheral and semi-peripheral areas, the dominant coalition was that between semi-feudal landed interests and the comprador-bourgeoisie[16] monopolizing foreign commerce. In ideological terms the era of free trade was above all the era of classical liberalism. From a global point of view, British capitalism – which is usually considered the classic example of the capitalist mode of production – appears rather as the specific national expression of a class compromise between classes and class fractions whose nature was largely determined at the global level. The context of the early transition to capitalism and to bourgeois rule, which was not radically shaken until well into the twentieth century thanks to the imperial hegemony which Britain was able to secure on the world market, has determined the peculiarities of the British state and British civil society: the 'multinational' character of the British state, the peculiar nature of 'British' (or better, English) nationalism, the parliamentary form of political rule, the composition and orientations of British capital, and the nature of British labour relations are the most important of these 'British peculiarities'.[17]

The late nineteenth and early twentieth centuries (1870–1940) saw the internationalization of the circuit of money capital in the form of the enormous increase in foreign investments in railway stock and government bonds (in short, in portfolio investments). This internationalization of money capital produced quite different responses in various countries. The ruling class coalitions (often newly constituted) in many countries took a 'nationalist' position induced by the need to develop their productive forces behind protective walls. The ruling bloc in Britain, however, clung to its earlier 'internationalism'. The British case is in fact one of exceptional stability as regards the hegemony of one particular, internationally oriented fraction of capital. This is a reflection of the specific compromises that were struck between the older, aristocratic fraction of the ruling class and the newer class fractions of the commercial and industrial bourgeoisie and the working class.

In other countries, too, the essential trait was the nature of the class compromise between finance capital and the landed classes. Between the 'financial oligarchies' of different nationalities, and indeed among bankers in particular, a cosmopolitan community existed: the financial and commercial bourgeoisie was from the very outset *international*. The landowning class however (certainly

31

if we are speaking of a feudal aristocracy or of a class of capitalist farmers and not of capitalist absentee landlords) is by virtue of its ties to the land a far more *national* class. The landed aristocracy developed into a capitalist, absentee landlord class, drawing income from its land but investing these profits in commercial, financial, and sometimes even industrial enterprises. Thus a strong coalition of interests developed between these two dominant sections of the overall capitalist class – the commercial and financial bourgeoisie and the landed capitalists – who both shared an essentially imperial and outward-looking view of the world. The 'national' space in Britain was left to the more directly productive classes, the numerically small agrarian population (small as a result of its great efficiency) consisting of capitalist farmers and rural workers, and the industrial classes: the industrial bourgeoisie and the urban proletariat, especially the masses outside the reach of the rising Labour movement but inside that of 'national unity'. There was thus no 'socialization of nationalism' as E. H. Carr expressed it (Carr, 1945).

The dominant sections of the British bourgeoisie were never faced with the necessity to come to terms with their own proletariat in order to conquer a position on the world market, as the German and American bourgeoisies had to (cf. Cain and Hopkins, 1986, p. 508). Owing to the *logic of priority* (the consequence of having been the first to industrialize and the first to conquer – in fact to constitute – the world market) the British bourgeoisie could in this way become the most international of all, a quality which was affected by the relative shrinking of its empire after 1870 only superficially until the Second World War.

Because in other countries finance capital was forced to compromise with these 'national' class fractions, it often accommodated the state-led emancipation of industrial capital. In order to defend its capital's interests on the world market, the state in these cases tended towards sphere-of-interest foreign policies and nationalism. Owing to its orientation towards the state and protection, industrial capital in these cases can be characterized as the *state-monopolistic generation* in the bourgeoisie. The 'national compartmentalization' of the world economy reached its zenith with the collapse of the world market during the 1930s, forcing even the internationalist British bourgeoisie into imperial retrenchment.

After the Second World War, internationalization again became the dominant tendency in the world economy, manifested through the internationalization of the circuit of productive capital – that is, through the enormous expansion of the activities of multinational corporations. Under the influence of the increasing internationalization of American industrial capital, the outlook of productive capital, typically expressed by the 'state-monopoly tendency', was 'liberalized' both in terms of the national class compromise underpinning it and in the international sphere. This synthesis between classical liberalism and the state-monopoly tendency, termed *corporate liberalism*, was also shared by reformist sections of the working class in Europe. The hegemony of an internationalized New Deal capitalism, based on the Fordist regime of accumulation, eventually vindicated Lenin's observation that ' "American ethics" ... have, in the age of finance capital, become the ethics of every large city in any country' (Lenin, [1917] 1978, p. 55). In the case of Great Britain, the postwar liberalization under American auspices facilitated the restoration of City domination over economic and monetary policy: in fact the City became even more detached from the domestic economy than it had been before. During the nineteenth century, the predominance of the City had been based on the productive superiority of British industry and on the almost absolute British hegemony in the world market. During the interwar years, the predominance of the City (particularly strong until 1932) was based on the domination of Britain in the empire and Commonwealth, and on the central role the financial markets of London played in the circuit of Atlantic capital. At that time it was still thought by many that London could regain its traditional hegemony over world finance. At the end of the Second World War even Keynes for a while thought that this was still possible. It soon became clear that this was not the case. The City could be resurrected partly because legislation in the United States prohibited American banks from deploying their full potential early on. The City's renewed internal dominance was shaped and conditioned by American hegemony in the world system, and by the international spread of Fordism actively pursued through the Marshall plan.

By the mid-1970s, American hegemony, the Keynesian welfare state and the Fordist mode of accumulation were in a triple crisis. The first response to the crisis, which assumed the form of a profitability crisis, on the part of the multinational corporations was to intensify the internationalization, which resulted in what came to be known as the 'new international division of labour'. Gradually, the initiative in this restructuring movement passed to the states in selected Third World countries and international financial institutions funding a wave of 'indebted industrialization' (Frieden, 1981). Eventually, by the late 1970s and early 1980s, the flight forward of international capital came to a grinding halt in the international debt crisis, which forced the international bourgeoisie to reconsider its options, and which confirmed the stranglehold which finance capital (the great banks and the IMF) had established over productive activities around the world. The ideological and political expression of this development was the rise of international neo-liberalism with the election victories of Mrs Thatcher in 1979 and Mr Reagan in 1980.

CHAPTER 2

The rise and fall of British hegemony

The making of the British class structure

In the following two chapters, our analysis will concentrate on the long-term perspective of the secular decline of Britain as a great power. The tone of the debate has been decisively influenced by the publication in 1964 of Perry Anderson's article on 'The origins of the present crisis'. Ever since that date, an important debate has periodically filled the pages of the *New Left Review* regarding the peculiarity of the crisis in Britain and its origins in distant British history. The fundamental question in the debate has been the characterization of British class and state structures, especially in the nineteenth century, and the implications for contemporary Britain. The Anderson/Nairn 'thesis' (also supported more recently by Ingham and by Cain and Hopkins) has thus been very stimulating and fruitful, and still evokes indignant reactions (cf. Brown, 1988).

Let us first summarize the position of Anderson and his colleagues, before trying to assess the extent to which the different positions might be reconciled. The Anderson/Nairn thesis can be summarized in four important British 'peculiarities':

- the nature of the British state;
- the 'fusion' between aristocracy and bourgeoisie;
- the international orientation of the commercial and financial bourgeoisie;
- the 'pre-industrial' ideological outlook of the working class.

These characteristics of the British class structure, shaped in the eighteenth century and reproduced in the nineteenth century, congealed towards the end of the nineteenth century instead of being transformed in the face of the surge of imperialist rivalry threatening Britain's monopolies in the world markets. This was not due to any lack of foresight on the part of a complacent ruling class, but rather to a careful calculation on the part of the hegemonic power bloc. The view that the dominant groups in the British ruling class were somehow unable to understand the signs of the time, that they were socially atavistic, seems inadequate in the face of historical reality: the choices made were, *for the dominant groups*, the ones maximizing profits in the given circumstances. Nevertheless, these choices carried with them implications which would eventually surface in the course of the 1960s as the immediate causes of the 'British disease'.

In the following pages we shall look at the genesis of Britain's 'peculiarities' and try to delineate their precise character and meaning in more detail.

The rise of British capitalism

Towards the end of the seventeenth century, the internal dynamic of English society, and at the same time the dynamic of the emerging capitalist world economy, climaxed in a rapid capitalization of the British economy, first in agriculture, later in industry.

In the countryside, it was the gentry in particular who came to be the torchbearers of the social changes breaking up the old order. Contradictions arose between *rentier* landowners, particularly the peerage, on the one hand, and capitalist farmers (mainly gentry and upper yeomanry) on the other. There was a marked difference in social outlook between these two fractions of the landowning classes. The capitalist farmers, whose entire existence depended on their commercial success, were very competitive and consequently were later to evolve into the main force behind the agricultural revolution. The *rentier* landowners, on the other hand, were not well disposed towards competition, because the management of their estates was not their principal occupation (Scott, 1982, p. 39).

The so-called commercial classes (the bourgeoisie proper) also showed signs of fractionation during the seventeenth century. Towards the end of the century 'there was a tendency for a fraction of extremely wealthy government financiers to be separated from the rest of the commercial class. This fraction – the so-called "moneyed interest" – entered into a profitable alliance with the landed magnates for the purpose of political rulership' (Scott, 1982, p. 43). However, in spite of incipient fractionation of the ruling classes as a result of the rise of agricultural capitalism, there was a fundamental unity of interests *vis-à-vis* what was commonly referred to as the lower orders, the 'meaner sort'

(Moore, 1967, p. 17). After the Glorious Revolution of 1688, the Whigs established a stable political regime which was to last for a century without serious challenge. Throughout the eighteenth century the interlocking between the commercial bourgeoisie and the landed aristocracy remained very close, and England was ruled by a 'committee of landlords'.

The process of the capitalization of agriculture through enclosures and the dispossession of peasants and smallholders went hand in hand with the amassing of wealth derived from foreign trade and colonial enterprise. These two historical processes are the cornerstones of what Marx called the primitive accumulation of capital.

The nature of the British state

The state in England played a central role in this process of the dissolution of feudal relations in agriculture. Nevertheless, the British state never truly became a modern industrial capitalist nation-state. The process of the formation of fairly homogeneous nation-states is a process intimately linked up with the rise of *industrial capitalism*. The early commercial bourgeoisie arose precisely in the towns whose autonomy shielded it from the grip of the feudal aristocracy, and therefore this newly emerging class had very little attachment to land, or to a particular area. In fact, it found its livelihood in providing the commercial links between different semi-autarchic areas, and needed the greatest possible freedom of movement to perform this role. Of course, in the stage of late commercial capitalism, the need for protection of commercial interests from competition has contributed towards the rise of the 'absolutist' state. Heide Gerstenberger has stressed the fact that state functions were executed before the capitalist nation-state existed as such. These 'proto-functions' included the *merkantile Aussenvertretung* (mercantile external representation) of the commercial bourgeoisie on the world market, with its consequent imposition of taxes and genesis of state debt, the legal guarantee of exchange relations, and the violent creation of a proletariat (Gerstenberger, 1973). But these episodes are really only the prehistory of the constitution of the bourgeois nation-state, and concern a state-form adequate to the original accumulation of capital.

It was only with the rise of industrial capitalism that the bourgeoisie was fully 'nationalized'. The 'long' nineteenth century, stretching from the French Revolution to the Treaty of Versailles, is the age of the formation of bourgeois nation-states, particularly in Europe, but also in the New World (the South and North

37

American Civil Wars can also be placed in this context). The regions in Europe formerly consisting of federations of city-states (the Low Countries, Germany, Italy) were also caught up in this process of 'nationalization' of capitalism, together with the 'external' island region of Japan. The most important exceptions (apart from the colonial areas subject to European domination) were Great Britain and Russia. In semi-peripheral Russia the process of industrial capitalist development and of the break-up of the imperial order (unlike the break-up of the Ottoman Empire) was arrested by the October Revolution, which has conserved the multinational Russian Empire in the new form of the multinational Soviet Union.

In hegemonic Great Britain, the multinational, pre-industrial state, which was by comparison with late feudal or absolutist European states quite strongly unified and advanced in the seventeenth and eighteenth centuries, was also retained through the nineteenth and twentieth centuries, precisely because Great Britain so dominated the world markets that the British commercial and financial bourgeoisie could make do with very little *merkantile Aussenvertretung* in the age of industrial capital. The historic consequence of Britain's hegemony on the world markets in the nineteenth century was that the British ruling class never went through the process of 'nationalization' to the same extent as the ruling classes of most of its competitor nations. The British bourgeoisie always pursued its interests in a transnational context (cf. Cain and Hopkins, 1986), whether in the context of the free trade imperialism of the nineteenth century, of the empire and Commonwealth of the first half of the twentieth century, or of the special relations and the integration of the Atlantic economy after 1945. At each crucial junction (both after the First World War with the return to the Gold Standard, and after the Second World War with the restoration of Sterling convertibility with all that that implied) the British bourgeoisie, which had shown tendencies towards prudent 'nationalization' in the preceding crisis-ridden period, was effectively 'denationalized' again, and the hegemony of the internationally oriented historic bloc restored.[1]

The logic of priority

The notion of 'temporal priority' is a key concept in the story of Britain's decline. Although we must avoid the implication of an 'ideal' type of capitalist development against which the British case is measured,[2] 'having been the first' (the first bourgeois revolution, the first industrial power, the first capitalist ruling class, the first industrial proletariat, the first industrial-capitalist hegemonic world power) has left its marks on the class structure, the politico-institutional structure of the British state (with its unwritten and thus in a way non-existent Constitution), and the prevailing ideological climate. 'The distinctive climate of modern British society', writes Tom Nairn,

> is a mercantile, old-bourgeois 'Weltanschauung' and not a neo-capitalist one. Many of its impulses are frankly hostile to 'capitalist' ideas in this narrower, more modern sense; and, of course, this is one important reason why the working class, which has its own motives for hatred of such factory-capitalist virtues, finds traditionalism palatable. (Nairn, 1979, p. 54)

Most successful manufacturers during the first half-century of the Industrial Revolution descended from marginal groups, such as the Quakers, a situation which has persisted up to the present day.

The French Revolution provided an effective shield behind which English manufacturers were able to prosper. The upper classes closed ranks around patriotic slogans against the radicalism threatening their privileges. The Napoleonic Wars and the consequent protection from continental competition allowed English industrial capital to expand rapidly and turn England into the workshop of the world in the following century. During the same decades, the British effectively destroyed all industry (particularly textiles) in India by levying heavy import duties on Indian cotton. It was only when Indian competition had in this way been disposed of that the British manufacturers became free traders. The free trade considered such an integral ingredient of the nineteenth century *Pax Britannica* was thus not a 'natural' development, and needed deliberate intervention by the British state to come into being until as late as the 1830s and 1840s (cf. Polanyi, 1957, pp. 135–41).

The class structure of the Pax Britannica

The struggle with France for hegemony in the world system left an important imprint on the character of British capitalism. *Politically*, the change was not very great: political power remained firmly in the hands of the old power bloc, consisting of the landed aristocracy and the 'moneyed interest'. *Economically*, however, the changes which the years 1789–1815 brought were far-reaching. English industrial capitalism emerged from the Napoleonic Wars clearly as the driving force of British, and indeed world, economic development, first in textiles (particularly cotton), then in railways.

French domination of the continent had driven British industrial and commercial capital to seek expansion across the Atlantic Ocean instead of across the Channel. As a result of French occupation, Holland's role as foremost creditor was also taken over by England. London had, by 1815, replaced Amsterdam as the most important financial centre of the world economy. Britain thus acquired dominance in the financial field as well as in the productive and commercial fields. In the century between 1815 and 1914, Britain was a net capital exporter in all but three years (1840, 1842 and 1847). Total British capital exports in this century amounted to almost \$20 billion[3] (Mikesell, 1962, pp. 35–7). However, the export of capital quickly led to a compensating flow of income from abroad, which in the case of Britain overtook the outflow of new capital from 1875 onwards (Pollard, 1985, p. 493). It should come as no surprise that, on this wave of foreign investments, the 'merchant banks', which specialized in the financing of foreign trade and the funding of foreign government bonds and railway stock, rose to prominence. The merchant bankers, many of foreign origin, 'formed a distinct fraction within the broader commercial class' (Scott, 1982, p. 80). British merchant bankers, most prominently Barings, financed the opening up of the American West. They played an essential role in the economic unification of the United States, and towards the end of the nineteenth century, after the Civil War had resolved the struggle between Southern agricultural and commercial interests and Northern industrial interests in favour of the latter, they enabled the USA to become a serious imperialist rival. Significantly, the role of Barings as the financier *par excellence* of Atlantic trade was by this time taken over by the American financial empire of J. P. Morgan.

The rise of the iron and steel industry on the basis of the export of railway equipment represented a new stage in the development of industrial capitalism in Britain, and was the basis for the rise of a new generation in the industrial bourgeoisie with interests which were quite distinct from the interests of the cotton barons in Lancashire.

> A merchant or trader, even in a quite undeveloped country, can fairly quickly dispose of cotton piecegoods where there is a large population of consumers, and raw materials to be bought in exchange. But railway equipment is an investment. From the very start, the railway-export business involved heavy exports of capital, and often of men too, for the duration of the job. (Brown, 1970, pp. 55–6)

Within the ranks of the bourgeoisie, there developed a split between those in London and the surrounding counties, active in brewing, stock-jobbing, merchanting, warehousing, retailing and shipping, and the manufacturing bourgeoisie concentrated in the north, active in mining and industry. Even here, there soon developed a division between the 'greasy, dirty' activities such as coal mining, iron and steel production, and chemicals, and the 'clean, gentleman-like' industries such as food, drink and tobacco (Anderson, 1987, pp. 34–5).

The expansion of the railway systems at home and in the USA thus brought together the financial community engaged in raising the capital for this enterprise, and the *rentier* landowning class increasingly providing the funds (Scott, 1982, pp. 82–3). Landowners frequently left the management of their estates to tenant farmers, who in turn employed rural labourers, and were thus able to live in the city and pursue other interests such as speculation with urban real estate (cf. Anderson, 1987, pp. 30–1). Throughout the first three-quarters of the century, this power bloc, which became ever more tightly knit, held all the reins of power in what Nairn has aptly described as the 'patrician' British state.

Closely linked to this power bloc were the great maritime companies such as P&O and Cunard, and the commercial and financial interests primarily engaged in the India and China trades such as the Matheson family (Van der Pijl, 1984, pp. 36–7). In the British state apparatus, the Royal Navy and the Colonial Office were the strongholds of 'free-trade imperialism', providing essential support and protection for the economic interests concerned.

The heyday of British industrial capital

The rapid expansion of British naval and industrial power notwithstanding, it took several decades before Britain truly ruled the waves and free trade could be adopted wholeheartedly. From about 1840 onwards, and accelerating after the repeal of the Corn Laws and the Companies Act of 1844, industrial capital expanded swiftly. Between 1850 and 1870 industrial production in Britain doubled. British exports accounted for approximately 40 per cent of world trade (which was about the same as the combined share of France, Germany and the United States), while world trade between 1840 and 1874 increased fivefold (Brown, 1970, p. 62).

British manufacturers shared in the spoils of empire, as transpires from data on the numbers of half-millionaires from different walks of life. Landed wealth still accounted for almost four-fifths of the number of deceased wealth-holders in the period

41

1809–59, but this proportion dropped to half in the years 1858–79, and continued to drop after that. The proportion of 'commercial wealth-holders' increased steadily, and the number of manufacturers among these was quite substantial (Scott, 1982, pp. 87–8). The middle decades of the nineteenth century were a time not only of prosperity but also of social advancement for industrial capitalists all around. In the large industrial cities such as Manchester, Birmingham and Leeds, industrial capital expressed its political interests through the newly formed chambers of commerce. Industrial capital particularly showed its strength in the successful campaign to repeal the Corn Laws.[4] The rise of manufacturing capital was also represented in the important changes in the political and social structure of the country. The manufacturers pressed succesfully for the amendment of the Poor Law (revised in 1834), which had hitherto prevented the full rise of an industrial working class on whose unimpeded availability they depended (Polanyi, 1957, p. 137).

The electoral reform of 1832, which brought a certain measure of popular influence, was another important milestone: eventually it led to the establishment of two separate bourgeois political parties. From their first headquarters, the Carlton Club, the Tories built their party into the mouthpiece of landed interests, and consequently condemned themselves to almost thirty years of opposition during the period of industrialist ascendancy (Gamble, 1974, pp. 16–17; Blake, 1985, pp. 1–28). The Liberal Party, operating from the Reform Club set up in 1836, dominated the period between the 1830s and the 1860s: the Whigs supported the campaign for the repeal of the protectionist Corn Laws, and by doing so became the spokesmen for the interests of the industrial- and free-trade-oriented bourgeoisie. Consequently, industrial and commercial capitalists played a prominent role in the Liberal Party, and the Rothschilds and several representatives of Jardine Matheson, for example, sat among the Liberals. When John Vincent speaks of the 'heroic element in Parliamentary Liberalism, its Radical industrialists', he refers to about three dozen industrialists who

> sighed for a higher and better civilization, which they conceived chiefly in terms of the material welfare of the labouring classes, and saw in Liberal politics a chief means of achieving this ... [They] defined their Liberalism in terms of social welfare more than did any other group in the party – more prominently than the working-class leaders themselves. (Vincent, 1972, p. 74)

However, the Liberal Party in this period was by no means composed chiefly of industrialists: aristocrats were the largest single group among the Liberal MPs, although their predominance in the case of the Tories was much greater.[5] The political activity of industrial capitalists was usually restricted to the local level. The local chambers of commerce in such industrial centres as Manchester, Birmingham, Glasgow, Belfast and Leeds were the most important organizational focus of these activities (Scott, 1982, p. 98), but at the national level the representation of industrial capitalists was and remained minimal.[6]

Although two different political parties arose in the middle of the nineteenth century broadly expressing the interests of separate fractions of the capitalist ruling class, the distinction did not become exclusive, and never led to a rigorous social divide between landed, moneyed and manufacturing interests. On the contrary, the nineteenth century was marked by an 'osmosis between business and the landed aristocracy' (Moore, 1967, p. 36). There was a great deal of intermarriage between members of the old and new ruling classes, the educational system was reorganized in order to allow the bourgeoisie to take up its rightful place and provide its children with a 'gentlemanly' education, and commercial interests tended to merge: capitalists bought into land – first financiers and merchants, later industrialists – and landed aristocrats became more and more involved in commercial and financial activities.

Certain distinctions persisted, however, and these were later to prove quite important. Within the bourgeois class, the distinction between industrial capitalists on the one hand, and others (merchants and financiers first of all, but people such as plantation owners and brewers as well) on the other, continued to exert its influence, and was to gain importance in the face of growing foreign competition after the 1860s.

Until the 1860s industrial capital in Britain had expanded rapidly and had in fact built up the basis upon which financiers and merchants could also expand. However, British manufacturers never extended their predominance into the social, cultural and ideological fields. Eventually even their economic predominance was to suffer: the last major technological breakthrough to have been effected by British industry dates back to the 1860s, in the steel industry (Burn, 1940). The heyday of industrial capital in Britain must therefore be situated in the middle decades of the nineteenth century, and effectively came to an end in the early 1860s. The British industrial bourgeoisie had not been able to transform its economic predominance into a hegemonic position in the power bloc, and failed to initiate the structural innovations that would have been able to contribute to the reproduction of its economic predominance (cf. Leys, 1985, pp. 21–3).

The aristocratization of the bourgeoisie

From the 1860s onwards, the children of the manufacturers showed a growing tendency to enter an 'aristocratic' career. This development was facilitated by the fact that the industrial bourgeoisie gained access for its children to the public schools to which the greater part of the aristocracy also sent its children. This was of great importance, since 'the criterion for inclusion in the hegemonic class is ... socialization in the "regulating institutions of assimilation" – the public schools' (Anderson, 1966, p. 13n). The impulse to emulate the lifestyle of the aristocracy was thus strongly reinforced (cf. Wiener, 1981).

The gradual acceptance of the industrial bourgeoisie by the older fractions of the ruling class was shown by its increased participation in Parliament. By 1885, 38 per cent of MPs were from industry and commerce, against 32 per cent from the professions, 12 per cent from the forces, and 16 per cent from the landowning class (Scott, 1982, p. 105). As a consequence, the proportion of new peerages awarded to representatives of the bourgeoisie (albeit primarily commercial and financial) rose as well. In the years around 1840, 10 per cent of new peers were non-landowners; after the turn of the century, this proportion had risen to 43 per cent (Scott, 1982, p. 109). The social advance of manufacturers at the more modest level of knighthood was even stronger: between the 1880s and the First World War the number of knighthoods awarded to men from business and the professions trebled (Scott, 1982, p. 110).

The 'aristocratization' of the British bourgeoisie[7] proceeded so harmoniously because of Britain's early and therefore slow industrialization. The aristocracy (the class of capitalist land-owners) survived the industrial bourgeois onslaught, while the bourgeoisie gained access to political power and social status, because there was a process of mutual adaptation. 'In return for accepting the hegemony of the values and life-style of the landed class, the most prominent manufacturers were to be admitted as full members of the status group of "gentlemen" ' (Scott, 1982, p. 104). The result of this process of mutual adaptation was the implantation within the bourgeoisie of the idea that industry was an occupation to be fled as soon as possible. The acquisition of an estate (for status purposes) and of a position in finance or trade, or in the state apparatus (particularly in the Navy,

Colonial Office or Foreign Office), and later in the professions, by the middle of the century replaced the original manufacturing activity. The remaining impulses to British industrial innovation came from socially marginal groups such as Quakers, Jews, and immigrants, especially from central Europe. Some of what became the largest British companies were founded by immigrants (Imperial Chemical Industries, for example, was founded by a German, Alfred Mond).[8] In so far as British capitalists were still investing in industry, they concentrated on trade and distribution, infrastructure (such as railways), and extractive industries such as mining and plantations. British capitalists had grown 'wary of close involvement in the vulgar ... business of making things' (Tylecote, 1982, p. 45). Even successful marginal manufacturers soon switched to such gentlemanlike occupations as banking (the Quaker banking families Barclays and Tukes, for example) as Barratt Brown inadvertently reminds us (Brown, 1988, p. 30).

The genesis of Britain's late-nineteenth-century class structure is to be understood as a complex process of class formation. The introduction of capitalism in Britain proceeded because certain fractions of the feudal aristocracy adopted capitalist modes of agricultural production in response to the demand for wool in Flanders. In their struggle against remaining feudal and royal prerogatives, these capitalist landlords led the way in the formation of a new *historic bloc* arising out of the coalition between landed and commercial/financial capitalists. The comprehensive concept of control to which this historic bloc subscribed – that is, its definition of the general interest – was still largely defined in aristocratic terms: it was formulated before the Industrial Revolution propelled the industrial manufacturers into an economically prominent place. In this manner, the process of capitalist class formation acquired aristocratic overtones which could persist because of Britain's supremacy in the world markets during most of the nineteenth century.

The industrial bourgeoisie shared one common interest with the fractions represented in the ruling coalition: the effective subordination of the working classes, both agrarian and industrial. This common interest provided the main basis (besides the industrial expansion facilitated by the fact that Britain was 'the workshop of the world') for the 'compensations' which induced the industrial bourgeoisie to accept its subordinate position. This was clearly shown in 1848, the year of European revolution, when aristocracy and bourgeoisie united in the defeat of the Chartist movement.

Britain's imperial decline

The crisis of British capitalism as it revealed itself from the late 1860s onwards is also, and especially, the crisis of the specific underlying structure of an archaic state and the class system which protects it. The historic bloc in England has been, since the English Revolution, the coalition between the (originally agrarian) aristocracy and the 'middle class', the non-industrial part of the bourgeoisie. The central elements of the comprehensive concept of control supported by this coalition were: the capitalization of agriculture; the common class interest *vis-à-vis* the working class; and the successful expansion of the empire, at first largely informally, and then, from the 1870s, formally, in response to growing inter-imperialist rivalry.

The industrial bourgeoisie was unable to maintain the momentum of its mid-century rise which had found its expression in the repeal of the Corn Laws, and instead found itself locked up in the straitjacket of the 'patrician state'. Instead of adapting to the new competition on the world market, the ruling classes in England responded by strengthening their hold over the state, and by formalizing the empire.

> During the very period when industrial backwardness began to present itself as an inescapable problem, between the 1870s and 1914, and foreign competition began to overwhelm England's economy, the archaic mould of society and state was greatly reinforced there ... the ruling elite compensated by extended control of the world's money market by building up a financial centre in the City of London ... Thus, one part of the capital of England was in effect converted into an 'offshore island' of international capitalism, to a considerable degree independent of the nation's declining domestic capitalism. (Nairn, 1977, pp. 23–4)

What was at work here was the 'logic of priority': precisely because England was the first country to industrialize, the industrialization was incomplete, and the power bloc compensated for this 'failure' by extraversion, by one-sided external expansion through the vehicle of 'liberal City-imperialism'.

The decline of Britain definitively set in during the decades after the 1860s. Industrial production in Britain doubled between 1870 and 1913; in Germany, industrial production increased fivefold in the same period, while in Russia the increase was ninefold. In 1870, Britain still produced more than Germany, Russia and France combined. By 1880, these three countries together had surpassed Britain, in 1893 Germany alone already produced more steel than Britain, and in 1913 German steel production was more than twice as high as British steel production (cf. Mitchell, 1978).

The British reaction to this did not take the form of a vigorous drive for industrial modernization. Instead, the British upper classes seemed 'inherently bound to find the "imperial" alternative more attractive than the "industrial" one' (Tylecote, 1982, p. 47). The empire provided protected markets which Britain could continue to keep largely for itself even when its productive superiority had long since been lost. In this way the very fact of hegemony 'impeded the structural reorganization necessary to emerge strengthened on the other side of the late nineteenth-century downturn' (Bergesen, 1982, p. 32). Foreign competition and foreign protectionism notwithstanding, the dominant sections of the British ruling class clung to their free-trade posture, convinced that their enormous colonial, commercial and financial advantages could withstand the onslaught of imperialist rivalry.

The protection of the sea routes, trading posts, and colonial state apparatuses necessary for the continuation of British imperialism, even in its free-trade version of most of the nineteenth century, of course came at a cost. Indeed, the cost to British society as a whole may have surpassed the gains. By the end of the century the income from foreign and colonial trade amounted to £18 million, and the income from foreign investments £90–£100million (Hobson, [1902] 1968, pp. 55–6). British expenditure on armaments and war exceeded £69 million in 1900 (Hobson, [1902] 1968, p. 65). British taxpayers thus in fact subsidized the income of the British investors. As John A. Hobson remarked, 'increasing public expenditure, apart from all political justification, is a direct source of gain to certain well-organized and influential interests, and to all such Imperialism is the chief instrument of such increasing expenditure' (Hobson [1902] 1968, pp. 96–7).

The issue of mounting nationalism, dialectically expressed in the rise of Germany, Italy and Japan and the intensification of inter-imperialist rivalry on the world markets, caught up with 'multinational' Britain in two complementary ways.

On the one hand, nationalism swept through Britain's nearest colony, Ireland. The Irish question very nearly caused the breakdown of the state order of the UK, and it brought down the Liberal Party. On the other hand, Britain too was affected by a strong social imperialist movement, attempting to integrate the working class into the effort to expand and consolidate the empire and

47

safeguard its markets against foreign competition (Gamble, 1981, pp. 170–4). The basis for the concept of social imperialism had been laid in 1867 when Disraeli developed the slogan of 'One Nation'. With this slogan, the Tories were able to break out of the limitations which their narrow class base as the party representing the landed interest had imposed on them. The electoral reforms forced the Tories to develop their own version of a general interest, and this Disraeli did through his 'One Nation' project. From then on, the Tories could claim to be a *national* party. It was Joseph Chamberlain who expanded the 'One Nation' project into a fully fledged social imperialist strategy in the 1880s and 1890s. The fact that the Liberals had split over the Irish question gave the social imperialist forces the upper hand in the formulation of government policy.

The exchange of certain tariff preferences between Great Britain and Canada, later followed by other dominions, in 1898, showed that Britain had joined the ranks of its aggressive imperialist competitors (Bukharin, [1917] 1972, pp. 77–8).[9] In this period there was increased activity by such pro-imperialist organizations as the Imperial Federation League and the United Empire League. The protectionist movement found a strong leader in Joseph Chamberlain. In a speech in 1896 as Secretary of State for the Colonies, Chamberlain confirmed the role the state played, or at least would have to play, in the defence of imperialist interests:

> all the great Offices of State are occupied with commercial affairs. The Foreign Office and the Colonial Office are chiefly engaged in finding new markets and defending old ones. The War Office and the Admiralty are mostly occupied in preparations for the defence of these markets and for the protection of our commerce ... that Government deserves most popular approval which does most to increase our trade and to settle it on a firm foundation. (quoted in Woolf, 1919, p. 7)

But Bukharin had been too anxious to demonstrate the tendency towards 'nationalization' of the world economy. Eventually, the discussion about protectionism vs. free trade was decided in favour of the free traders. Between 1903 and 1906 free trade liberalism prevailed, and financial and commercial capital maintained its predominance over industrial capital. With the movement for tariff reform in 1905, 'the political hour of heavy industry seemed finally to strike', but the movement was defeated because it was unable to gain the support of the old liberal capitalists in such industries as textiles, coal and shipbuilding, who at this time 'remained loyal to Free Trade', (Anderson, 1987, p. 43; see also Cain and

Hopkins, 1987, p.7). Only in the 1930s, when Britain could no longer ward off the pressures of imperialist competition, was this old liberal fraction of the bourgeoisie temporarily subordinated to the fractions favouring protection.

In the case of Great Britain, continued adherence to the principles of free trade in the face of protectionist competition abroad spelled disaster. As Polanyi remarked, *laissez-faire* economic liberalism consisted of three elements:

> The three tenets – competitive labor market, automatic gold standard, and international free trade – formed one whole. The sacrifices involved in achieving any one of them were useless, if not worse, unless the other two were equally secured. It was everything or nothing. (Polanyi, 1957, p. 138)

For the time being however the British bourgeoisie continued its internationalization strategy based on the gold standard and adherence to free trade, although in fact international trade was no longer free. The City was satisfied only with the whole globe as its operational terrain, and would not accept the limitation of its operation to the formal boundaries of the empire (cf. Brown, 1988, p. 33).

British foreign investment

The cohesion of Britain's empire rested on British trade and on British overseas investments, especially in the Atlantic area. Before 1870, most British capital exports went to countries or areas outside the British Empire (especially to the United States and Europe). After 1870, the geographical distribution of British foreign investment gradually changed. In the decade 1860–70, 36 per cent of British investments had gone to the countries of the empire; this percentage rose to 47 per cent in the years 1901–10. Of the funds going to the empire, the percentage going to the White Dominions (Canada, Australia, New Zealand and South Africa) increased from one-third to two-thirds. At the same time the part of investment going to America declined from 27 to 21 per cent, while the share going to Europe dropped from 25 per cent to no more than 5 per cent (Brown, 1970, p. 110). Whether British investment went mostly to the colonies or to other areas (such as the United States and South America) is largely irrelevant when one is trying to ascertain whether or not British foreign investments have been harmful to domestic industry. This question is directly relevant for one of the central themes of this book: the relations between the different fractions of capital, in this case primarily those between the City and British industry.

As already mentioned, the outward flow of capital during this period was enormous. The weight of British foreign investment in the nineteenth and early twentieth centuries can hardly be overestimated. Authoritative estimates about the share in total British capital holdings by British capital abroad vary from 28 per cent (by Hobson and Feis) to 43 per cent by Cairncross (Pollard, 1985, p. 491). British overseas investments in 1870 accounted for over 60 per cent of all international investments. In 1914 the British share still stood at 44 per cent (Pollard, 1985, p. 492). As for absolute figures, in 1914 British foreign investments amounted to £4,100 million, French foreign investment amounted to £1,900 million (20 per cent), German foreign investment was £1,200 million (13 per cent), and American foreign investment ran up to £700 million (7 per cent) (Kenwood and Lougheed, 1983, p. 41).

What were the sources of these capital exports? For one thing, they did not arise out of a trade surplus: the nineteenth century shows a consistent balance of trade deficit, which grew from an annual average of around £10 million between 1815 and 1825 to an annual average of £175 million during the years 1901–5 (Brown, 1970, p. 75).

Before the 1870s, there was a net outflow of new capital from Britain. Capital exports at that time were at least partly financed out of domestic profits. On the other hand, the flow of foreign investment gave rise to a corresponding flow of investment income. After the early 1870s the inflow of capital (in the form of dividends, interest payments and amortization) generally surpassed the outflow: new foreign investments were now financed out of the income from earlier foreign investments. In the decade of the 1870s, net foreign lending amounted to £544 million, while net property income from abroad amounted exactly to the same amount; in the years 1900–13, net foreign lending had risen to £1,650 million, and net property income from abroad had risen to £1,988 million (Pollard, 1985, pp. 493–4).

This investment income, which contributed to an overvaluation of the pound, concealed the steady loss of competitiveness of British industry because it prevented balance of payments deficits from developing into urgent political problems (cf. Parboni, 1981, p. 97).

One important consequence of the enormous export of capital and the return flow of investment income was that the City of London became fully geared to the provision of commercial and financial services not just to British merchants and investors, but to merchants and investors the world over. This was a logical consequence of the fact of British productive supremacy rather than of any conscious effort by the British state to establish monetary hegemony. The maintenance of this role for the City after imperialist competition stiffened from the 1860s onwards did, however, require state intervention in the form of the formalization of the empire. The Sterling balances which the colonies were required to accumulate ensured continued British control, particularly over the trade surpluses of India and over South Africa's gold (Ingham, 1984, pp. 96–127).

The City was so internationally oriented that the *Economist* in 1911 complained that 'London was more concerned with the course of events in Mexico than with what happened in the Midlands' (quoted in Pollard, 1985, p. 500). The amount of capital raised by industrial firms on the London capital markets in the years 1911–13 covered only 10 per cent of manufacturing industry's capital needs, and this sum of £5 million per annum represented less than 3 per cent of British capital export in these years (Pollard, 1985, p. 500). There is considerable agreement that the financial structure in Britain was unfavourable for domestic industrial expansion. The provincial banks, traditionally close to industry, were subjected to the dominance and discipline of the City, and through that to the discipline of the international financial markets (Ingham, 1984, pp. 166–7). Finance capital, the *national* coalescence of industrial and banking capital in the form of holding companies, did not develop in Britain (cf. Overbeek, 1980), and this led to dissatisfaction among industrial capitalists over their access to credits.[10]

The relative weight of City interests in the concrete configuration of the British ruling class tended to be reflected in a concept of control based on the money-capital concept and pervaded with liberal internationalism, which clearly induced bankers to neglect domestic possibilities in favour of foreign undertakings. And even if these overseas investments were of an industrial nature, as Barratt Brown (1988, pp. 30, 36) rather unconvincingly argues, the effect upon the *domestic* balance of forces would be largely the same: they strengthened the commercial and financial interests, and weakened the industrial interest *in Britain*.

The incorporation of the labour movement
Because Great Britain was the first country to industrialize, it was the first country to see the growth of an industrial proletariat, and was also the first country where trade unions were able to

secure some minimal legal protection and recognition. However, trade unionism arose before industrial production in Britain had entered the stage of mechanized factory production. The organizational structure remained primarily based on crafts, and not on industry-wide representation. Trade unions were not, by and large, a 'national' phenomenon, making demands on the national political institutions of the state. This has had far-reaching implications for labour relations in the UK. Precisely because the working class was locked out, because no fraction of the power bloc had any serious interest in a coalition with the working class, traditions of class co-operation, other than on the shopfloor, were hardly established at all, and remained confined to small segments of the working class where they were established (cf. Kilpatrick and Lawson, 1980).

The second half of the nineteenth century saw the emergence of an industrial proletariat, a class of factory workers, who joined the earlier sections of the working class, the artisans who had completely dominated the first half of the century and remained an important part of the working class until well into the interwar period. This first large proletariat was also the first to secure a number of basic trade union rights. The process of recognition of working-class rights was not the result of any clear bourgeois strategy, but rather came about by constant concessions without disturbing the overarching order of the British state (cf. Gamble, 1981, p. 83).

The official recognition of trade union rights came with the 1871 Trade Union Act; the Trades Union Congress (TUC) doubled its membership in the years 1869–73, from 250,000 to 510,000 (Kilpatrick and Lawson, 1980, p. 86). The following two decades saw the steady rise of real wages: the working class was deflected from radical confrontation through the benefits of social imperialism, which included not just higher wages but increased possibilities for emigration to different parts of the empire as well.[11]

The early recognition of working-class rights precluded the emergence of a revolutionary tendency in the labour movement. It also facilitated the preservation of trade union structures and practices which had largely originated in the proto-industrial stage of capitalist development, before the stage of mass production which was introduced in Britain in the 1920s. This led to a peculiar combination of trade union characteristics: a high degree of industrial organization, great workplace strength, and decentralized bargaining, but also the continuation of craft union practices and a serious political weakness at the national level (cf. Kilpatrick and Lawson, 1980, pp. 87–8; Anderson, 1987, pp. 49–50).

It was only in the course of the 1890s that the relation between capital and labour on the organizational level became more strained. The campaign by the employers against union strength resulted in the famous Taff Vale decision of 1901 which rescinded the legal union rights which had been won thirty years earlier. This finally induced the TUC to establish the Labour Representation Committee, thus transmitting working-class demands to the political level for the first time. Thus emerged the threat of a political organization of the working class, aggravated by the extension of the vote to a large part of this class. The increasing separation between civil society and state which this development implied made clear the necessity for the ruling class to develop a comprehensive concept of control – a notion of the general interest in which the working class could find compensation for its social and economic deprivations.

This political crisis, which concerned the accommodation of bourgeois rule to the rise of a mass party of the working class, was resolved in and by the First World War, which established the contours of the later social democratic welfare state (cf. Leys, 1986, pp. 231–2; also Middlemas, 1979). The basis for this development was laid by the Liberal government which came to power in 1906. Between 1906 and 1913, a whole series of Acts was passed, ranging from legislation on school lunches to unemployment pay and from accident insurance to trade union rights. To these measures, the name of David Lloyd George is particularly connected. It was his vision, his concept of *control*, which aimed at defusing the dangers of the rise of a socialist mass movement through large-scale social reforms, which aimed to satisfy a number of working-class demands without endangering the rule of capital and the protection of private property rights.

During the war, this development was taken an important step further in the sense that it brought the direct integration of the Labour Party into the state through its representation in Parliament, the extension of social security, and the expansion of the scope of state intervention in the economy. The Labour Party was thus committed to the fortunes of British capitalism through social imperialism and nationalism.

The wartime needs for planning and state co-ordination meant that the days of the nightwatch state, if they had ever existed, were certainly over after 1914. Stringent controls were imposed over the most important industrial sectors, the first import duties (the McKenna duties of 1915) were levied, and in response to the stimulus from the government, British employers organized for the first time: the Federation of British Industries (FBI) was founded in 1916.

The war also induced the traditional ruling elites to become more co-operative *vis-à-vis* the working class whose allegiance to the needs of the nation (and the empire) was badly needed. During the five years of the war, TUC membership almost doubled (from 1.6 million to over 3 million), and the Labour share of the popular vote increased from 7.7 per cent in the last prewar election in 1910 to 23.9 per cent in 1918 (Beer, 1969, pp. 145–6).

The war further fostered the tendency toward concentration and centralization of capital to such a degree that a Standing Committee on Trusts was installed which reported (in 1918) that 'oligopolistic trends existed widely in the British economy and would soon "control all important branches of British trade" ' (quoted by Harris, 1972, p. 39).

The productive apparatus in Britain, particularly heavy industry, was greatly expanded during the war, and also immediately after, in order to cope with the demand that had built up during the war. This expansion of productive capacity (essentially on the prewar technical basis) led to enormous overcapacity and to heavy debts in industrial enterprises. The ensuing depression of 1919–21 led on the one hand to a large increase in mergers and takeovers: in this period 234 firms disappeared annually in this way, with a total value of over £300 million; this was approximately four times as much as in the preceding three-year period, and twice as much as in the following three-year period (Aaronovitch and Sawyer, 1975, p. 124). On the other hand, the big banks (after a process of rapid concentration in the preceding decades only five independent big clearing banks had survived) became involved in the management of those industrial companies – in particular the railway companies – so heavily in their debt (Stanworth and Giddens, 1975, p. 12).[12]

Centralization of capital and bank involvement in industry notwithstanding, important differences remained as to the most desirable internationalization strategy for British capital. This debate was not restricted to the question of free trade vs. protection, but also extended to imperial policy in more general terms, and to the problem of how to handle the working class, which became more radical under the impact of the revolutionary movements on the European continent.

The two most obvious strategies with respect to Britain's relations with the empire (economically, politically and militarily) were those of imperial protection and of resumed free trade imperialism. Although the British ruling class clung to the maintenance of the empire and clearly expected to return to business as usual, the immediate prewar period and the war itself had already established the fact that Britain would not be able militarily to guarantee the integrity of the empire. As First Lord of the Admiralty, Churchill had told Australia and New Zealand in 1914 that, should the worst come to the worst, 'the only course of the five millions of white men in the Pacific would be to seek the protection of the United States', and a few years later a Canadian author summed up the state of affairs: 'All roads in the Commonwealth lead to Washington' (both quoted in Barraclough, 1967, p. 73). The 'dwarfing of Europe' relative to its two flanking powers (Russia and the United States) had become irreversible. The ambiguous relationship between Britain and the United States which would dominate the years after 1941 had thus already been established thirty years earlier: Britain depended upon the US for the ultimate protection of its imperial interests, but would have to pay a heavy price for that protection, viz., the admittance of the US into most of its sphere of influence.

This strategic debate over Britain's international position after 1919 eventually concentrated on the question of whether or not Britain should return to the Gold Standard, which had collapsed in 1914. The end of the war brought the first of many balance of payments crises, which now sharpened the contradictions between domestic industrial capital and the financial and commercial interests in the City. The City strongly backed the return to gold, which was necessary for its leading role in international finance, in which American capital was making rapid headway now that the US had become an important creditor nation. A large majority in the FBI on the other hand opposed this step, which would entail a revaluation of Sterling by at least 10 per cent, because this policy would be detrimental to British industrial exports. Instead, the FBI favoured a policy directed at protection of Commonwealth markets (Winch, 1972, p. 128).

The City prevailed in this strategic confrontation, and the Chancellor of the Exchequer, Winston Churchill, embarked on a course of deflation aimed at restoring the international value of Sterling to its prewar level. British industry, and in particular those older branches that had provided the bulk of British industrial exports since the nineteenth century, was hit hard, and attempted to transfer the costs of this policy to their workforce (cf. Dunford and Perrons, 1983, pp. 309–10).

The downfall of the Liberal Party

The early postwar years brought the demise of the Liberal Party as an alternative governing party in Britain. The aftermath of the war and conjunctural effects have played an important role in this decline (cf. Wilson, 1966). However, the more structural factor was that, given the extension of the popular vote and given the rise of the Labour Party (which the Liberals could no longer contain as they had done in the late nineteenth and early twentieth centuries), the British electoral system only left room for one bourgeois political party: the Labour Party would sooner or later easily win a comfortable majority if the non-socialist vote were split down the middle between Liberals and Conservatives. As it turned out, the social imperialist programme of the Tories proved better able than the reform policies of the Liberals to constitute the core of a comprehensive concept of control which would enable the ruling class to remain so politically.

In the 1922 election the Liberals (Independents and Coalition Liberals together) gained 31 seats from the Tories, and only 2 from Labour, while losing 34 seats to the Tories, and 48 to Labour: during this election, therefore, the Liberals lost almost one-third of their seats (165 in 1918, 116 in 1922) to Labour, while maintaining a rough balance with the Tories. The elections of 1923 brought gains for the Liberals: 158 Liberals were elected, because of a net gain of 53 seats from the Conservatives, and a further net loss of 10 seats to Labour. Clearly, the Liberals continued to lose to Labour, while the balance with the Conservatives was unstable. The final blow for the Liberals came in the 1924 election, which brought them a net loss to Labour of only 8 seats, but a net loss to the Conservatives of 107 seats (Wilson, 1966, pp. 393–4). From now on, the Liberal Party could no longer pretend to be an alternative bourgeois governing party; the struggles between competing concepts of control would henceforth be fought out *within* the Conservative Party.

The Conservative Party, which now established itself definitively as the political party of the ruling class, was divided over the strategy to be followed in the face of the intensification of working-class struggle. Three fractions within the Conservative Party struggled for dominance (Gamble, 1981, p. 92):

(1)   the 'confrontationist' fraction, represented by Lord Birkenhead, wanted to smash the Labour Party completely;
(2)   the 'social imperialist' fraction, led by Leo Amery, aimed at the formation of a 'national' movement transcending class boundaries on the basis of a more strongly knit 'Commonwealth and empire';[13]
(3)   the 'corporatist' fraction, led by Stanley Baldwin, followed the strategy of the incorporation of the Labour Party and the TUC into the organs of the state.

The struggle between these fractions was to be decided in a matter of a few years, in which the militant tendency in the British working class was annihilated through a mixture of confrontation and incorporation.

Towards the General Strike

The result of the prevalence of the classic liberal economic preferences of money capital in the postwar years was a period of violent class struggle in Britain. 'The 1920s saw the prestige of economic liberalism at its height ... No private suffering, no infringement of sovereignty, was deemed too great a sacrifice for the recovery of monetary integrity' (Polanyi, 1957, p. 142). During the war, which was being fought at their expense (through a decline of real wages by one-fifth and through curtailment of their recently acquired union rights), the British workers had begun to organize on a larger scale: in 1913 trade union membership had stood at 4 million, in 1919 this figure had doubled to 8 million. It was in this period that the shop steward movement arose and amassed such power that Lloyd George was for some time afraid that the workers would establish a system of Soviets (workers' councils) following the example of the revolutionaries in Russia (Glyn and Sutcliffe, 1972).

As so often later, the coal miners would prove to be both the vanguard of radicalism and the main victims of the ruling-class victory in the confrontation. In the coal industry, worker militancy reached its zenith during the campaign for the nationalization of the coal mines and for higher wages and shorter hours, especially when the government-appointed Sankey Commission supported the demand for nationalization. In March 1921, the government announced that it would not follow the recommendations of the commission, which encouraged the mine owners to cut wages. The miners went on strike, but eventually lost, partly for lack of outside support. From then on, wage cuts, lengthening of working hours, strikes, and police action to break them, were a daily affair. In the years 1920–4, average nominal wages declined by 38 per cent; in the period 1919–26 the annual average number of days lost because of strikes and lockouts amounted to 40 million (Allen, 1972, p. 106).

In this period of vehement class struggle unemployment never sank below 10 per cent of the work force, which emphasizes the offensive nature of working-class militancy in these years. During the short-lived Labour government of 1924–5, there was some respite, but the Tory government of Prime Minister Stanley

Baldwin and Chancellor of the Exchequer Winston Churchill pursued such a rigorously deflationary policy that it forced the trade union movement to take a desperate step: the General Strike of 1926 was the result. It seemed at the time that Britain was on the brink of revolution. The *British Gazette* (for which Churchill was responsible) declared: 'There can be no compromise of any kind. Either the country will break the General Strike or the General Strike will break the country' (quoted in Gamble, 1981, p. 253n).

The TUC leadership and a great part of the rank and file lacked the determination to carry the General Strike through. The years since the start of the war had instilled an incipient attitude of class co-operation in several industrial sectors, which affected the willingness of the workers in these industries to participate in a prolonged General Strike. Further, the TUC leadership had to some extent been co-opted into the national councils and was unwilling to risk wholesale defections by dissatisfied union members. As a consequence, the TUC's leadership undertook no serious mobilizing efforts, and after just a few days withdrew its support for the movement. The period of fierce class struggle of the early 1920s came rapidly to an end. The miners held out for six more months, but were in the end forced to accept the terms of the employers. The General Strike in a sense represented at once the climax of this intensified class confrontation and also its end. The defeat of the strike movement removed the obstacles to the return to the Gold Standard by making possible mass redundancies, wage cuts, and longer working days. The workers' movement was defeated: the number of strikes dwindled and union membership was almost halved to 4 million within a few years.

With the 1927 Trade Disputes and Trade Unions Act the government cashed in its victory. Sympathy strikes and strikes intended to impose hardship on the community were outlawed, and the system established by Labour and the TUC by which union members automatically paid a political levy to the Labour Party unless they opted out was changed into a 'contracting-in' system. Finally, civil service unions were prohibited from affiliating to the Labour Party or the TUC (Hain, 1986, p. 83–4). In this way, the stage was set for the emergence in the labour movement of 'responsible elements' as they were called by the Conservatives and the bourgeois press, or by reformist and corporatist elements as their position can also be characterized. The defeat in the General Strike and the ensuing changes that were effected in the balance of forces in the working class created the conditions determining the shape of British politics in the following decade.

CHAPTER 3

Between New Deal and fascism: depression, war and transition in Britain

The Great Crash of 1929 led to intensified international trade conflicts, eventually culminating in the abolition of the Gold Standard and the establishment of rivalling and in some cases protectionist trading blocs.

The internal socio-economic and political responses to this breakdown of the international capitalist economy varied greatly between different capitalist countries (Gourevitch, 1986). In Germany extremely protectionist and counter-cyclical economic policies were combined with reactionary political and social practices and nearly full militarization. In the United States and Sweden, on the other hand, political liberalism was combined with the first prototype of the welfare state and with a strong orientation toward international free trade (particularly after 1936). In Great Britain, economic policy throughout the depression could be characterized as 'neo-orthodox': protectionist but pro-cyclical (currency devaluation, tariffs, cartellization). Traditional orthodox liberal solutions were not followed to the full in any of the important capitalist countries.

The debates over the desired response to the great crisis and the surge of protectionism signalled the arrival of a new dominant class coalition in the capitalist world. The coalition of the first two generations of the bourgeoisie, the *financial/commercial aristocracy* hegemonic since the beginning of the nineteenth century, and the old *liberal bourgeoisie* dominating the first wave of industrialization in Britain in textiles and coal, had still prevailed in the struggle over the return to the Gold Standard. The old staple industries, however, were not able to restore their prewar prosperity, both because of the changed structure of world demand and because of their diminished competitiveness. When the crisis hit, these industries were so severely affected that the old liberal bourgeoisie could not effectively defend its position.

Instead, on the wave of protectionism engulfing the globe, a third generation of the British bourgeoisie came to the fore: the

59

state monopoly bourgeoisie, – that is, the iron and steel capitalists (and other heavy industrialists) with their almost 'natural' preferences for restriction of competition and protection and their dependence on state orders and state backing. This newly prominent fraction of the British bourgeoisie was able to claim a share of power as a result of the development of global capitalism in the 1930s. From 1931 until the advent of the Second World War it occupied a relatively strong position *vis-à-vis* the City, whose room for manoeuvre and general influence suffered from the conditions pertaining both at home and abroad.

The position of the emerging *corporate liberal bourgeoisie* based in the industries producing mass consumer goods, which had crystallized during the 1920s, developed rather ambivalently. Economic development behind protective tariffs favoured the new mass production branches, which boomed during the 1930s (the so-called Depression Boom). As these new branches developed, their share in overall employment also grew; the impact of the new sections of the working class thus arising in the overall composition and outlook of the labour movement was considerable, and strengthened reformist tendencies. However, conditions were such that Great Britain did not experience a New Deal. As we shall see, the corporate-liberal bourgeoisie proved unable to articulate its fractional interests into a concept of control that could also express the interests of other fractions of the bourgeoisie or of the working classes.

The turn to protectionism

The Great Crash of 1929, followed by a turn towards protectionism in the world economy, acutely undermined the conditions for the international expansion of British capital which had been restored at such cost to their position before the First World War. The redefinition of Britain's position in the world economy had already been debated, but these debates now suddenly acquired an urgency unknown before. The outcome of the struggle over protectionism, and over the *form* of protectionism that should be adopted, would be decisive for the industrial structure in Britain and for the degree to which industrial modernization would take place in Britain.

The most eloquent defenders of protection were to be found in the Conservative Party. The thought of protective tariffs was not alien to the Conservative tradition (Beer, 1969, pp. 282–7): at the beginning of the century, Joseph Chamberlain had campaigned for the adoption of protectionist measures. However, in spite of these tendencies, the free trade orientation prevailed. In 1924 the

Empire Industries Association was formed with the purpose of promoting imperial trading policies. In 1929 more than 200 Conservative MPs were members of this association, among them Leo Amery (Beer, 1969, p. 286). The free trade fraction in the Tory Party was led by Winston Churchill (the former Liberal). Chamberlain's son Neville, who became Chancellor of the Exchequer in the National Government of Ramsay MacDonald, took up his father's project again and became the torchbearer of the protectionists.

The Great Depression that set in in 1929 intensified the call for protection: parts of the business community which had until then not spoken out in favour of protection now joined the rising tide. That the state monopoly fraction of the British bourgeoisie, with its interests in the heavy industries, favoured protection had already been clear for some time. But now others too recognized the inevitability of some form of protectionism, given developments in the world economy. Tory MP Leo Amery was joined by Sir Alfred Mond (of Imperial Chemical Industries) in founding the Empire Economic Union, which enlisted the support of the Federation of British Industries and other employers' organizations. In the course of 1930 important parts of the City also went over to the protectionist faction. In the autumn of the same year, both Churchill and the Trades Union Congress declared themselves to be in favour of a more protectionist course as well. When the government of national unity took office in August 1931, full plans had already been prepared for the turn towards protectionism, and the government was determined to go ahead (Beer, 1969, pp. 287–92; also Mowat, [1955] 1971, pp. 366–72).

The turn towards protectionism was precipitated by the international monetary crisis, and the resulting exacerbation of the fundamental underlying weakness of the pound and of the position of the City. The dominant position of the City of London in international finance prior to the First World War had rested on the productive superiority of British industry. That productive superiority had passed to other countries, most notably of course to the United States. The 'struggle' between London and New York for financial hegemony in the years 1919–29 could not possibly have been decided in London's favour, and this became very clear when the City proved unable to surmount the reduction in its income resulting from the autarchic tendencies in the world economy (Ingham, 1984, pp. 187–8).[1]

In 1929, Labour was voted into office. With respect to monetary policy, this change of government did not in the least imply any change. On the contrary, the Labour government tried to cope with the increasing difficulties by applying exactly the same orthodox deflationary policies which the Conservatives had applied, and with as little success. In 1931 the situation became acute. Labour's Chancellor, Philip Snowden, intended to prepare public opinion for the severe austerity measures he felt were necessary. But the unintended effect was far stronger: foreign suspicion as to the health of the pound and the safety of deposits in London contributed to the run on the pound which had already got underway. Snowden (with the help, by the way, of Neville Chamberlain) had created a bogey man to which his own government fell victim (Mowat, [1955] 1971, pp. 379–85; Miliband, 1972, pp. 171–3). Bankers and *rentiers* called for extreme financial orthodoxy as a precondition for 'help', and the responsible government leaders (Snowden and MacDonald) simply refused to consider any option but obliging the bankers' call for discipline.[2]

In the end, the issue of severe cutbacks in unemployment benefits was forced by J. P. Morgan & Company. When the final request for American credit had been made, the government waited for the reply from New York. The telegram from Morgan arrived on Sunday, 23 August, demanding austerity measures and City approval for them as conditions for the loan (Mowat, [1955] 1971, p. 392). Twenty-five hours later, the Labour government had fallen and Britain had a National government committed to the restoration of J. P. Morgan's confidence.

After a period of serious pressure on the pound, Britain finally left the Gold Standard, joined at such social costs only six years earlier, in September 1931, and created the so-called Sterling Bloc.[3]

The next step in the gradual transition to protectionism was the Import Duties Act, designed by the Secretary of the Board of Trade, Sir P. Cunliffe-Lister, to protect British industry from foreign competition, which was put to Parliament by Neville Chamberlain in February 1932. Its main provisions were a general 10 per cent *ad valorem* tax on all imported manufactures and the establishment of the Import Duties Advisory Committee (IDAC) (Pfaltzgraff, 1964, p. 334).

The next logical step against foreign competition was taken at the Ottawa Conference of the British Empire and Commonwealth from July to September 1932. The result was the setting up of the system of Imperial Preferences: the colonies and dominions gained free entrance to the British markets for roughly 80 per cent of their products, British products were to be accorded preferential treatment on dominion markets, and Britain would maintain the 10 per cent tariff on manufactures from third (non-Commonwealth) countries for at least five years. At the same time, Great Britain's foreign lending became subject to political control through an unofficial embargo on the issue of foreign loans on the British market (Carr, 1939, p. 126). This underlined the relative weakening of financial interests in the City *vis-à-vis* the coalition of social imperialist and national forces. The City was heavily involved in financing the national debt, and the Ottawa arrangements also served to ensure that the Dominions could continue to pay interest on their debts (Cain and Hopkins, 1987, pp. 9–10, 14). Expansion of foreign operations did not figure prominently in City activity during these years.

The result of these measures was an extensive reorientation of British trade and investments. In 1925–9, 28 per cent of British imports came from the empire, as against 39.5 per cent in the years 1935–9. For the destination of British exports, the figures for the same years are 42 and 49 per cent. The percentage of British capital exports, which had declined sharply after the First World War and did not exceed 20 per cent of the level of 1913, going to the empire and Commonwealth (except for Canada which significantly did not belong to the Sterling Area) went up from 33 per cent in 1913 to 43 per cent in 1930, and to 50 per cent by the end of the decade (Brown, 1970, p. 111).[4]

Corporate liberalism in the 1930s

The insulation from world market pressures by the Ottawa system was a necessary condition for the rise to prominence of the mass production industries, because hitherto imperialist imperatives had dictated policies detrimental to the interests of the mass production industries during the 1920s.

However, the developments of the decade were to show that the relative 'nationalization' of the British economy during the 1930s was *not* a *sufficient* condition for the successful introduction of Fordism, either on the level of the firm in the sphere of the relations of production, or at the national level in the sphere of Keynesian welfare economics. The alignment of class forces as it had taken shape in the century leading up to the Great Depression of the 1930s made it almost inevitable that the coalition supporting the neo-orthodox option would prevail. Several critical moments were of crucial importance in checking the forces supporting the social democratic or Keynesian option, while at the same time the reactionary variant of corporatism (in the shape of Mosley's fascism) failed because of the traditional liberal outlook of the British bourgeoisie and did not attract a large following.

A central point of debate in this period was the direction which industrial restructuring should take. Three positions were discernable: anonymous regulation (a self-regulating market, as supported by the classical liberals), private regulation (practically synonymous with cartellization), and public regulation (by the state) (see Jacobs, 1988, pp. 17–40).

In its programme, *Britain's Industrial Future* (1928), the Liberal Party called for self-governing industries and the granting of statutory powers for majorities within industrial branches so that they could enforce collective discipline on the minority of firms. The influence of Keynes in the drafting of this corporatist programme was clearly recognizable (Harris, 1972, p. 54).

In the Conservative Party the most outspoken protagonist of new organizational forms in industry was Harold Macmillan, who on several occasions during the 1930s advocated forms of central planning (Beer, 1969, p. 297). Macmillan wrote down his *étatist* ideas on these matters in *The Middle Way* (1939). But he was clearly in a minority position within his party. The majority of Conservatives was not attracted by the proposals put forward by either Keynes or Macmillan, for it was not prepared to break with (neo-)orthodox liberal economic policies. Indeed, the breakup of the Gold Standard *had* enforced a break of sorts; however, in Britain this did not lead to the implementation of demand-stimulating policies but rather to a combination of elements of traditional economic liberalism and of reactionary corporatism as practised in Germany and Italy.

The campaign for the restructuring of industry was most vigorously led by the Industrial Reorganization League. In this league, corporate-liberal politicians like Macmillan worked together with corporate-liberal businessmen. Perhaps the most prominent of these was Sir Alfred Mond (later Lord Melchett). As President of Imperial Chemical Industries (formed during the wave of centralization of British capital in 1926) Mond became the most important spokesman for the newly rising industries of the 1920s. In these industries, the organic composition of capital was much higher than in traditional industries (such as textiles); and so the importance attached to continuity of production by the employers was much higher than that accorded to a low wage bill. In many of these industries, the principles of scientific management (Taylorism) were introduced and a beginning was made with the reorganization of production and consumption which came to be known as Fordism (Dunford and Perrons, 1983, pp. 324–31; Blackburn, Coombes and Green, 1985, pp. 41–9). Capitalists in the new spheres of production tended to attach a high value to maintaining reasonable working relations with their workers and with the trade unions. Apart from the chemical industry, this holds particularly for the electro-technical and automobile industries. Quite a few of the capitalists from these branches played a major role in the pursuit of modernizing industrial policies during the depression years. The 1930s saw regular conflicts between these modernizing industrialists on the one hand and representatives of older industries and of other fractions of capital on the other.

Were a reflationary and interventionist programme to have been tried with any chance of success, it would have been under the auspices of the new Labour government headed by Ramsay MacDonald, which took office in 1929. Ideas for such programmes were plentiful: the most outspoken and developed programme was that of Sir Oswald Mosley, whose ideas drew upon the thinking of Keynes. The 'Mosley Memorandum' dealing with new ways of attacking unemployment was however defeated in Cabinet in May 1930. Mosley resigned (and was succeeded by Clement Attlee), and, after losing his uphill battle against dominant orthodoxy in the Labour Party, in 1931 formed his New Party.[5] The mainstream of the Labour Party at this point clung to liberal economic orthodoxy – not only while it remained in power until August 1931 but also thereafter (cf. Skidelsky, 1977b, pp. 36–7).

Notwithstanding the orthodox policies of the Chancellor of the Exchequer, Philip Snowden, the pressures on the new government were heavy from the start, resulting in several successive crises, the worst of which took place in February 1931. In July, the international financial crisis began to be felt in London as well, and resulted in a run on Britain's reserves. The situation worsened in August, and the Labour government (as recorded above) was pressurized by Morgan and the Bank of England into 'balancing' the budget. In particular it was required to cut back on unemployment benefits to help save the pound. This caused the fall of the government.

The opposition, though joyful over the downfall of the Labour Cabinet, had been reluctant to see Labour leave the centre of power completely and return to the opposition benches. The representatives of corporate liberalism (both in the Tory Party and in the Liberal Party) as well as of the state monopoly tendency were aware that the economic measures needed to restore the pound would cause great social tensions, and some form of Labour commitment to these policies would make it much easier to execute them. Thus, when consulted by the King, the Liberal leader Sir Herbert Samuel advised that 'the necessary but unpalatable economies affecting the working class could best be imposed by a

Labour government' (Mowat, [1955] 1971, p. 391; see also Miliband, 1972, pp. 186–91). MacDonald remained in the National government, as did Snowden, but the great majority of Labour did not follow and went into opposition.

On the social front, the British working class began to recover from the shocks of the General Strike of 1926 and MacDonald's 'betrayal' of 1931. One indication for this is the level of union membership. The total membership of the TUC had declined from 4.7 million in 1925, on the eve of the General Strike, to a record low of under 3.7 million in 1933. In 1938, the membership total reached 5.1 million. For these same years union membership as a proportion of total employment was 37 per cent, 27.4 and 37.8 per cent respectively (Middlemas, 1979, p. 215). This recovery was facilitated by the fact that the corporate liberal tendency in the Conservative Party led by Baldwin followed a conciliatory line towards the moderates in the union movement (McBride, 1986, p. 337), and was further reinforced by the rise of the 'new unions', such as the Amalgamated Engineering Union (AEU), the Transport and General Workers' Union (TGWU, Ernest Bevin's union) and the General and Municipal Workers' Union (GMWU) whose membership was concentrated in the newly industrializing regions in the south and south-east and in the midlands (Middlemas, 1979, p. 218).

How was it possible, one may ask, that in the Labour Party, and indeed in the whole Labour movement, orthodox views remained dominant for a long time? The answer is that the long wave of class formation of the era of classical imperialism had not only produced a power bloc dominated by the liberal internationalist bourgeoisie with its money-capital concept of control, but at the same time it had produced an industrial working class which by and large subscribed to this concept as well. In this respect it is significant that the breakup of Labour did not involve a difference over the general direction of economic policy: rather, the proposed cuts in unemployment benefits were the cause of the rupture in the party. Herbert Morrison, for example, had during his short term in office prepared for the nationalization (effected in 1933) of the London public transport system. His plans, however, envisaged no change in the way the system was to be run: the leadership and management of the nationalized transport system was left to the old managers, and no trade union representatives were included on the board.

This attitude of prominent Labour leaders led to some heated discussions as to the general direction of Labour's socio-economic policies, particularly with regard to (future) nationalized industries. On the one hand, the majority in the Labour movement demanded a strong voice in the running of these public industries, while on the other the majority at the same time declined to accept formal responsibility, fearing for its freedom of industrial action. The ambiguous plans formulated in these years had to await practical implementation until the postwar period (Middlemas, 1979, p. 220).

In 1928, an initiative by Sir Alfred Mond led to talks between a joint committee of employers and the General Council of the TUC. The talks were named after the two delegation leaders, Mond for the FBI and Turner for the TUC, but most of the talking on the side of the TUC was done by Ernest Bevin, who was greatly influenced by these meetings (Taylor, 1975, p. 317). The report resulting from these talks, as well as the Macmillan Report a few years later,[6] was in itself rather ineffectual but provided an early instance of joint industry–union action against the dominance of the City of London over financial and economic policy. The report demanded that 'government should provide its own national credit policy' and called for 'a means to review the arcane operation of the Gold Standard itself' (Middlemas, 1979, p. 206).

A second important result of the report was the acceptance by the TUC of 'adaptation' of real wages to the economic situation. As a result of this 'social contract *avant la lettre*' real wages remained unchanged during the years 1932–7, while they had actually increased by 7.8 per cent between 1929 and 1932 (Glyn and Sutcliffe, 1972, pp. 32–4). Of course, this stability of income did not extend to the unemployed. During all the years from 1921 to 1938, at least one in ten British workers was out of work. Unemployment particularly hit the workforce of the older industries, concentrated in peripheral areas in Wales and Scotland. By 1932, 34.5 per cent of coal miners, 47.9 per cent of steel workers, and no fewer than 62 per cent of shipbuilders and ship repairers had lost their jobs (Hobsbawm, 1969, pp. 208–9).

The stability of real wages during the Depression, in such marked contrast with developments elsewhere in the imperialist countries, was made possible by the sharp decline of agricultural prices on the world market. The price of wheat, for example, fell by two-thirds (Dobb, 1973, p. 335). This is particularly important because ever since the early nineteenth century Britain had relied heavily on imported foodstuffs.[7]

The corporate-liberal class coalition had hesitatingly supported imperial protectionism with the objectives (in the trade unions) of protecting jobs and cheap foodstuffs and (in mass production industry) of industrial modernization. It was from this perspective that people such as Keynes, Boothby and Macmillan, along with important FBI spokesmen and with such TUC leaders as Ernest Bevin, had supported protective tariffs and expansionary measures for the domestic economy (Winch, 1972, p. 7).

Although this was certainly not intended by the imperialist coalition of Beaverbrook and Chamberlain, the changes of 1931 and 1932 resulted in conditions which propelled the economic basis of the corporate-liberal fraction forward. The political strength of the corporate-liberal fraction of the bourgeoisie in Britain was however not yet sufficient to displace the dominance of the coalition of older generations in the British ruling class.

The strength of the state monopoly bourgeoisie

During the 1920s the power bloc had been dominated by the coalition of the financial and commercial bourgeoisie and the old liberal industrial bourgeoisie which had enforced the return to the Gold Standard. The strong deflation caused great dissatisfaction among the new industries which opposed the measure both because of its directly negative impact on their own competitive position and also because of the consequences for labour relations.

The onset of the Great Depression in 1929 and the consequent events reaching a climax in 1931 changed the composition of the power bloc. The old liberal industry fell victim to the worldwide surge of protectionism, and faced a serious struggle for survival. In the wake of the breakdown of the international monetary and commercial order, the financial and commercial bourgeoisie was forced to concede more freedoms to industrial capitalists, mainly those based in the iron and steel industries and related branches. In these circumstances, it was only logical that the corporatist and restrictionist elements in the corporate liberal synthesis should still have the upper hand over the liberal element. Thus the efforts by Sir Alfred Mond, who was as it were the personification of the true corporate liberal in the 1930s, to establish tripartite arrangements and institutions governing economic policy remained without much impact. By contrast, his colleague and right-hand man in the ICI boardroom, former Nobel Industries Chairman Sir Harry McGowan, involved himself in projects much more in line with the preferences of the state monopoly bourgeoisie, and had much more success. His involvement (and that of the Midland Bank, of which he was also a director) in the cartellization and reorganization of the gas and electricity corporations and his later complaints over the cost of coal (harmful to the interests of iron and steel firms and chemical producers) exemplify this.

As a matter of fact, taken as a whole, ICI was one of the main bulwarks of the state monopoly bourgeoisie during the 1930s. No doubt the strong ties with German capital (going back to the beginning of the century and preserved through family relationships) were partly the reason for this: in Germany, of course, the position of this fraction of the bourgeoisie was much stronger than in Britain (Brady, 1945). Another reason is that for ICI the mass production of consumer products such as plastics had not yet become important; the bulk of production was in the sphere of intermediary products, much the same as the iron and steel industry.

There were other prominent businessmen and politicians in the 1930s with strong ties to the state monopoly capitalists in Germany. One of them was Oliver Lyttelton (later Viscount Chandos), who combined his position as chairman of Associated Electrical Industries with directorates in the German firm Metallgesellschaft (until the outbreak of war), Alliance Assurance, the British Metal Corporation, the Imperial Smelting Corporation, and Rio Tinto Zinc: his nickname might well have been Mr Non-Ferro.

Another case in point was that of Neville Chamberlain. The ties of the Chamberlain family to German capital were established by the directorship in Siemens (electrical engineering) through a solicitor and in Mannesmann Rörenwerke (steel tubes) through a cousin (Bode, 1975, p. 46). Sir Neville himself was a director of Birmingham Small Arms of Elliott's Metal Company, in which firm he owned a considerable amount of stock. When Elliott's was merged into Imperial Chemical Industries in 1926, Chamberlain became a stockholder of ICI, an interest which he shared with his later Chancellor (and fellow Appeaser) Sir John Simon (Haxey, 1939, p. 54). Most of these men met each other regularly as members of the 'Cliveden Set', meeting in the Astor family residence and in the Anglo-German Fellowship. They formed the hard core of the Appeasers faction.[8]

In 1938 it became clear that war with Germany was fast becoming inevitable, notwithstanding the Munich 'agreements'. At the same time the recession of 1937–8 put a brake on the Depression Boom. The government hesitatingly embarked on a rearmament programme which was intended to have a beneficial effect on the general economic situation as well as on the military position of the country. Defence spending, which had risen from £103 million in 1932–3 (amounting to 12.9 per cent of total budget) to £137 million in 1935–6 (17.7 per cent), rose to £186.7 million a year later (22.4 per cent) (Mowat, [1955] 1971, p. 571). In 1938, Britain spent £358 million on armaments (7 per cent of national income, over quarter of the government budget). From the military point of view, this rise in expenditure was not nearly enough to offset the German lead: Germany by 1938 had spent £1,710 million on armaments, or a quarter of its national income (Mowat, [1955] 1971, p. 628). Economically, British rearmament proved to be a relative 'success': full employment was reached in 1941.

The arrangements that were set up during the war in order to centralize the war effort not only proved successful with respect to the conduct of the struggle against Nazi domination in Europe, but also helped many capitalists to overcome their innate fear of state interference in and planning of the economy: it transpired that capital could profit by state regulation and still in the final instance remain in control. This experience would be used in the immediate postwar years, when a government propelled by quite a different ideological fervour came to power.

The war, and the shadows it cast ahead, gave the predominance of the state monopoly fraction and the corporate liberals close to it a new dimension. Of course the Appeasers in the end had to leave the political stage, but the industrial interests they represented were in many cases indispensable for the war effort. The War Cabinet of National Unity, though composed of all three main parties, was dominated by the Conservatives politically, and by the representatives of British industrial capital in terms of class background. Almost all 'wartime controls' dealing with problems caused by the war effort were dominated by the direct representatives of the industries concerned. In this sense, 'Big Business moved directly into the organs of control', as Aaronovitch has remarked (1955, p. 76). Sir John Anderson (of Vickers) became Lord President and Chancellor of the Exchequer, Oliver Lyttelton became Minister of Production, and Sir Andrew Duncan (of the Iron and Steel Federation) Minister of Supply. The Ministry of Food was dominated by Unilever. The same principle was applied to the Ministry of Manpower, led by trade union leader Ernest Bevin. The control of aluminium was run by the British Aluminum Company, the iron and steel control by the Iron and Steel Federation, the control of non-ferrous metals by the British Metal Corporation, the control of sulphuric acid by ICI, and so forth (Aaronovitch, 1955, p. 76). In this regard, a pattern was established that was to be retained until well into the 1960s.

The structure of the British economy during the 1930s

What changes occurred in the structure of the British economy in this period? As a result of the insulation from the world market and of the changing composition of the power bloc, the spread of the intensive mode of accumulation in Britain followed a unique trajectory, in the sense of being propelled forward and being restrained at the same time. For a while during the 1930s, the spread of Fordism appeared to proceed apace, but some of the conditions which were to contribute to its retardation after 1945 were already visible, and also developed swiftly.

During the 1920s, those branches of industry whose expansion rested primarily on the production of relative surplus value (such as chemicals, automobiles, household appliances) had been small and without much influence, although they were already the fastest growing branches. During the 1930s, this *corporate-liberal fraction* profited greatly from the peculiar situation then existing. Because of its conditions of accumulation – large scale of production, high organic composition of both capital and labour – it had increasingly advocated a conciliatory policy towards the working class, while also actively favouring state attempts to rationalize basic industries such as transport and energy. There was a considerable expansion of employment in the sectors producing durable consumer goods: Britain even became the second largest car-producing nation. In this sector of the economy, real wages were rising, and there was a good measure of social peace.

The *liberal internationalist fraction* of the British bourgeoisie bore the brunt of the collapse of world trade, which caused stagnation in older industrial branches and regions and mass unemployment (up to 45 per cent at times in coal mining districts).

The *state monopoly fraction* of the British bourgeoisie also suffered severe problems in the early years of the Depression. This fraction proved able, however, to exploit its *political* strength by enlisting state support for cartellization of the basic industries.

The declining industries

The situation in Britain's traditional industries had been deteriorating for a long time, certainly since the war. But the Depression meant a qualitative break: the situation turned from bad to disastrous. Private capital was unable to handle the situation: the industries concerned, such as cotton and textiles, coal mining, and transport, were characterized by competitive market relations, and in this situation it is up to forces outside the industries concerned, often the state, to take on the task of reorganization, rationalization and modernization. With regard to coal, for example, there was a very early initiative shortly after the General Strike: 'a group of the more forward-looking members of the FBI ... like Sir Peter

Rylands [an ex-President] and Sir Alfred Mond, proposed schemes for the regrouping of the coal mines on the model adopted by the Rheinisch-Westphälische syndicate' (Middlemas, 1979, p. 205).

During the 1930s, the British government indeed instigated various programmes of this kind, which always involved concentration of production, limitation of output, and sometimes nationalization. Although the government vaguely hoped that its policies would contribute to rationalization of Britain's basic industries, in fact the route followed effectively thwarted any meaningful progress, because it left the capitalists of the industries concerned in charge. These were only interested in the immediate protection of their profits, not in a long-term programme to improve their international competitiveness. Behind the comfortable tariff walls of imperial preference, real modernization was put off for an indefinite period, and in its place came *government-induced voluntary cartellization*. Although superficially these industries seemed to be under public regulation, they were thus in fact mostly privately regulated.

In the coalmining industry the first cartel schemes were introduced in the years following the General Strike, culminating in the Coal Mines Act of 1930. This Act involved a voluntary scheme of production cutbacks and of production quotation among sectors and firms (Youngson, 1960, p. 99). Several studies and surveys of the coal industry in the interwar years showed that output per manshift and profits per ton were lower in Britain than in competing coalmining countries, and costs were higher. The most important factor was the relatively low degree of mechanization in British mines: in 1936 the average rate of mechanization (the percentage of total output mechanically cut) was 55 per cent for Great Britain, against 97 per cent for the Ruhr area in Germany (Heinemann, 1944, pp. 89, 103).

The Coal Mines Act of 1930 did little to improve the situation. One problem about which the Act in itself could not do much was the changing pattern of energy consumption: the role of coal declined as the supply of cheap oil increased. This development was already noticeable in the interwar years even though its full force would be felt only after 1945. The strategic importance of coal for the maintenance of empire (as fuel for the Navy and merchant fleet) greatly diminished in these years, and with it the interest of the City in financing investment in the mining districts.

The cartel's aims were to reduce output and improve profitability. The coal owners themselves, however, were made responsible for executing this task, and they tended to divide the production quotas evenly over all mines irrespective of their distinct levels of productivity. The Act therefore did not provide an incentive to eliminate inefficient pits (Burn, 1958, pp. 117ff.). As is so often the case, cartellization proved a serious obstacle to technological progress.

The lack of investment in the coal industry during the 1930s was further caused by the attitude of the financial world. Heinemann's indictment of the role of the City of London in this respect is a strong one:

> There is no lack of money in the City of London, but modernising our basic industry is too long-term and unprofitable a proposition for rentier financial institutions. The total money advanced by the London clearing banks to the coal industry in 1938 was only 18 million pounds – *i.e.*, 1.5% of the total money advanced. The entertainments and amusements group was lent three times as much as the coal industry. Retail trade got four times as much as coal. This was the schedule of priorities on which our ruling oligarchy was working in 1938. Well might Mr. Keynes suggest that it was unwise for us as a nation to let the development of our basic industries take place as the by-products of a casino. (Heinemann, 1944, p. 119)

The Act did reduce the length of the working day – if not to the seven-hour day which had been won by the miners in 1921 and lost again in the aftermath of the General Strike – but it failed in its aim of stimulating national wage bargaining. Obstruction by the mine owners also caused the failure of the Coal Mines Reorganization Commission, whose task was to effect concentration of production. In 1938 the government attempted, through a second Act, to redress the situation, but again largely in vain. As a result, prices were too high, and productivity lagged behind that in other countries.[9]

In the shipbuilding industry production capacity had been reduced by about one-third in the course of the 1930s, leading to local unemployment levels of up to 80 per cent.

> But little was done to increase the specialization and concentration of production on particular types of ships with a view to achieving scale economies or to improve the technical efficiency of the industry, while the cuts in existing types of capacity did not have to go further because of the increase in demand generated by the approaching war. (Dunford and Perrons, 1983, pp. 319–22)

In other staple industries and basic sectors the situation was hardly any better. Concentration and cartellization, usually arising out of government initiatives, were the rule everywhere. In 1929, the Bank of England successfully urged the formation of the Lancashire Cotton Corporation, which controlled 9 million spindles at the time of its establishment, and very quickly destroyed half of them (Aaronovitch, 1955, p. 52). In 1936 the Lancashire Cotton Corporation merged into a national cartel. In 1933 electricity companies were nationalized and merged on the recommendation of a committee chaired by Lord McGowan of ICI; in the same year, the urban transport systems in London were brought into public ownership. In 1939, finally, civil aviation was concentrated.

The British iron and steel industry was (just like coal) once essential for British imperialism, dominating the world markets for railway equipment, heavy steel plates used in shipbuilding and so forth. However, it steadily became less important under the impact of increasing competition and foreign protection, and was already behind technologically when the First World War arrived (Brady, 1950, p. 204). In the first years of the Depression profitability in the industry, in which there was fierce competition, approached the red figures. The government intervened in 1932: upon advice from the Import Duties Advisory Committee (IDAC) a tariff of 33.3 per cent was imposed covering a great number of iron and steel products. The British iron and steel industry thus had an important advantage in its own home markets. Partly in response to this, the European steel cartel was formed in 1933 by France, Belgium, Luxembourg and Germany, and this development led to pressure from British iron and steel firms for even higher tariffs. In 1934 an agreement was reached. The British government agreed to an increase of the import duties on iron and steel products to no less than 50 per cent, in exchange for the establishment of the British Iron and Steel Federation (BISF).

The BISF was to operate as a producers' cartel, aimed at reorganization of the industry and restoration of profitability. Conditions were fairly favourable: competition from abroad was effectively shut out, and demand was increasing as a result of the Depression Boom in consumer durables. In the course of the 1930s steel production in Britain approximately doubled, a result which was further achieved only in Germany (and Japan) as a result of massive rearmament programmes. In 1935 the BISF reached agreement with the European steel cartel over a carve-up of the world market and the formation of an international steel cartel.[10] By 1937 profitability in the iron and steel industry had again been raised to about 12 per cent (Burn, 1961, p. 47).

During the latter half of the decade, some new investments were made: between 1936 and 1939 76 of the 246 existing furnaces were scrapped, and 48 new ones built. The average production of British blast furnaces increased from 62,000 tonnes in 1934 to 68,000 in 1937 (Brady, 1950, p. 207). In international terms, however, this modest productivity gain did not result in an improved competitive position. Average production of blast furnaces in 1937 reached 81,600 tonnes in Belgium, 127,700 tonnes in Germany, and over 250,000 tonnes in the United States (Brady, 1950, p. 207).

Productivity in the steel industry in Germany was approximately 15 per cent higher than in Britain on the eve of the Second World War, while the US steel industry was almost 70 per cent more productive in melting and rolling, and more than 250 per cent more productive in blast furnaces (Burn, 1961, p. 64).

According to most observers, the principal reasons for this failure to reorganize the British iron and steel industry during the 1930s must be sought in the structure of the industry and the *modus operandi* of the British Iron and Steel Federation.

It requires little perspicacity, and but small knowledge of recent history, to recognize here a supercartel of the type which not even the Germans succeeded in effecting for any major industry until the rise of the Nazis in the early thirties. There is a close analogy, in fact, between this organization and that of the *Reichsgruppe Industrie* as it was developed by the Nazis. (Brady, 1950, p. 195)

The most revealing instance of the way in which the organization of the British iron and steel industry impeded technological progress is the history of the first continuous wide-strip mill in Britain (producing thin sheet steel to be used by the motor car industry among others). The initiator of the project, Sir William Firth of the steel firm Richard Thomas, first proposed, in 1935, to build the mill in Lincolnshire, but was pressurized by the government to locate the plant in a Welsh valley plagued by unemployment: Ebbw Vale. Due to its inland location and to certain design problems, the company soon needed outside financing. The City, however, through the Governor of the Bank of England, required that the BISF be represented on its board and that the company accept the BISF production quotas which of course meant the loss of the competitive advantage of the firm (the Steel Company of Wales). The City's interest in this case was prompted by its heavy financial involvement in many iron and steel firms since the recession of the early 1920s. The BISF also succeeded in blocking realization of a second modern steel plant at Jarrow (Burn, 1961, pp. 54–8; Dunford and Perrons, 1983, pp. 318–19). When the wide-strip mill in Ebbw Vale became operational in 1939, the control committee counted among its members as watchdogs of the BISF and the Bank of England Sir Andrew Duncan (director of both) and Lord Montagu Norman (Governor of the Bank). The arrival of the Second World War put an almost complete stop to whatever innovation had still been possible. In the years 1939–45 only four new furnaces were built and eleven were scrapped (Brady, 1950, p. 207), and the new furnaces were much smaller than new American furnaces of the same period (25–30 tonnes as against 60–100 tonnes: Burn, 1961, p. 17).

To summarize, we have seen that the old staple industries in Britain had been hit after the First World War by a deteriorating international competitive position, due on the one hand to the decreased weight of these industries in twentieth-century capitalism, and on the other to increased foreign competition on foreign and domestic markets. These problems were aggravated by the overvaluation of the pound between 1925 and 1931, and by increased international protectionism after 1930. During the 1930s attempts were made, usually through government initiative, to reorganize the problem industries. Management of the reorganization schemes, however, was entrusted to the representatives of the industries themselves, and these were quite satisfied to reduce output and to erect high protective tariffs to maintain a reasonable rate of profit: the iron and steel capitalists were particularly successful in this respect. Little attention was paid to technological developments elsewhere, and those attempts at important technological innovation (such as the continuous wide-strip steel mill) which did take place were thwarted by the conservative financial world and the conservative and restrictionist cartel leaders. The inescapable result was that much excess capacity was retained.

The Fordist industries

In sharp contrast to the situation in the old industries, which were hard hit by the impact of the Depression, the new industries which had sprung into life during the 1920s flourished behind the protective tariff walls of imperial preference. Mass production of durable consumer goods such as vacuum cleaners, bicycles, refrigerators and motor cars got under way in earnest.

Competitive relations in these newer industries differed sharply from the state-induced cartellization in the older sectors: the predominant form of market organization was that of oligopoly. The trend toward monopolization in Britain was not new, although it had become noticeable rather late in comparison with developments in Germany. Before the First World War, such great monopolies as Royal Dutch/Shell (1907) and Courtaulds (1913) had already come into existence. By the end of the war, the alarm in certain government circles over this trend toward monopoly 'was sufficient to prompt the creation of a standing committee in 1918 to examine business concentration. The report concluded that oligopolistic trends existed widely in the British economy and would soon "control all important branches of British trade" ' (Harris, 1972, p. 39).

The 1920s brought two more waves of rapid centralization, in the years 1919–21, and again in the second half of the decade (Aaronovitch and Sawyer, 1975, p. 124). It was during this second wave that several of the great monopolies were formed that even today determine the face of British imperialism: Imperial Chemical Industries (1926), Vickers/Armstrong (1927), and Unilever (1929). During the 1930s, concentration in most industries continued, tainted by the restrictionism caused by the Depression. In 1935, 'in forty of the main industries, the three biggest firms controlled ... over 60 per cent of total production' (Aaronovitch, 1955, p. 21). Notwithstanding this rapid concentration of capital, however, the degree of monopolization in Britain during the 1930s never reached the level it had reached in Germany and the United States (cf. Dobb, 1973, pp. 342–8). Aaronovitch mentions three reasons for this retardation: the protection of the empire markets providing safe profits without the need for heavy investment, the low wages and hence the limited domestic market, and the rapid growth of British foreign investments (Aaronovitch, 1955, p. 20).

Perhaps the most important new industry to reach maturity in the 1930s was the motor car industry. From the early 1920s, motor manufacturing in Britain had grown rapidly, aided by the 1915 McKenna duties of 33 $1/3$ per cent.[11] The number of independent firms decreased from 198 in 1913 to 96 in 1922, and to 20 in 1939. In this last year 90 per cent of all passenger cars were produced by six firms: Austin, Morris, Vauxhall, Ford, Rootes and Standard. As Duncan Burn remarks, 'the industry [was] in so strong a phase of expansion during this period that it was relatively little affected by the slump' (Burn, 1958, p. 3). Thanks to the introduction of assembly-line production techniques (by Austin and Morris in the 1920s, by Vauxhall and Ford in the 1930s) productivity rose quickly, and the price for an average new motor car decreased from £684 in 1920 to £210 in 1938;

even so, the British car industry continued to need the support of protective tariffs both on its home market and on its growing export markets in the Commonwealth, for production costs and prices in the American car industry with its far larger scale of production were much lower. Another factor adversely affecting the competitive strength of British motor manufacturers was the peculiar structure of taxation: the so-called horsepower tax (a tax progressing with increasing motor power) forced British manufacturers to specialize in small cars and thereby to give up competition with the American motor industry (Plowden, 1973, pp. 164 ff.).

For the time being, the *de facto* protection offered by the McKenna duties and the horsepower tax were sufficient to enable the British motor industry to flourish on the basis of the home market. Output increased from 35,000 cars in 1920 to 182,000 in 1929, and to 341,000 in 1938. Employment also rose sharply in this new branch, which was concentrated in areas without previous industrial traditions. In 1938, the industry employed over half a million workers. 'As a result, the industry's growth played a major role in the modernization of the economy and in reshaping the geography of the country and the regions in which it was implanted' (Dunford and Perrons, 1983, p. 330).

For other modern industries such as electrical engineering, rayon, and chemicals, the story is much the same: modern production techniques were introduced, tariffs protected the growth of the domestic market, employment in these new industries increased. In the electrical engineering industry output more than doubled between 1924 and 1938, as did employment (from 156,000 to 325,500). Finally, the building industry also experienced a modest boom, especially in the private sector catering for middle-class tenants and owner-occupiers.

An important aspect of the development of these new industries was the role of American direct investments in Britain. The turn to 'imperial protectionism' was not in the least a reaction against the threat of American penetration in British spheres of influence, as American capital was the single most important competitor for British capital in many parts of the world. However, American penetration was not restricted to the empire and Commonwealth, but also reached into the British heartland itself where it played an important role in establishing bases for Fordism in Britain.

American investments in Britain started to grow particularly after the First World War. This American offensive in British markets (paralleled by incursions into the Commonwealth markets) was a response to the incipient protectionism of the British which was seen in the McKenna duties of 1915, followed by the Safeguarding of Industries Act of 1921, which aimed at the protection both of industry in Britain and of essential sources of raw materials such as oil (cf. Carr, 1939, p. 123).

In the motor car industry, one of the first and most successful American companies in Britain was the Ford Motor Company, which was established in Manchester in 1908, and had become the largest car producer in Britain by 1913. General Motors followed suit in 1927 when it bought Vauxhall, while Chrysler eventually established an interest in Britain through Rootes. By the end of the 1930s the three biggest American motor companies had thus also become three of the six biggest car producers in Britain.

In the electrical engineering industry, also in the forefront of the transformation of the British economy along proto-Fordist lines, the involvement of Westinghouse (with its interest in English Electric – cf. Morus, 1956, p. 141), and particularly of the General Electric Company (USA), was enormous.[12] The British electrical industry presented a true mirror-image of the internationally operating electrical cartel, which essentially divided the world market between General Electric (USA) and the Dutch firm Philips (in Germany, General Electric (USA) controlled AEG and had a sizeable interest in Siemens).

In the chemical industry American influence was somewhat less pronounced, but in this area there was a strong German connection instead. Through its interest in Nobel Industries (the firm of McGowan), acquired in 1925, Dupont de Nemours (the leading chemical monopoly in the USA) was linked directly to Imperial Chemical Industries (established in 1926), as in Germany Dupont had an interest in IG Farben (formed in 1925). These direct capital links were reinforced and complemented by the international cartel which came about on the initiative of ICI (Aaronovitch, 1955, p. 89). ICI was also involved in a cartel agreement with IG Farben, Standard Oil and Royal Dutch/Shell regarding the synthesis of oil from coal.

American investment in Britain reached a record level in 1929, leading to increased fears of an 'American invasion' and to 'Buy British' actions. In September 1928 the annual stockholders' meeting of General Electric Ltd, upon receiving the news that 60 per cent of its stocks were in American hands, decided to deprive foreigners of voting rights (Lewis, 1948, p. 165; Dunning, 1958, p. 40). According to American sources, Britain in 1929 had 169 manufacturing units with an American interest of 25 per cent or more, the combined interest amounting to US $268 million, which was 55 per cent of all American capital holdings (including portfolio investments) in Britain at the time (Dunning, 1958, p. 43).

During the early 1930s total American foreign investments decreased, but in Britain they continued to grow, primarily as a result of imperial preference. The number of American subsidiaries increased from 169 in 1929 to 224 in 1936, the new investments mainly financed out of retained profits and locally borrowed capital (Dunning, 1958, pp. 45–7; Wilkins, 1974, p. 172).

The balance of depression

The nineteenth-century Victorian economy collapsed during the first decades of the twentieth century. It could be argued that in fact this fall had started in the 1870s, with the increasing imperialist competition between Britain and the newly emerging powers. However, in Britain the debate over free trade vs. protection was decided in favour of the free traders for the time being, and the Victorian economy lived on for a while longer.

It could also be argued that the First World War signified the end of British free trade imperialism with the increased role of the state in the economy and the retention of certain protectionist tariffs after the war. But Britain returned to the Gold Standard and to free trade once more, even though the world market was less and less 'free'. The costs of this policy were borne by the old liberal bourgeoisie (in lower profits), and mostly by the working class (in lower wages, longer hours, high unemployment).

The shock of the collapse of the world economy after 1929, however, proved too much. The liberal world order came to an end, and this time the disturbance was so serious that the option of maintaining a free trade posture suddenly became a totally unrealistic proposition. The strongholds of economic liberalism, the City and the Liberal Party, suffered serious blows. The City would eventually recover after the Second World War, but the Liberal Party would never again become a credible alternative for important sections of the British electorate.

The period of the 1930s and the war years was one of transition. The liberal order had vanished for good, but it was not quite clear what was to take its place. On the one hand, the situation in Britain seemed similar to that in the United States. The growth of mass production and mass consumption was, by pre-1929 standards, quite spectacular, and the requirements of war favoured the rapid growth of the 'new industries' even more. Along with the rise of the new industries, the reformist tendency in the labour movement gained strength, and experiments in tripartite consultation achieved a degree of sophistication unknown elsewhere in Europe (or America) except for Sweden.

And yet, in contrast to the developments in the United States, mass consumption remained restricted to a limited segment of the domestic market: British car workers did not earn nearly enough money to buy the products they were turning out. Consumption of the new durables was for all practical purposes restricted to the higher-income, white-collar workers and the 'middle classes'. Likewise, the contours of tripartite corporatism were clearly visible, but were for the most part just contours without much inner substance.

Four factors can explain this state of affairs:

(1) The reorganization of the basic industries, and particularly of the iron and steel industry, failed, thus leading to high input prices. During the 1930s, the strength of the state monopoly tendency had effectively prevented rationalization. Only the war created more favourable conditions for reorganization, and destroyed the capacity of the capitalists in the basic sectors to ward off the imminent subordination of their industry to the needs of the 'new industries'. In the process, part of the state monopoly fraction of the bourgeoisie was incorporated into the new class fraction now coming to dominate British industry.[13]

(2) The dominant consensus during the 1930s remained that of liberal orthodoxy, which was only left in the field of foreign trade. Demand stimulus, one of the essential ingredients of the Keynesian policies to be pursued after 1945, was not put into practice during the 1930s.

(3) The resulting relatively small scale of production prohibited full exploitation of the possibilities for cost reduction.

(4) Protection from international competition through imperial preference and international cartellization created very few incentives to increase efficiency and to introduce technological innovations in production. The war economy proved a continuation of this situation: increased demand was met not by new investment, but by intensified use of existing capacity.

The long decline: determination vs. contingency

The characteristics of the British class structure, shaped in the eighteenth century and reproduced in the nineteenth, congealed towards the end of the nineteenth century instead of being transformed in the face of the surge of imperialist rivalry threatening Britain's monopolies in the world markets. This was not because of any lack of foresight on the part of a complacent ruling class but rather because of a careful calculation on the part of the hegemonic power bloc. The choices made were, *for the dominant groups*, the ones maximizing profits in the given circumstances. Nevertheless, these choices carried with them implications which would eventually surface in the course of the 1960s as the primary causes of the 'British disease'.

Should the continued decline of Britain be seen as the unavoidable and historically necessary outcome of the decline which started during the third quarter of the last century? Or should we rather adopt a voluntaristic view of history, emphasizing the contingency of historical processes and the role of strategic action by historical actors?

In my view, structural determinations do play an important role. The task of the political scientist is to analyse the precise manner in which structural forces and consciously pursued strategic action of social forces become intertwined. The room for manouevre for consciously operating forces *vis-à-vis* structural limitations becomes particularly great and therefore also particularly relevant for an *explanation* of the course of events when the structure itself (the economic, political and ideological order) enters a phase of crisis. Such was precisely the case from 1929 onwards, when the international economic and political order was severely shaken. World trade broke down, the Gold Standard was abandoned by more and more countries, unemployment exploded to levels unheard of for decades, and the world entered a period of renewed inter-imperialist warfare. From this period onwards, the factors of decline outlined here continued to affect the fate of Britain, but on their own they can no longer fully explain the further decline of Britain.

Does this mean that the 1930s were a watershed, a fundamental qualitative break with the past?

From the point of view of the development of capitalism and of capitalist relations *in* Britain, there was indeed a qualitative break with the preceding liberal era. For the first time in almost a century the direct hold of internationalized money capital over British industry slackened, as the City was forced to a retreat into empire, while the Depression Boom limited the need of industrial capital for outside finance. The domestic market experienced a boom that stood in sharp contrast to the situation in many other leading capitalist economies. New industrial sectors came to the fore, changing the balance of forces between different economic sectors, and in their wake also transforming the composition of the working class. In the wake of the Great Depression, the role of the Liberal Party as the main party of opposition to the Tories was finally taken over by the Labour Party, thus reflecting the end of the *laissez-faire* free trade era of which the Liberal Party had been the torchbearer. The Liberals' only hope of carrying out their projects of economic recovery (such as those of Keynes) lay in the power of numbers which only the Labour Party could now muster.

But *from the point of view of the development of advanced capitalism as a world system* the 1930s were a decade in which a number of problems which had contributed to the decline of Britain could not be resolved, and their persistence laid the basis for the aggravation of these problems from the late 1950s onwards. In that sense, the 1930s *re-produced* the foundations for the continuation of decline after the war.

Through the adherence to orthodoxy by the National government, the Treasury and the Bank of England retained full control over fiscal and monetary matters, thus further enhancing the conservative tendencies in British industry. Out of the global crisis of 1929–32, which was not really resolved until after the Second World War, emerged a *new global structural reality*, namely Fordism. The relative failure of Britain to internalize Fordism in the postwar era provides the focus for the following two chapters.

CHAPTER 4

The redefinition of Britain's global position 1941–73

Global Fordism

In the following chapters we leave the domain of the *longue durée*, of explanations in terms of secular trends in British history, and turn our attention to the medium-term perspective, in which we are concerned with the stage of development of capitalism which is characterized by the gradual generalization of mass production and mass consumption, for which complex of developments we shall employ the term 'Fordism'.

Most of the theories dealing with the study of stages of capitalist development, characterized by particular accumulation regimes, can be situated both in the middle of the time 'scale', employing as they do mainly a medium-term time horizon, and in the middle (although the variation is somewhat greater here) of the 'space axis', for in practice their validity is mostly limited to the core areas of the world system. This does not mean that these theories do not make any meaningful statements about other parts of the world system. However, as a rule they do not start out from a system-wide approach, but instead take as their main focus of analysis the core area of the world economy, and consider other parts of the world primarily in terms of their relation to or importance for the centre. This concentration on the core countries flows from the emphasis in these theories on the *internal dynamic of growth* which is characteristic of Fordism.

In the following chapters, we shall be concerned to show that it is essential to take into account the global dimension as well: stages of capitalist development are characterized not only by particular forms of organization of the production process, and by particular forms of the regulation of social relations and by particular state forms, but also by particular patterns of organization of the global political and economic relations. It is in this context that we can give specific historical meaning to the notion of 'cycles of hegemony', which in the context of world systems theory suffers from a mechanistic and ahistorical interpretation.

The first Marxist theorist to analyse the transition to the new stage of capitalist development into which the US economy gradually entered in the 1920s was Antonio Gramsci. In particular, Gramsci theorized about the new production methods being introduced in the United States. In the first place this concerned the 'scientific management' methods of Frederick Taylor, which produced a 'gap between manual labour and the "human content" of work' (Gramsci, 1971, p. 308). Next, Henry Ford introduced mass production techniques based on parcelling of production tasks and coupled to high ('consumer') wages paid to the workers.

The intensity of production which this implied led Ford and other American industrialists to concern themselves with maintaining a stable, skilled labour force. This concern led them to interfere in the personal lives of their workers as well as regulating their working lives: disciplinary 'problems' such as irregular sexual relations and alcohol abuse specifically came under scrutiny. For Ford's methods to be generalized,

> a change must take place in social conditions and in the way of life and the habits of individuals. This, however, cannot take place through coercion alone, but only through tempering compulsion (self-discipline) with persuasion. Persuasion should also take the form of high wages, which offer the possibility of a better standard of living, or more exactly perhaps, the possibility of realising a standard of living which is adequate to the new methods of production and work which demand a particular degree of expenditure of muscular and nervous energy. (Gramsci, 1971, p. 312)

The term 'Fordism' does not only refer to the large-scale introduction of mass production techniques in such industrial sectors as the automobile industry. If we accept that capital is a social relation instead of simply a quantity of accumulated wealth, restructuring production along Fordist lines indeed means a new technical basis of the production process, but at the same time it also means a restructuring of the working class (in terms of education, skills, consumption patterns, and so on), and it entails a reorganization of labour relations both at shop floor level and at company and even industry level. When we look at the implications that follow from the new technological basis on which industrial production was founded, we see that the kind of products requirred from industrial branches changes, and with it the structure of the relations between different branches of industry. These new forms of organization of the labour process, of labour relations and of the industrial structure, are what 'Fordism' in the Gramscian sense means.

In the 1960s and 1970s the developments which Gramsci could only vaguely foretell had become the dominant reality throughout the developed capitalist world. Not only had a fundamental change occurred in the social conditions of production and in the 'way of life', but the role of the state underwent a fundamental transformation as well. These changes were reflected in new theoretical currents. In the German language area, the debate was dominated by discussions of the origins and functions of the capitalist state (cf. Holloway and Picciotto, 1978). In the Anglo-Saxon world, the discussion centred more on corporatism and the specificities of the Keynesian welfare state. In France, Aglietta and later Lipietz and others focused on the crisis in what they called the postwar 'regime of accumulation', designated as 'Fordism'. Here, the notion of Fordism came to denote

> a series of major transformations in the labour process closely linked to those changes in the conditions of existence of the wage-earning class that gives rise to the formation of a social consumption norm and tend to institutionalize the economic class struggle in the form of collective bargaining ... It marks a new stage in the regulation of capitalism, the regime of intensive accumulation in which the capitalist class seeks overall management of the production of wage-labour by the close articulation of relations of production with the commodity relations in which the wage-earners purchase their means of consumption. (Aglietta, 1979, pp. 116–17)

'Fordism' is seen by Aglietta as equivalent for the *intensive* mode of accumulation, which succeeded the *extensive* mode of accumulation.[1]

Regimes of accumulation consist of a particular mode of accumulation (a mode of organizing the production process), and of a mode of regulation of the social environment of production (or the productive relations on a public, societal level). In the French discussion, 'Fordism' is therefore not only the term employed to denote these characteristics of the production process, but at the same time refers to the 'social structure of accumulation', the ensemble of regulatory agencies and practices at the level of society which are created in response to the problems threatening the smooth operation of the Fordist mode of accumulation. In particular, such elements as collective wage bargaining, the provision of social welfare benefits guaranteeing a minimum living standard and a minimum social consumption level, wage indexation, tripartite representation in advisory bodies, recognition of trade union rights and so forth, make up the Fordist *mode of regulation*.[2]

To complete the picture of Fordism as a stage of development of global capitalism, we should add a third dimension. In its concrete historical manifestation, the Fordist stage of capitalist development *in its totality* is characterized not only by its specific forms at the level of the organization of the production process and its specific state form and form of social organization, but also by the global organization of the capitalist system. In concrete terms, the global dimension of Fordism is found in American hegemony in the post-1945 world. If we want to analyse the ways in which Fordism was introduced in a particular country, we are therefore also, and in a sense first of all, concerned with its position in the 'international division of labour', the 'insertion' of the national economy (or branch) in the world market, and, secondly, with the location of the national class structure in the overarching global class structure and the position of the individual country in the hierarchy of the global state system.

The 'Fordist' stage of development of capitalism can therefore be characterized as Fordism when considered at the level of the organization of production, as the era of the Keynesian welfare state when looked at from the level of society and state, and as the *Pax Americana* when looked at from the perspective of the overall organization of the capitalist world system. In fact, what we are discussing here are superimposed dimensions of reality, where 'facts' pertinent to one dimension only acquire their full meaning if they are considered against the background of the other dimensions. An account of the spread of Fordism in Britain after 1945 would be almost meaningless without an evaluation of the British 'performance' in international perspective and without an analysis of the way in which the development of the British political economy is dialectically intertwined with the development of global capitalism in this period.

In *Labour in Power 1945–1951*, Kenneth Morgan enumerates four main policy areas in which postwar Labour governments were particularly successful or to which they were particularly committed (Morgan, 1985): these were nationalization and industrial modernization; the welfare state; decolonization and the creation of the New Commonwealth; foreign affairs and defence. These four areas cover the three dimensions of the Fordist stage of

87

capitalist development fairly well: the nationalization programme was Labour's intended contribution to the radical modernization of British industry and its labour relations; the project of the welfare state clearly fitted the social (or state) dimension of Fordism; while the two remaining areas together cover the restructuring of the British role in the world capitalist system.

These areas have been central not only for the immediate postwar Labour governments but more generally for the whole period up to the mid-1970s. With the partial exception of the Churchill–Eden governments of 1951–7, all governments up to (and in many ways including) the Heath government of 1970–4 have attempted to carry through policies intended to quicken the pace of Fordist development.

In this chapter we shall start with the changes being sought by or forced upon Britain with regard to its position in the imperialist system (its insertion in the world economy) and with the constraints this entailed for domestic policy formation.[3]

Postwar reconstruction of the global order and the birth of the 'special relation'

The British adaptation to the realities of American hegemony in world politics has been a slow and painful process, starting with the wartime concessions to the USA, the postwar acceptance of American commercial and military supremacy, the dissolution of the British Empire, the experiences of the Suez expedition, and the difficulties involved in restoring the 'special relation' after Suez. Britain's relation with Western Europe provided another source of continuous debate, closely interlinked however with the question of the 'special relation'.

The whole period of the late 1940s through to the 1960s is indeed coloured by the tension between the 'special relation', the need for a strong partnership with the United States as the ultimate guarantee for Britain's position as a late imperial power, and the need for closer associations with Western Europe where the fastest growing markets were located for Britain's Fordist industries. The determining factor would prove to be this asynchronous relation between the developments in the sphere of the 'basis' (economic relations with Western Europe) and in the 'superstructure' (the persisting foreign policy orientation appropriate to a bygone era).

The Lend Lease Act, the first tangible expression of the special relationship, passed Congress on 11 March 1941, but was hardly used during that year. One of the conditions which had been attached to the Act, however, already foreshadowed what was to come: Britain was required to stop exports competing with American exports. For the time being, this was not such a great problem: British exports by 1943 amounted to only 29 per cent of what they had been in 1938 (Taylor, 1975, p. 623).

In August 1941, the first of many conferences between Roosevelt and Churchill resulted in the adoption of the Atlantic Charter which set out the principles and conditions of Anglo-American co-operation. The charter bore the imprint of the strong position of the Americans and underlined the necessity for the liberalization of postwar international economic relations. Subsequent Anglo-American conferences repeatedly exposed the ambivalent position of Britain: it needed the relation with the US in order to survive the war and to cling to the empire, but at the same time it was forced to promise to abandon its principal instrument of domination over the empire (imperial preference) in exchange for American aid. The Anglo-American Lend Lease Agreement of February 1942 gave as its central purpose the need to fight the common enemy (America had entered the war when the Japanese attacked Pearl Harbor in December 1941), but also stipulated that Great Britain should agree to free trade after the war (Taylor, 1975, p. 647).

For more than three years, Lend Lease remained the basis for American aid to Britain, which totalled $27 billion (approximately 11 per cent of total US war expenditure), while British reciprocal aid to the US totalled $5.7 billion (9 per cent of the total war effort).[4]

In 1945, the end of the war also brought Lend Lease to a quick end. Three important events were responsible for this abrupt end to the Anglo-American partnership: the death of Roosevelt, the end of the war in Europe, and the electoral victory of Labour.

The replacement of Wallace by Truman as vice-presidential candidate had already been a sign of Roosevelt's universalism weakening, and Roosevelt's death allowed Truman and the forces that supported him in 1944 to consolidate further the inward-looking orientation now getting the upper hand. Germany's capitulation shifted American attention to the Pacific where Britain's role was minor, and when the left-wing Labour government took office in July 1945 fears of advancing socialism contributed to the sudden stopping of Lend Lease on 21 August 1945.

Notwithstanding the enormous war efforts which almost exhausted the country (and forced it to liquidate a great proportion of its foreign assets), Great Britain at first seemed to retain its position as a major power, particularly because Britain's economic position in the immediate postwar years was comparatively favourable. The most important factor explaining the rapid recovery and growth of British production after 1945 was without doubt the situation on the world market: the combination of great demand, little competition, and effective protection from (American) competition by imperial preference and the inconvertibility of Sterling, and by the dollar shortage. These factors, although they were weakened after 1949, continued to operate until around 1955, when German and Japanese competition regained momentum. The successful export drive was not based on a technical revolution resulting in enormous productivity gains, such as the war brought about in the US (cf. Brady, 1950, pp. 496–7), but rather on the very specific circumstances prevailing on the world market after 1945 and on the particular position of Britain.

The international economic position of Britain had changed dramatically in the 1930s and during the war. Britain had become to a large extent self-sufficient: the import share of the domestic market for manufactures fell from 24 per cent in 1931 to only 4.7 per cent in 1950, 'granted that it was imperial rather than national self-sufficiency' (Radice, 1984, p. 124). Britain's international financial position had also undergone a drastic change: between 1938 and 1946, the stock of foreign investments decreased from £4.5 billion to £3.4 billion, the Sterling balances deteriorated from minus £800 million to minus £3.5 billion, government debts were incurred to a total of £1.5 billion, and the gold reserves decreased from £800 million to £600 million (Youngson, 1976, p. 150). In all, then, a positive sum of £4.5 billion in foreign assets had been transformed by the war in a negative total of £1 billion. The income from foreign investments and other invisible income, traditionally making up for the trade deficit, was decimated.

Britain's overriding aim after the war was to redress this state of affairs and resume its 'rightful' place or – as Keynes set out in the objectives in negotiating the 1945 American loan needed to replace Lend Lease – to recover 'for London its ancient prestige and its hegemony' and avoid being left 'hopelessly at the mercy of the United States' (Brett, 1985, p. 137–8). Britain succeeded in the first objective precisely by accepting the second, undesirable but unavoidable, consequence. It was able to maintain the integrity of the Commonwealth and the Sterling Area only with the aid of the 1945 American loan,[5] but had to pay the price of the untimely return to convertibility in 1947 which led to a very severe crisis. From the transfer of the shares of the American Viscose Corporation (a subsidiary of Courtaulds) as collateral for the 1941 loan by the Reconstruction Finance Corporation, to the aborted return to convertibility in July 1947, the essential relation between the US and Britain was continuously reaffirmed: Britain attempted to regain at least part of its earlier prominence, but was able to do so only within the confines defined by her acceptance of US hegemony.

The terms of the American loan were not welcomed by all fractions in Britain. The Tory corporate liberals in particular had many reservations about the wisdom of the policy being pursued. Robert Boothby considered the agreement to be an 'economic Munich' (Childs, 1979, p. 23), and Harold Macmillan criticized the proposed multilateral trade system as a return to nineteenth-century free trade (Harris, 1972, p. 83), a prospect abhorred by most corporate liberals. In fact, however, multilateralism did not mean a return to nineteenth-century free trade. As Ruggie emphasizes, multilateralism above all meant adherence to the principle of non-discrimination, which was to become the foundation of the GATT, the General Agreement on Tariffs and Trade. A certain degree of infringement on free trade was allowed in the new system, both to defend domestic industrial expansion and to retain certain preferential arrangements with (former) colonial territories. This American concession later led to repeated clashes between the different member countries of GATT, but it was a central element in the overall compromise that was struck in 1945, and that, in the final analysis, 'reflected the extraordinary power and perseverance of the United States' (Ruggie, 1983, p. 213).

Another central element in the compromise shaping the postwar international economic order was the agreed necessity to raise the standard of living in Europe, both as a preservative against communist contagion and also as a precondition for the transatlantic expansion of Fordism. It was the Marshall Plan, first publicly proposed by Marshall in his speech of 5 June 1947, which put the crown on the replacement of the *Pax Britannica* by the *Pax Americana*, begun prior to the First World War but temporarily halted by the imperial retrenchment of the 1930s.

A look at the use of the Marshall funds in Britain is instructive as it shows that, contrary to the expressed aims of the plan, they were used more to underpin the international financial position of Britain than to support the modernization of the domestic industrial structure. The most direct contribution to the modernization of production is the financing of machinery and equipment: for all recipient countries, 10.2 per cent of total aid was used for this purpose, and in the case of France the percentage was 11.9 per cent; but in Britain it was only 8.8 per cent (*Statistical Abstracts of the United States*, 1954).

When we include data on the use of the counterpart funds[6] the difference is far more striking. In the case of France more than 90 per cent of the counterpart funds were spent on 'production and other purposes' (that is, supporting the 'real' economy); the percentage was roughly similar in Germany and Italy. For the Netherlands the figure was much lower, but still considerably higher than that for the UK, where *all* counterpart funds were either left unused or were used for debt retirement (Brown and Opie, 1954, p. 244). Comparatively speaking, then, in the case of Britain the Marshall programme was not so much directed at strengthening the productive base of the economy, but rather at improving the external financial position.

We have seen that the war left Britain financially dependent on the United States. The US took advantage of Britain's dependence to press for concessions in the sphere of access to imperial markets, and with considerable success. Nevertheless, the US did agree to the resurgence of Sterling as an international reserve currency and to a degree of British autonomy.

One could ask why the United States allowed Britain even the little autonomy it did. The answer, it is suggested, is that Britain proved a reliable partner in the reconstruction of the postwar international economy and the containment of communism: 'while Keynes and Dalton were capitulating to the Americans to gain $3.75 billion and thus stave off an unacceptable austerity, the government was to spend almost $8 billion between 1946 and 1951 on overseas military and other programmes' (Brett, 1985, p. 141).

The reconstruction (under US-imposed limitations) of the Sterling Area, to which these decisions amounted, had two long-term consequences (Brett, 1985, p. 146–7).[7] It facilitated and encouraged a large outflow of capital, which came on top of foreign military expenditures and the loss of reserves resulting from the untimely return to convertibility in 1947: between 1946 and 1951, private investment abroad reached almost £1,300 million (of which three-quarters went to the Sterling Area), while overseas public investment amounted to £345 million in the same period.[8] Secondly, being the centre of the Sterling Area required a continuous balance of payments surplus and consequently high interest rates.

After international monetary relations had been restructured in 1949, this problem during the 1950s and 1960s manifested itself in the infamous 'stop–go' cycle with its disastrous effects on the development of the domestic economy. This problem, to some extent the 'normal' situation for any capitalist country, was far more severe in the case of Great Britain because it tried to preserve the role of reserve currency for Sterling.

This second consequence had two implications for power relations between capital fractions and state apparatuses. First, the preservation of Sterling's reserve role formed the basis for the City's postwar revival as an international financial centre. Second, the Bank of England and the Treasury again won enormous power in the area of economic policy formation (Ingham, 1984, pp. 204–6).

It cannot be emphasized often enough, however, that this renewed predominance of the institutional strongholds of the money-capital concept came about under quite different auspices. The City's renewed internal dominance was shaped and conditioned by American hegemony in the world system, and by the international spread of Fordism actively pursued through the Marshall plan.

Britain's relationship with Europe

In this context (of adaptation to American hegemony and attempted maintenance of the empire) the debate regarding British foreign policy did not involve the question of whether or not there was to be a special position for Britain, but rather how best to shape the special position that very few people seriously doubted. Two principal positions were discernible within the Labour foreign policy establishment.

One position, after initial hesitations adhered to by Ernest Bevin, was in fact very similar to the orientation outlined by Winston Churchill. According to this view Britain owed its special position after the war to the fact that it was the only country which was part of three of the most important and powerful international groupings: the Commonwealth, the Atlantic axis between Britain and the United States of America, and Western Europe. Even though Britain was not a power of the same rank as the USA and the Soviet Union, thanks to this unique position it would be able to pursue and defend its own worldwide interests and play a role in the shaping of the postwar world by the superpowers. It was essential, given this line of reasoning, for Britain to maintain its position as leading power of the British Commonwealth, and its 'special relationship' with the United States. Unity in Western Europe was to be actively supported, but from the outside: Britain would endorse Western European unity as a buffer between itself and the Soviet Union. This position has been dubbed the 'Churchill option' (Zeeman, 1983b), and was institutionally supported primarily by the Treasury, the Board of Trade and the Commonwealth Office (cf. Kölling, 1984). The anti-Soviet and anti-communist nature of this view was overriding.

The Foreign Office during these early postwar years supported another view of Britain's place in the world: it favoured the formation of a strong West European group under British leadership, which would be able to deal with the USA and the USSR on an equal footing and which could co-operate with the Soviet Union in opposing possible German *revanchism*.[9] In fact, the Foreign Office option found strong support in the Labour rank and file, where sympathies for the Soviet Union were still strong (the Labour Left had campaigned intensely for the early opening of a second front in order to relieve German pressure on the Eastern front). This forced the new Foreign Secretary, Ernest Bevin (notwithstanding his personal Atlantic orientation) to take a neutralist stance and to insist upon Soviet participation in any proposed European settlement. But, in practice, Bevin continued the Churchill line in foreign policy and even took a leading part in the onset of the Cold War, by his attitude at Potsdam, for example, by the British intervention in Greece, and by British policies in Germany.[10] In fact 'the sources of policy were not Labour manifestos but Churchillian texts' (Epstein, 1954, p. 133). The first (isolated) success for the adherents of the West European group was the conclusion in March 1947 of the Anglo-French Treaty of Dunkirk (cf. Zeeman, 1986). Its success, however, was shortlived.

In all accounts of the postwar years, 1947 is seen as the turning point. The start of the year brought a very severe winter in Britain and a serious fuel shortage as a result. Problems were aggravated by the disastrous return to convertibility in the summer, and the first signs of renewed economic decline became visible. Internationally, the situation also deteriorated quickly. In Eastern Europe, pro-Soviet forces were slowly ousting non-communist forces from the coalition governments formed after the war. In the US, the first postwar recession seemed on the way, leading to increasing anxiety over the need to break open foreign markets. The advance of anti-imperialist forces (in Greece, Turkey, Iran) and the strong position of the communists in Western Europe (particularly their participation in government in France and Italy) lent support to those forces in the State Department pleading for a more activist American foreign policy. Britain's announcement (in February 1947) that it would leave Greece provided the final stimulus. First, the Truman doctrine was announced; then, Under Secretary of State Dean Acheson made a speech which preluded the plan for aid to Europe; finally, on 5 June, Marshall announced the plan named after him.

The meeting between Molotov, Bidault and Bevin of 27 June–2 July regarding Marshall's proposals was decisive. On the basis of that meeting, the Soviet Union decided that, given the conditions regarding liberalization set by the USA, it could not agree to participation in the Marshall plan. When the Soviet Union and its allies failed to take part in the Paris conference later that month, the fate of Europe was sealed: the separation into two blocs was indeed a fact, and the rationale behind both the position of the Labour Left and the 'Foreign Office option' had disintegrated.[11]

Bevin was no longer held in check and was now able to formulate his Churchillian vision in his famous Western Union speech to the Commons on 22 January 1948, followed in March 1948 by the Brussels Treaty (signed by Britain, France and the Benelux countries), which was openly directed against the Soviet Union. The treaty of 4 April 1949, establishing the North Atlantic Treaty Organization (NATO), completed the demise of the 'European' road for Britain, and the wholesale embrace of the Atlantic road (cf. Barker, 1971; Melissen and Zeeman, 1987). From that time onwards, Bevin's first worry was to 'commit[ting] the US to European defence' (Newton, 1985, p. 178).[12]

The Conservative Party did not in the main disagree with Bevin's conduct of foreign policy. On the issue of the 'communist threat', there was no disagreement whatsoever, and support for a strong military alliance with the USA was general.

Policies with regard to West European unity and to the international monetary and commercial regime, however, were not supported by all tendencies in the Conservative Party. At the London Party Conference of 1949 there emerged a strong lobby for British involvement in Europe: Duncan Sandys advocated this line, so did David Eccles, and Harold Macmillan felt that Britain's future was to be found in Europe (Gamble, 1974, p. 185). Macmillan in fact was also a prominent member of ELEC, the European League for Economic Cooperation, which had been formed during the war in London, and counted many prominent corporate liberals amongst its membership. The British National Committee of ELEC consisted of Sir Harold Butler (President), Macmillan, Lord Layton, Sir Roy Harrod, David Eccles, and Alexander Loveday (cf. Rebattet, 1962, pp. 5–6). Although these voices were strong, 'Britain's residual Imperial interests guided the policy of the new Government' (which was to come to power in 1951), and Anthony Eden was the 'leading spokesman' of this tendency (Gamble, 1974, p. 186). The imperialist fraction, however, was divided over the issue of American commercial hegemony. The imperialist diehards aimed their fire principally at the GATT, which precluded the maintenance of imperial preference, and which had also been a condition on Lend Lease and the American loan of 1945. These diehards (Julian Amery being one of their most prominent spokesmen) still clung to the conception of Britain leading the Commonwealth to independent superpower status, and were prepared to confront the US head on. Their position, however, was far weaker than it had been in the early 1930s. One reason was that, unlike the situation in 1931, industry did not support a new imperialist scheme; the second, related, reason was that many former imperialists, although still giving precedence to the Commonwealth over stronger ties with Western Europe, had come to the realization that a condition for maintaining at least a reasonable measure of influence in the world was the acceptance of American hegemony. Therefore, the campaign against GATT had little success.[13]

Early European integration projects

Given the predominance after 1947 of the Churchillian conception of Britain's role in the world, it was no surprise that when the French minister Schuman on 9 May 1950 announced his plan for pooling the European coal and steel industries, British reactions were generally negative (Anouil, 1960, pp. 56–64). There were only a few exceptions, such as the promising new Tory MP Edward Heath who devoted his 'maiden speech' to the need for Britain to 'participate in the discussions on the Schuman Plan' (quoted by Camps, 1964, p. 315). Mainstream Conservative opinion was fearful of the expressed hope that the European Coal and Steel Community (ECSC) might represent the first step towards further economic (and eventually political) integration.

The Labour Party and the trade union movement were mostly opposed to the scheme for fear that their priority of full employment would not stand up to the rationalizations foreseen in the Schuman Plan. The opponents thus found themselves united in their intense dislike of the supranational dimension involved in the Schuman Plan. When the West European countries met in June 1950, Britain did not take part in the discussions. The only projects for European co-operation in which Britain was willing, in the next decade, to participate were intergovernmental organizations such as the Council of Europe, or organizations which could ensure American involvement in Europe, such as the Organization for European Economic Co-operation (OEEC, 1948) and NATO (1949).[14]

In 1950 the Pleven plan for a European Defence Community (EDC) was proposed, for which a treaty was signed in 1952. After coming to power in 1951, Eden made it clear that Britain would not be able to join in view of her other commitments, but in order to appease France's fears of German supremacy he proposed to link the EDC to the ECSC and to the Council of Europe. The French Assembly in the end refused to ratify the EDC. Eden was determined, however, to achieve the 'pacification' of Western Europe, that is, to resolve the Franco-German security problems. Eden's view by now was that successful long-term resistance to Soviet pressures depended on continental West European defence co-operation within the context of the Atlantic Alliance. To that purpose he proposed in 1954 the enlargement of the Treaty of Brussels to encompass Italy and the Federal Republic of Germany; Britain promised to maintain its forces on the Rhine. This new plan was successful, and after its adoption France also gave up its resistance to German membership of NATO. The pacification of Western Europe was thus achieved through the West European Union (WEU).

In February 1955, the association between Britain and the ECSC was signed. At that point in time, it still seemed possible that Britain and Europe would resolve their differences. The essential moment at which Britain might have joined Europe but did not was at the conference taking place in Messina in June 1955, at which Belgian Foreign Minister Paul-Henri Spaak proposed for the first time the formation of a European customs union. Britain did not participate and, remarkably enough, Harold Macmillan, then Foreign Secretary, showed no particular interest in participating.[15] The Messina conference was treated by Britain as essentially an economic one: at the preparatory discussion in Brussels, the Six were represented by foreign ministers, Britain by a representative of the Board of Trade (Camps, 1964, p. 47–8).

The British decision not to participate seriously in the preparations for the European Economic Community was a momentous one: it in fact implied that Britain relinquished the opportunity to rationalize its industrial structure in a period in which the international conjuncture was still favourable. Later, when Britain finally did attempt to join the EEC, conditions had changed for the worse.

Suez and the special relationship

What would occupy the minds of Britons much more for the time being were the development of Britain's imperial position and clashes with the USA over British policy in this respect. The first serious setback came in Iran where the Anglo-Iranian Oil Company (AIOC, later British Petroleum) had the monopoly over the exploitation of oil reserves. In 1951, the nationalist government of Prime Minister Mossadeq rejected proposals (made after a long silence on earlier Iranian initiatives) for a 50:50 joint venture, and nationalized the AIOC. Great Britain proved unable to resolve the matter, and was forced to turn to the United States for help. In 1953 the CIA removed Mossadeq from office and installed the Shah. Britain was left without any influence to speak of: the British were allowed back into the Iranian oil business, but this time as the junior partner in a consortium dominated by American oil companies. The establishment of the Baghdad Pact (with Iran, Iraq, Turkey and Pakistan) followed the same pattern: its role was defined by the American anti-Soviet posture of the Eisenhower years.

Immediately after this episode, new problems for Britain's international position appeared. In the summer of 1953 King Farouk of Egypt was deposed and Naguib became President, and in February 1954 Gamal Abdel Nasser became the new Egyptian leader. In the next two years, Nasser regularly collided with the different Western powers, who refused to arm him, and eventually also refused to finance the Aswan Dam. This latest rebuttal led Nasser to the nationalization of the Suez Canal Company on 26 July 1956. The canal represented a considerable British interest: Britain owned 44 per cent of the Canal Company, and 25 per cent of British overseas trade went through it. The Eden government first tried to reach a negotiated solution through the United Nations, but in October agreed to Franco-Israeli plans for concerted military action against Egypt. The Israelis attacked on 29 October, the French and British followed two days later.[16]

The Suez expedition was opposed from different sides: by Labour, by many Commonwealth countries (such as India), by the US and the UN, and by such people as Robert Boothby, Keith Joseph (outside the government) and Lord Mountbatten (Childs, 1979, p. 89). Harold Macmillan, who had become chancellor in the meantime, supported the action, at least at the beginning.

The execution of the operation against Nasser was far from perfect, but in the end the fundamental and fatal weakness was that France and Britain had not recognized the American position.

Rightly sensing the dangers of communist expansion, and understandably fearing the consequences of a third world war, the US government began to support the cause of those seeking an end to colonialism. This impulse, springing from a desire to shield the Third World from Soviet imperialism, together with a realistic appreciation of the importance of Middle East oil, led the US to use its power ruthlessly to bring the Franco-British action to an ignominious halt. (Chalfont, 1986, p. 9)

Massive speculation against the pound further confirmed that the British government had made a serious miscalculation: in November alone Britain lost $280 million as a result of speculation, leading to an acute balance of payments crisis. It was this reason that brought the chancellor, Macmillan, to oppose further prolongation of the adventure, the more so because British withdrawal from Egypt had been made (by the Americans) a condition for the IMF loan which Britain needed (Childs, 1979, p. 90). The Suez fiasco made even the most dogged imperialists realize that Britain was no longer a great power: 'another prop of Britain's imperial mission had gone forever' (Gamble, 1974, p. 175).

When Macmillan succeeded Eden his first priority was the restoration of a working relationship with the United States, and then to overcome the remaining influence of the imperialist wing of the Conservative Party. On a personal level, the first task proved easy enough: Eisenhower and Macmillan had worked together in North Africa during the war and Eisenhower welcomed the opportunity to renew the partnership (Calvocoressi, 1979, p. 210). Britain also proved itself to be a reliable defence partner for the US: in May 1957 the first British H-bomb was exploded, and in the same year the long range V-bombers came into service. As a result the American MacMahon Act (prohibiting the sharing of nuclear expertise) was relaxed for Britain. On this basis of renewed Anglo-American understanding Macmillan could in earnest embark on his mission to liquidate what was left of the British Empire, which was indeed achieved without very serious problems for the British government. Decolonization came too late, however, to serve as a catalyst for the modernization of the domestic economy, as had happened in the Netherlands and France (cf. Van der Pijl, 1978; Baudet and Fennema, 1983).

Internally, the position of the imperialist wing of the Tories had deteriorated still further, discredited as it was by the Suez débâcle, and weakened by the erosion of the material basis for its views. Having laid these foundations (a stronger Atlantic connection and with the dissolution of the empire firmly under way), Macmillan could begin to restructure Britain's relations with Western Europe.

The move towards Europe

A new appraisal of Britain's relations with Western Europe was urgently needed. The reasons are neatly summarized in a number of propositions with which Boyd opens his book, *Britain's Search for a Role*:

(1) Between 1958 and 1975 the 'importance' of the link with Europe for Britain increased, while that of the connection with the United States decreased.

(2) The increase in 'importance' of Europe for Britain came first and most markedly in the economic sector.

(3) In the military sector, the 'importance' of the United States remained well above that of Europe for the British.

(4) The 'importance' of Europe for Britain in the political sector increased as her own economic and military capability decreased.

(5) As Britain's economic and military capability decreased, her bargaining ability, that is, her 'importance' to the United States and to the European Community, decreased.(Boyd, 1975, pp. 8–9).

The structural changes which took place in Britain's international trade are well known: the share in world trade of manufactured products increased, and the fastest growing market for these products, and therefore for the output of Britain's internationalizing Fordist companies, was to be found in the Common Market:[17] its share in British exports rose from 13.9 per cent in 1958 to 21 per cent in 1963. The UK share of EEC imports increased from 8 to 10 per cent in the same period (Boyd, 1975, pp. 56, 63).[18]

But recognition of changed realities still did not go so far as to persuade important sections of British capital of the inevitability of EEC membership. A special committee of the FBI reported in 1956 that to join the EEC would mean the 'forfeiture of the preferences at present enjoyed by Commonwealth countries on their exports to the UK'. Although 'the aggregate benefits still accruing to British Industry as a whole from the imperial preference system were probably not substantial ... [they were] nevertheless still important to some industries'. The conclusion was that Britain should not join the Common Market ('the FBI and European integration', quoted in Pfaltzgraff, 1964, pp. 249–50). This position was reiterated at the FBI's 1958 conference. There was less opposition to the plan, proposed in November 1956, to create a European free trade area, in which Britain and the EEC could join, without Britain having to give up its ties with the Commonwealth. Reginald Maudling was appointed to negotiate with the EEC, but in January 1959 the plan failed definitively, because such a free trade area involving the EEC would have destabilized the intricate compromise on which the building of European unity was based.

In the meantime, the pressures from British industry needing access to the European markets became stronger. In 1959, William McFadzean of BICC became the new President of the FBI, and after the failure of the EFTA plans he established contacts with the Dutch Chamber of Commerce in order to look at the possibilities of Britain becoming more closely associated with the EEC (Lieber, 1970, ch. 4). In 1960, the FBI established a special Export Council for Europe, to help counter the worsening of Britain's trading position. More and more firms invested in Europe in order to jump the EEC external tariffs. ICI invested £100 million in the expansion of its subsidiary in Rotterdam in 1961 (Schneider, 1968, pp. 102–3), and ICI director Paul Chambers was one of the most active protagonists of British membership of the EEC (Sampson, 1965, p. 503). British direct investment in the EEC increased rapidly in this period: in 1958 5.5 per cent of new British foreign investment went to the EEC, in 1963 this had risen to 16.9 per cent, and, after varying between 10 and 20 per cent in the years between, it reached 42.5 per cent in 1971 (Boyd, 1975, p. 68). Apparently, Britain's multinational companies could wait no longer. In July 1961 the FBI, dominated now by the big corporations, declared itself in favour of EEC membership (Pfaltzgraff, 1964, pp. 269–71). In its report of that year the Westminster Bank prophesied that Britain's share in world trade would continue to fall if Britain did not join, and the *Banker* expected, in that case, a fall-off of American investment in Britain (Pfaltzgraff, 1964, pp. 288–9). As we know now, both these prophecies have come true.

Before Britain could apply for membership with any hope of success, there were two obstacles: opposition within the Cabinet would have to be overcome, and American approval for the move was necessary.

Relations with the United States improved steadily. After Britain's attempt to develop its own missile (the Blue Streak) – intended to guarantee British nuclear independence – had failed, Macmillan went to Eisenhower and got from him the promise that Britain would get the new American missile, Skybolt, being developed at that time (in March 1960), in return for the use of a Scottish base for submarines carrying the Polaris missiles.

Having secured his position with America, Macmillan went on, in July 1960, to execute a major Cabinet reshuffle, putting noted pro-Europeans in key positions: Duncan Sandys became Secretary for Commonwealth Relations, Christopher Soames became Secretary for Agriculture (important for dealing with possible objections from the farmers), and Edward Heath became Lord Privy Seal and negotiator with the EEC. These shifts were, according to Miriam Camps, 'astute strategic moves' (Camps, 1964, p. 314). The imperialist *Daily Express* got wind of a 'sensational secret report' prepared for the Cabinet in July 1960, dealing with the supposed political necessity of British membership of the EEC, and called it a 'blueprint for disaster' (Camps, 1964, p. 293).

The outcome of the American elections of November 1960 finally cleared the last obstacle: Kennedy's foreign policy actively supported British membership in the EEC. The US remained firm on one point however (a logical consequence of its preference for global free trade arrangements such as the later GATT rounds of tarriff reductions), and insisted that the Commonwealth should remain outside EEC tariff walls (Beloff, 1963, pp. 101, 106–7). The new American position was made clear when Macmillan visited Kennedy in April 1961, and that opened the way for Macmillan's decision to apply for EEC membership.

The British application was announced on 31 July 1961. It was strongly supported by the United States administration. The universalist Kennedy offensive resulted in the articulation of a new concept of 'Atlantic partnership' in which a united Western Europe, including Britain, was an essential pillar, both in an economic sense and in a political sense (with regard to East–West relations and with regard to the restructuring of Western relations with the emerging Third World). As Kennedy himself formulated it on 4 July 1962, he wanted to 'discuss with a united Europe the ways and means of forming a concrete Atlantic partnership, a mutually beneficial partnership between the new union now emerging in Europe and the old American Union founded here a century and three quarters ago' (quoted by Beloff, 1963, p. 161). This, however, was not General de Gaulle's view of Europe's future. It was precisely Britain's success in restoring its special relation with the US – highlighted by the Nassau agreements on military and nuclear co-operation giving Britain Polaris missiles in place of the cancelled Skybolt – which also provided strong grounds for France's fear of an American Trojan Horse being introduced, and led to the eventual French veto in 1963.

Macmillan's role in the redefinition of Britain's international position had been played out: he had successfully removed both the domestic and the American obstacles in the way of his vision of British entry into Europe, only to fail because his very success had created a new obstacle inside the EEC.

In 1964 the Conservatives were succeeded by Labour. Many Labourites, particularly on the left, had been against EEC membership, but the Wilson government brought to power many of the corporate liberal Gaitskellites, some of whom had for a long time been in favour of British membership in the EEC. Roy Jenkins, for example, together with Sir William Beveridge, belonged to the Federal Union, founded in 1938, which was in favour of a political link between Britain and Western Europe. From 1961 to 1963 he led the Labour Common Market Committee, in 1963 replaced by the Labour Committee for Europe. From 1965 to 1969, he was also active in the Campaign for a European Political Community (in 1967 renamed Campaign for Europe), which interest he shared with, again, Sir William Beveridge, the Liberal Lord Gladwyn (director of S. G. Warburg & Co.), and Shirley Williams, another right-wing Labour activist.[19]

The new Labour leadership also realized, as Macmillan had, that in order to be able to achieve anything meaningful the consent of the American administration was essential. Harold Wilson took it upon himself to defend Labour's election manifesto in the *New York Times* (Miliband, 1972, p. 353), and immediately after coming to office he went to Washington, in the company of Patrick Gordon Walker (Foreign Secretary) and Denis Healey (Minister of Defence), to obtain America's blessing (Miliband, 1972, pp. 370–1). There was, after decolonization and after the acceptance of possible EEC membership within the context of the Atlantic partnership, still one more logical conclusion to be drawn from the Suez débâcle: Britain's military role 'East of Suez' was a millstone around the country's neck and had to be abandoned for the restructuring of Britain's position in the world to be completed.

In 1965, Edward Heath, the new Conservative leader, attempted to get the withdrawal from 'East of Suez' accepted as Tory policy. He was supported by the nationalist (as opposed to imperialist) wing of the party, personified by Enoch Powell. But he was unable to overcome the objections of the party's imperialist wing, and could not move as quickly as he wished (Gamble, 1974, pp. 164–5). It would be the Labour government that would in the end start the withdrawal from the East. In 1968 it was forced to adopt a deflationary programme including budget cuts amounting to £700 million, and to make this package somewhat more palatable for the rank and file the government at the same time undertook the obligation to start withdrawal from Singapore, Malaysia and the Persian Gulf by March 1971 (instead of some time between 1973 and 1977, as had been the position until then). On the request of the Prime Minister of Singapore the date was postponed until December 1971. The shadow spokesman for Defence, Enoch Powell, agreed, although most other Conservatives were still unwilling to acquiesce in these plans. Nevertheless, when the Tories returned to power in 1970 the withdrawal was not cancelled: both major parties had finally accepted that Britain's role in the world was no longer imperial (Miliband, 1972, p. 368; Calvocoressi, 1979, pp. 216–7).

In 1967 the Labour government for the second time applied for British membership of the Common Market. Again the attempt foundered on a French veto. By 1969, however, both the domestic and the international situation had changed so decisively that British governments had no choice but to pursue the European option until they were successful. In particular, the following shifts had made this course inevitable.

The Foreign Office had once been in favour of intimate British involvement in West European unification, but had returned to the Churchillian view after 1947. Suez, however, set in motion a process of fundamental reappraisal of the place of Britain in the world, resulting by the mid-1960s in the conviction that Britain could only hope to maintain even second-rate power status if it were to join the EEC (cf. Jessop, 1980, p. 70–4).

Secondly, there was a shift in international reactions to Britain's wish to join the Common Market. For one, there was now unqualified American support: Kennedy's ideas of Atlantic partnership were an important factor in propelling Britain forward towards Europe. Also the political changes taking place in France after 1968 diminished French resistance: in 1969 de Gaulle was succeeded by Pompidou, and, more important, the Atlanticist Liberal Giscard d'Estaing as Minister of Finance came to dominate French economic policies. Thus, when the most European of British politicians, Edward Heath, became Prime Minister in 1970 conditions were as favourable as they had ever been. The 1971 application by Britain was successful, and on 1 January 1973 Britain became a member of the European Community.

A third factor which had aided this development had been the change in the position of the City–Treasury axis, resulting from the changing position of Britain in the world economy.

The world market and the British political economy in the 1950s

The multinationalization of the British economy

One of the purposes of the Marshall plan was to facilitate American investment in the recipient countries. In the case of Great Britain, this objective was certainly pursued successfully. Between 1943 and 1950 American direct private investment in the UK increased from $519 million to $847 million, while in the same period total direct American investment in Europe declined from $2,025 million to $1,720 million. The British share of American direct investment in Europe thus increased from approximately 25 per cent to almost half, to decline again to approximately one-third by 1971 (Moock, 1977, p. 27). In the countries of the Commonwealth, American direct investment started to surpass British investments from 1950. By the end of 1953, American investment in the British Commonwealth amounted to 43 per cent of all American foreign investment. The postwar period thus showed a strong increase in the rate of penetration of American capital in Britain and its traditional imperial backyard (Aaronovitch, 1955, p. 66).

American business in Britain during the 1950s grew much faster than British business. Between 1950 and 1958, UK manufacturing output increased by 16 per cent, while US investments in manufacturing industry in the UK increased by 151 per cent. Between 1958 and 1965 these figures were 33 and 143 per cent respectively (Moock, 1977, p. 32). In 1965, foreign direct investment in Britain (almost all American) amounted to 10 per cent of the net capital stock in the UK, and US firms were responsible for no less than 20 per cent of new net fixed capital formation (Murray, 1975, pp. 13, 16). The share of US firms in British exports was expected to rise to 25 per cent by 1980 (Poulantzas, 1975, p. 55).

Between 1958–60 and 1970–2, the average annual inflow of foreign capital in Britain increased from £122.7 million to £387.3 million. The share of American firms remained almost stable at approximately two-thirds, while the share of European firms increased slowly from less than 1 per cent to slightly over 10 per cent (see Boyd, 1975, p. 69). The total stock of American investment in Britain in these years increased from $2.147 billion in 1958 to $11.115 billion in 1973 (Boyd, 1975, p. 71).

But incoming American investment was not the only variable in the period under consideration. From the end of the war, British overseas investment had resumed, and it soon became an important factor again in the development (or underdevelopment) of the British economy. British direct investment overseas totalled £4.5 billion by 1953 (Aaronovitch, 1955, p. 109) and the flow of new investments continued: during the years 1952–8 the annual average of direct investment flowing out of Britain was £160 million (Youngson, 1976, p. 159), and between 1958 and the early 1970s new outward investment further increased to over £700 million annually (Boyd, 1975, p. 68). The EEC's share of British overseas investment increased dramatically faster than the United States': the US's share increased from 7.2 per cent in 1958–60 to 18.9 per cent in 1970–2, while the EEC's share increased from 7.8 to 31.9 per cent.

This rapidly growing stream of capital exports by 1965 amounted to over 30 per cent of total fixed capital formation by British companies, and was mostly undertaken by the largest firms: 80 per cent of direct foreign investment from the UK was by the fifty largest companies (Murray, 1975, p. 16).

The explanation for this massive resumption of capital export from Britain after the war must of course be multifaceted. For one, it reflects the country's postwar attempt to retain or regain imperial control over the remnants of the empire. To a large degree the internationalization of British capital was also a manifestation of the general trend towards increased internationalization characterizing the postwar Atlantic economy. Britain, or rather British capital, played a pivotal role in the constitution of the integrated Atlantic economy, and she was one of the first European countries to liberalize foreign exchange transactions. This partly explains why British capital internationalized considerably sooner than continental European capital.

Furthermore, the formation of the European Common Market provided an extra stimulus to British capital exports, particularly to Europe. Finally, the relative stagnation of the domestic market and its lower profitability have played a role. The defensive strength of the working class, its effective power of veto on the shopfloor, argues Jessop, 'stimulated the export of capital to areas where labour was more compliant, wages were lower, and the rate of exploitation higher' (Jessop, 1980, p. 35). The relative flight of capital from Britain in its turn reinforced some of the tendencies driving it out in the first place, as the Reddaway Report showed in detail (Reddaway, 1967).

The effects of City dominance for British monetary policy

During the period of the *Pax Britannica*, when Britain was still the 'workshop of the world', the international orientation of

British financial interests had presented no particular problem for the domestic economy: on the contrary, the expansion of industrial capital went hand in hand with, even depended on, the successful operation of the City of London as the dominant international centre of commerce and finance. In the era of classical imperialism the interests of domestic industrial capital and the City diverged, until in 1932 the collapse of the world market and the imposition of imperial preference reconstituted if not a harmony of interests, at least a tolerable *modus vivendi*.

After 1945, these conditions no longer prevailed. The price to be paid by Britain for American assistance after the war was the gradual liberalization of Britain's foreign economic relations. As we have seen, this led to penetration by American capital (through trade and investment) both in the countries of the Commonwealth and in Britain itself, and to a resumption of capital exports from Britain. In the process, the City regained its hegemony over other fractions of British capital. Increasingly, however, the role of the City in the world economy changed, and its place was now clearly defined by the contours of the Atlantic economy and the *Pax Americana* (cf. Cain and Hopkins, 1987, pp. 16–17), and by the dominance of those fractions of capital associated with that American hegemony – the internationalizing 'Fordist' industries such as automobiles, chemicals, and consumer electronics. In fact, it was precisely because of its successful adaptation to the new realities of dominance that the City could regain its hegemonic position in Britain. The City thus came to play a crucial role in the internationalization of British (and many non-British) multinational corporations with all its consequences for domestic industry and employment.

Colonial interests also became subject to a radical restructuring in the light of the new international balance of forces: first, the relative weight of colonial capital (extractive capital) diminished sharply after 1945 and the centre of gravity of surplus value production shifted more and more to the mass-producing industries in the industrialized capitalist economies; secondly, the role of colonial capital itself was restructured under the impact of American hegemony and decolonization. The restructuring of British colonial capital was reflected in the changing direction of British foreign investments, in the redirection of trade flows, and in the diversification of activities by colonial companies themselves. In fact, colonial capital underwent the same subjugation to the interests of manufacturing industry as did mining and iron and steel within Britain (and Europe).

Under the Conservative governments of the 1950s, relations between the City, the Bank of England and the Treasury were restored to their earlier self-evident normality, owing to the force of habit, the social background of the members of the government, and the newly reconfirmed hegemony of the City over the economy:

> government may develop relations of cooperation with a key producers group in which there is such a gentlemanly give and take that no mention and little thought of sanctions are occasioned. The Conservative government's relations with the City were of this character. (Beer, 1969, p. 327)

The dominance of the City, with its strong external orientation and its grip on the Treasury, caused the stop–go cycle so specific to the British economy of the 1950s and 1960s. (A good analysis of this phenomenon is to be found in Brett, 1985, pp. 148–56.) Every expansionary period quickly led (because of Britain's strong dependence on imports) to balance of payments problems (which were aggravated still further by Britain's overseas military expenditure and its capital exports). These Sterling crises could not be countered by devaluation and an industrial policy aiming at the restructuring of industry, because that would endanger the international role of the pound. Instead the crisis each time had to be met by deflation, which 'reinforced the conditions making for continued industrial decline' (Jessop, 1980, p. 30–3). But the expansionary phases did not lead to industrial restructuring either, because the peculiar balance of class forces in Britain prevented this: industrial capital was unable to articulate its interests on a political level, let alone to formulate a concept of the general interest which had a chance of gaining hegemony over the City's concept. There is some justification, therefore, in claiming that the City's role in the Atlantic economy, particularly after the completion of convertibility in 1958, 'placed real constraints on the range of domestic policy options' (Ingham, 1984, p. 215).

This then was the situation when the 1964 Labour government came to office: it was faced by immediate balance of payments problems, and by the inescapable reality of City hegemony over monetary policy. Nevertheless, the plans Labour had when arriving in the corridors of power were far-reaching. The new government created, alongside the Treasury, a second 'Super Ministry', the Department of Economic Affairs. Subsequently, a battle of competence developed between the established power of the Treasury and the new power struggling to emerge, the main issue being control over the general management of the economy.[20] As it transpired, the Labour government did not dare go against the pressures exerted by the City and the Bank of England, and deflated the economy once more.

In the meantime, however, the 'City' itself was no unchanging constant. Indeed, changes were taking place with increasing vehemence. In 1962, things did not to established figures in the City seem likely to change: in that year Hambro's Bank could still in all honesty consider the Eurodollar market to be a 'temporary phenomenon' (Ferris, 1970, p. 140). But relative newcomers in the City such as S. G. Warburg had already found out that the Eurodollar market was a very lucrative new development. Eurodollars first appeared in London in 1958, when all foreign exchange controls were relaxed, and the real growth of the market dates back to about 1960 (Ferris, 1970, p. 172–3). The 1960s showed an enormous increase of the size of the market, which even accelerated when the inflationary financing of the Vietnam War started after 1964.

The growth of this international money market increased the risks of a massive run on the pound. The sudden withdrawal of funds from London for purely speculative reasons might well have undermined confidence in Sterling for reasons having nothing to do with the soundness of Britain's domestic economy. This risk was 'the dark side of being an international money-centre where the local currency is weak' (Ferris, 1970, p. 173), and it 'has challenged the state's short-term stabilization instruments' (Murray, 1975, pp. 24–5). This became painfully clear in November 1967. Foreign currency manipulation by multinational companies played a decisive role in the immense speculation against the pound[21] which in the end forced the government to turn to the IMF and to devalue the pound (from $2.80 to $2.40). The new Chancellor, Roy Jenkins, faithfully executed the deflationary policies prescribed by the IMF, as his successor Denis Healey would again do nine years later.

The devaluation of the pound proved three important points.

(1) It showed that Britain's international commitments and position made it impossible to combine Keynesian domestic policies with external economic liberalism (Brett, 1985, p. 154).

(2) After devaluation the American firms that had profited from their hedging operations invested their profits in an expansion of their British subsidiaries. Murray concludes from this that devaluation only served to intensify Britain's incorporation in the world market (Murray, 1975, p. 43), but on the other

hand this fact also proves that in principle a policy of devaluation could indeed have led to domestic industrial expansion.

(3) The fact of devaluation, and the fact that it was effected with relatively little opposition from the City, showed that the growth of the Euromoney markets had made more and more City firms independent from, or at least less dependent on, the exchange rate of the pound, as long as exchange controls were not reinstituted.

The growth of the Euromarket led many clearing banks to taking an interest in merchant banks,[22] which had been very active in the Euromarkets from the beginning (Ferris, 1968, pp: 162–3). This movement of the clearing banks into merchant banking was in fact the start of a fundamental restructuring of British finance capital (cf. Overbeek, 1980), which was to contribute to the fundamental restructuring of the British political economy in the 1970s.

In the preceding chapter we traced the redefinition of Britain's global position in the years 1942–73. The first period, between 1942 and 1950, is the period of (planning for) postwar reconstruction of the global order. We have seen that Britain's position as a major power was secured after 1945, but in a radically different context than before the war: whatever Britain's role, it was circumscribed by the all-pervasive fact of American hegemony. Any remaining vision of an *independent* role was finally shattered by the events of 1956. After that, the way was cleared for a fundamental reorientation of Britain's foreign policy, in which membership of the European Community became the overriding goal. The failure to secure this membership in the years of the Macmillan government had serious consequences for the British *economy*, even though most big British *firms* were able to overcome these consequences through their strategy of large-scale internationalization.

The growing internationalization of the world economy helped the City of London to regain its dominance over other fractions of British capital. The City's role in the world economy came to resemble (even more so than before 1929), that of an offshore financial centre, detached from the domestic economy. Its interest in maintaining a high exchange rate for the pound (necessary to attract Sterling holdings from abroad) diverged sharply from that of Britain's industry, which was harmed in its competitive position on foreign markets. It was only with the growth of the Eurodollar market in the second half of the 1960s that the City's interest in a high exchange rate for the pound diminished.

Having sketched the context of the insertion of Britain's economy into the world economy in the 1950s and 1960s, and that of the restructuring of the international state system under American domination after 1945, it is now time to turn our attention to the domestic side of the coin, the attempts by successive governments to modernize and rationalize Britain's economy.

CHAPTER 5

The postwar Fordist offensives

In Western Europe in general, and in Germany and the occupied countries in particular, the war served as 'executioner of the crisis' (Goralczyk, 1975, p. 39). Western capitalism was thoroughly changed by the effects of the war, which created the conditions for a phase of rapid growth.

In Britain, the war did not have this effect, neither in a strict economic sense nor in a political sense. Established interests in Britain never lost control of politics: the important political parties and their leadership were not, as in the greater part of Europe, destroyed by (or corrupted and discredited by collaboration with) occupying German forces. Similarly, working-class organizations in Britain were not physically crushed or forced to operate underground. The war, and the national effort to win it, greatly strengthened reformist tendencies in British trade unions, while in most of continental Europe the revolutionary forces in the working-class movements were strengthened in the resistance against Nazi occupation.

In the course of the early postwar years, the balance of power was rather favourable to the forces of the Left. It was only after two or three years that these forces were isolated and immobilized, with American intervention playing a major role in the process (see, for example, Kolko and Kolko, 1972). The ousting of the French and Italian communists from the government and the 'solution' of the Greek Civil War completed the elimination of the immediate 'internal threat' from the Left.

Britain constituted an exception to this rule. The defeat in the General Strike had been a serious setback for the Labour movement, but during most of the 1930s and certainly during the war the situation of the British working class had steadily improved. The participation of the Labour Party in the National government during the war, and the pivotal role played by prominent trade union officials, instilled strong reformist tendencies into the working-class movement, in response to the willingness of most sections of the British bourgeoisie to put aside its traditional unco-operative attitude for the time

112

being. Hence, 'it was subjectively the only major proletariat in the world which suffered no serious defeat for the thirty years from 1936 to 1966 – an experience which profoundly modified the relationship of class forces in England' (Mandel, 1975, p. 179).

Further, the productive potential of the country, particularly in the basic industries such as iron and steel, underwent no such spectacular expansion as during the First World War. Rather than expand, rationalize and modernize the basic industries, the War Cabinet chose to import the necessary raw materials and finished products, if possible from the Commonwealth but if necessary from the United States. The war also left British industrial capacity, such as it was, intact. Although the extent of destruction on the continent should not be exaggerated, there was a significant difference. Britain emerged from the war with a productive apparatus that was heavily dated if not altogether obsolete.

For the time being, however, this state of affairs did not particularly occupy the minds of most Britons. The British voters, although acclaiming Churchill the victorious war leader, voted overwhelmingly against Churchill, the Conservative Party leader, because that party was generally held responsible for the very high unemployment of the interwar years. After the shock of the lost elections had subsided, Churchill could acknowledge the implications of this state of affairs: he was reported to have admitted: 'I'm not certain the Conservative Party could have dealt with the labour troubles that are coming' (quoted by Childs, 1979, p. 8). This was the job to be taken on by the Labour Party.

The postwar Labour government

The Labour government, elected by a landslide, was first of all bound by its promises of aiming for full employment and social security, and for a thorough (and badly needed) modernization and rationalization of the British productive apparatus. In this way Labour became the political party *par excellence* to be guided by a productive-capital concept. In its concrete historical manifestation of the welfare state and Keynesian economic policies, this became the dominant concept of control for the three decades to follow. In this section, we will look at two broad areas of postwar domestic policy which were only reluctantly accepted by the Conservatives: that of industrial policy (nationalization), and that of the establishment of the welfare state.

Nationalization

The successful introduction of Fordism required the subordination of basic industries to the needs of mass production of consumer durables. On the continent, this subordination was eventually effected in 1951 by the establishment of the European Coal and Steel Community (ECSC), which in one study was dubbed (because of the role of American intervention partly through the Marshall plan) 'An American Plan for Europe' (Van der Pijl, 1978). The formation of the ECSC, seen by many in Britain as the resurrection of the prewar European steel cartel (see, for example, Aaronovitch, 1955), must in fact be considered not as a sign of renewed strength of the steel barons, but on the contrary as the proof of their final elimination as an independent and powerful fraction of the European bourgeoisie, indeed as a supranational 'nationalization' of the basic industries (Bode, 1975). The state monopoly tendency thus lost its pre-eminence and was transcended by the rise of corporate liberalism. In Britain the nationalizations of the years 1945–50 were intended to perform the same function via an alternative and autonomous route.

The programme of nationalizations to which the Labour Party was committed by its election manifesto, *Let us Face the Future* (1944), was directed primarily at most of the basic industries. Before or during the war these industries had been brought under some form of public regulation. Both during these years, and also in the immediate postwar period, the capitalists of the industries concerned proved themselves incapable of carrying out the rationalizations and modernizations which were necessary if they were to recover to a minimum level of competitiveness. In particular, the basic industries would have to be reorganized according to the requirements of the fast-expanding modern industries with their mass production techniques. This applied first of all to energy-producing industries (coal, electricity and gas), transportation (road haulage, civil aviation, railways), infrastructure (the building of roads, harbours, and so on), and finally central banking. The plans to nationalize these sectors of business were widely accepted.

The method of implementing nationalization was a fairly simple one: it consisted in entrusting the nationalized industries to committees and councils made up of the capitalists concerned. Participation from the trade union movement was minimal: many in the unions were reluctant to accept responsibility for the conduct of what remained in essence a capitalist enterprise. In this way the Labour government inadvertently repeated the practices of the prewar cartéls in these industries, since most employers were interested in restriction rather than in restructuring what were hopelessly unproductive industries when compared to the United States (see Brady, 1950, pp. 205–11; also Burn, 1961). The employers were further helped in their restrictionist stance by the maintenance of price controls, which ensured that inefficient firms remained in business.[1]

In the case of coal, nationalization was not opposed vigorously: the coal owners had had their chance to reorganize and modernize their industry before and during the war, and they had not taken it. The miners strongly favoured nationalization and exerted strong pressures on the Labour Party to move quickly. The Conservatives neither opposed the Nationalization Act, nor did they promise denationalization of the coal industry once the voters returned them to office. However, beyond the pure act of nationalization, Labour had no clear plan as to what to do with the industry, and in fact the policies pursued were dictated by the circumstances of the day. In the immediate postwar years, the principal problem was to produce as much coal as possible, because demand was enormous and in early 1947 rose very sharply because of the unusually harsh winter. Investment in the coal industry rose considerably after nationalization. Yet, in the first years of its existence, executives of the National Coal Board sometimes felt desperate because productivity would not rise:

> We are putting in the pits day by day great masses of machinery, and it does not seem to matter what we do – output per man is not rising. The board are very much concerned. There is something wrong somewhere ... We think there is a slackening off all over and we are not going to get the advantage of the machinery. (quoted by Youngson, 1960, p. 193)

In the course of the 1950s the situation improved. The rationalizations carried through in the mining industry between 1947 and 1974 were arguably impressive (see, for example, Fine and Harris, 1985, pp. 167–202). They nevertheless left Britain with a structure of energy provision quite different from that in Western Europe. After a number of transition years (according to Fine and Harris this period lasted until 1956) a much stronger change to oil as the major source of energy would have been possible, and perhaps desirable.

115

By far the most important nationalization, and the one creating the strongest opposition, was that of the iron and steel industry. The story of the nationalization of the steel industry in Britain is an important one: it was an important cornerstone in Labour's general industrial policy, it became a major focus of inter-party conflict, and it also had repercussions for the attitude of Britain *vis-à-vis* the first serious European integration project, the European Coal and Steel Community.

Several factors can explain why nationalization in this case was so strongly opposed, and why it was undone so quickly after the Conservatives regained power.

First, and perhaps most important, the iron and steel industry was, generally speaking, a prosperous and profitable industry. The situation on the world market, where demand outstripped production, where major competitors such as the Germans and the Japanese were temporarily unable to pose a threat, and where the dollar shortage put a brake on American competitiveness, was very favourable. The successes of the immediate postwar years in the field of industrial development must therefore be ascribed in the first place not to any success of the interventions by the Labour government,[2] but more to the exceptional situation on the world market. The nationalization of such a profitable industry (even if only temporarily profitable) would possibly, it was feared, clear the way for the nationalization of other profitable industries. The Labour Party's policy statement of April 1949, entitled *Labour Believes in Britain*, contained proposals to nationalize life insurance, sugar (meaning the monopoly Tate & Lyle), cement (Portland Cement), meat wholesaling and slaughtering, water, and most minerals.[3] Under the provisions of this plan the government could also start public enterprises where private capital failed to 'act in the public interest', take over concerns 'which are woefully failing the nation', and buy up any firms it might want through the normal acquisition procedures (Miliband, 1972, pp. 299–300). The age-old plans fostered by the Labour Left to nationalize finance and banking, it was feared, might again be put on the agenda if a stop was not put to the nationalization drive now – hence, for instance, the campaign by the rightwing pro-business lobby organization, Aims of Industry, on behalf of Tate & Lyle.

A second factor was the hybrid character of the steel industry. An important part of the industry was in fact producing raw materials and semi-finished products which served as inputs for manufacturing industries which used steel, such as motor car production and engineering.[4] The subordination of this part of the steel industry through nationalization would probably not have been so seriously opposed, and motor car manufacturers, for example, had been complaining at least since 1934 about the high steel prices maintained by·the BISF. These corporate-liberal industrialists did not seem very worried about the dangers of 'creeping socialism', but rather welcomed the proposals for nationalization (Brady, 1950, p. 196; also Burn, 1961, p. 65, 68ff.).

Also, during the war the representatives of heavy industries (such as those producing armaments) had acquired a particularly prominent position in the state apparatus: the Ministry of War had been completely dominated by such men as Sir Charles Craven (Vickers), Sir John Anderson (later Lord Waverly, of Vickers and ICI), and Sir Ronald Weeks (a lieutenant-general, and president of Vickers) (Aaronovitch, 1955, pp. 101–2).

These two sections of the iron and steel industry ensured that their interests were not put in jeopardy. When the final Nation-alization Act was presented to Parliament, significant exceptions had been included. Two vertically integrated companies (which had internally carried out the subordination of the production of crude steel to final steel consumption) were explicitly left out: the Ford Motor Company, and Vickers, the owners of English Steel and Darlington Forge (Brady, 1950, pp. 217, 220). These revealing exceptions had been included at the last minute after direct intervention by the Marshall Aid administrator Paul Hoffman (who, significantly, was also a director of the American car manufacturer Studebaker). He threatened to halt all Marshall Aid funds going to the British steel industry (most of which, $27 million, went to the Steel Company of Wales, owners of the first continuous wide-strip rolling mill in Britain at Ebbw Vale) if the Act were passed in its original form (Brady, 1950, p. 189). Whether Ford and Vickers were explicitly mentioned is not certain; in the context, it is not impossible that they were.

A third factor is the circumstance that, unlike mineworkers, the steel workers were relatively indifferent to the issue of nation-alization: there was no radical rank and file pressure to pro-pel the case forward (Barry, 1965, p. 377). Perhaps the time factor is important here: if the government had tackled iron and steel immediately in 1945, it might have been in a stron-ger position than it now found itself (Miliband, 1972, p. 301).

Finally, many steel companies maintained a remarkable posi-tion in the network of interlocking directorships which had been established between 1946 and 1952. More than half of all inter-locks between industrial companies in 1952 involved steel compa-nies, with the Westminster Bank occupying a central position (see Stanworth and Giddens, 1975, pp. 15–18).[5] This high degree of interlocking reflects in the first place the difficulties which the industry had experienced two decades earlier, resulting in the involvement of the banks, and secondly the centripetal effects of the operation of the Iron and Steel Federation since 1934; lastly it can partly also be seen as an attempt to join forces in order to avert nationalization (Stanworth and Giddens, 1975, p. 16). This last motive undoubtedly also played a role in the positive initial reactions voiced by the British iron and steel industry to the Schuman plan for the ECSC, launched in May 1950 (Anouil, 1960, p. 49).

The case of the steel industry was also indicative for the role of the nationalization programme in a wider sense. The Labour Party's commitment to a productive-capital concept dated back either to prewar resolutions or to the 1944 election programme, entitled *Let Us Face The Future*, and was pushed forward primarily by the rank and file of the party. It was only supported to a limited extent by the party leadership. And in so far as Labour leaders (Morrison, for example) did propagate nationalization, they generally did not clearly specify in detail the goals to be served by nationalization. As a result, very little planning had been done at the time when Labour came into office. Emanuel Shinwell, who as Minister of Fuel was immediately responsible for the running of the nationalized coal industry, expressed his amazement over the absence of any plan as follows:

> For the whole of my political life I had listened to the Party speakers advocating state ownership and control of the coal mines, and I had myself spoken of it as a primary task once the Labour Party was in power. I had believed, as other members had, that in the Party archives a blueprint was ready ... I found nothing practicable and tangible existed. I had to start with a clear desk. (quoted by Allen, 1960, p. 271n)

In steel, the situation was no better. In 1947, productivity per man year in the USA was twice that of the British steel industry (Burn, 1961, pp. 270–1). There was, therefore, certainly an objective necessity for the sector's rationalization. But this should not tempt us to view the nationalization of the steel industry as 'the better solution because ... it more suited the class interests of capital, even though the class did not fight for that solution' (McEachern, 1979, p. 139), nor can we simply conclude that Labour's policy 'strengthened British capitalism in some essential regards' (Miliband, 1973, p. 97). Two qualifications are necessary here.

In the first place, the fact that *ex post facto* 'capital' proved able to live with nationalization and even to be better off in the end does not justify the thesis that at the time of nationalization 'the class interests of capital' were served by nationalization even though 'capital' itself resisted this 'better solution'. The nationalization of steel progressed *through struggle* and in the end 'capital' was able to adapt to the outcome of the struggle: no more, no less.

The second qualification concerns the parties to the struggle: it was not simply a struggle between the Labour movement wielding political power on the one hand, and 'capital' on the other. The most important struggle concerning the nationalization of steel, the most important clash of interests, rather, was that between two fractions of capital, or more broadly between two coalitions. The form in which this clash was resolved (nationalization rather than integration in the ECSC) was decided by a whole range of factors, such as the commitment of the Labour Party to nationalization and the general direction of British foreign policy after the war, which precluded British membership in a supranational European integration project. The clash of interests itself, however, was very similar to that in Western Europe, namely, the clash between older, pre-Fordist, industries such as textiles, coal, and iron and steel, and the 'modern', Fordist, industries. The view that the Labour government served 'the' interests of 'capital' is too simplistic. Rather, the Labour government, through its express objective of modernizing and rationalizing the British economy, of establishing a 'mixed economy' (*not* of establishing socialism),[6] can be said to have served the interests of those fractions of British capital whose prospects for rapid accumulation were intimately tied in with this modernization and with the successful introduction of Fordism throughout the whole British economy instead of just in a few isolated enclaves. Moreover, those interests which were served by the modernization programme (presumably those of the 'Fordist' industries) were not served in sufficient measure.

The abolition of many wartime controls in a way symbolizes the fact that Labour willingly gave up the instruments which might have enabled it to enforce the rationalization of the British economy and of industrial relations in Britain. It proved 'impossible to develop the wartime practice and understandings into forms of central bargaining like those of Germany or Sweden' (Middlemas, 1979, p. 398).

The establishment of the welfare state

In 1942 the Liberal William Beveridge had published his *Report on Social Security*.[7] In the report, measures were proposed to

119

combat the renewed occurrence of mass poverty and unemployment through a redistribution of income by means of a flat-rate contribution, thus implicitly rejecting socialist-inspired calls for a progressive-rate system (Taylor, 1975, p. 688). The Conservatives in the government were not very enthusiastic about the proposals, and it was only after serious and sustained pressure by Labour that the government reluctantly welcomed the report and made a vague promise to realize some of its proposals after the war (Taylor, 1975, p. 688).

Initial Conservative opposition to the Beveridge Report – and the gradual waning of Labour radicalism in the course of the war in fact intensified this – indicated that corporate liberalism had not developed into a truly comprehensive concept of control encompassing the sphere of foreign policy (Atlanticism) *and* the sphere of domestic policy, particularly with regard to the incorporation of labour into the very structure of British capitalism. The bleak result, in this area of postwar planning, was the 1944 White Paper on employment policy,[8] where it was stated that: 'The Government accept as one of their primary aims and responsibilities the maintenance of a high and stable level of employment after the war' (quoted in Winch, 1972, p. 279).

Beveridge himself was not at all satisfied with the result: he denounced the employment policies embodied in the White Paper as 'public works policy, not a policy of full employment', and reacted with a truly Keynesian tract, *Full Employment in a Free Society*. In it he stated that maintenance of full employment was a precondition for the prevalence of democracy. He further advocated, following Keynes, a considerable socialization of investment (housing, roads, schools, and so on) and of demand (through social security benefits), although not of production. The implementation of the main elements of the welfare state was taken up by the Labour government. The year 1948 saw the enactment of National Assistance, the passing of the National Insurance Act, and the institution of the National Health Service, together meant to provide a universal national minimum income.

In order to control and direct the development of the economy, attempts at planning were also undertaken. These attempts, however, never aimed at subjecting the market to social needs and criteria, and went no further than voluntary arrangements and, even in the nationalized industries, 'indicative planning' (Leruez, 1972). The working-class organizations, and first of all the TUC, were not interested (certainly not after 1944) in workers' control. In fact, the TUC and Labour were at best interested in 'public control', in combination with the continuation of management power in the firms. In its 1944 *Report on Reconstruction*, the TUC proposed an 'explicit industrial contract' along tripartite lines, but the Attlee government would not co-operate in this; it was not until 1962 that their proposals were (in a sense) embodied in the National Economic Development Council (Middlemas, 1979, p. 393).

In the area of fiscal policy, the Labour government set out at first on an expansionary course, hoping to facilitate both investment and private consumption in the same way that was later so successfully adopted in Western Europe and provided the basis for the postwar boom. Chancellor Hugh Dalton's 'cheap money' policy explicitly aimed at avoiding the deflationary recession (1921–2) which had followed the postwar boom of the years 1919–20, and to consolidate (or effect) the 'euthanasia of the *rentier*' (as prescribed by Keynes) (cf. Morgan, 1985, pp. 337–9; also Winch, 1972, pp. 294–5). The cheap money policy attracted criticism from the financial press and from the Bank of England because it led to a strong growth of domestic expenditure and a worsening of the trade balance. The attempt to restore the convertibility of Sterling in 1947 made it clear that it was impossible to maintain the value of the pound and at the same time to sustain the intended level of spending. The year 1947 turned into a year of disaster, and by autumn Dalton was forced to a return to austerity with his November budget: 'An expansionist, part inflationary policy had been cast aside, under extreme necessity. Dalton had fallen with it' (Morgan, 1985, p. 350).

Dalton's successor at the Treasury was Sir Stafford Cripps, who had only just (in 1947) become Minister of Economic Affairs. Because Cripps combined both posts, the Ministry of Economic Affairs, which had not yet been institutionally established, in fact became a department of the Treasury. In this way industrial policy was subsumed under monetary policy, which consolidated the restored domination of the Treasury over government policy (cf. Leruez, 1972).

The government, however, had not lost the (guarded) confidence of the trade unions. Cripps succeeded in February 1948 in reaching the first tripartite voluntary wage–price agreement, and for a year and a half wage restraint on a voluntary basis worked. The devaluation of the pound in September 1949, however, necessitated by the terms of the American loans and of Marshall Aid, terminated this short-lived experiment in corporatist wage regulation: the one-sided imposition of wage controls to which the devaluation forced the government was too great a strain for the incipient structure of tripartite organization.

121

However, thanks to the voluntary arrangements, industrial profits in this period were higher than ever (Rogow and Shore, 1955, p. 68).

The Labour experiment in expansionism found its definitive end when the Korean War and the costs of Britain's participation forced the government to even further austerity measures. The cuts affecting the National Health Service, the showpiece of Labour's achievement, prompted the Minister of Labour (Aneurin Bevan) and the Minister of Trade (Harold Wilson) to resign in 1950. The elections in that year confirmed that Labour had all but forfeited the support for its reform programme it had gained in 1945, and in 1951 its fate was sealed, even though Labour polled more votes (48.8 per cent) than the Conservatives (48 per cent) who owed their electoral victory to the collapse of the Liberals (from 9.1 per cent in 1950 to 2.5 per cent in 1951) as much as to the electoral system (Gamble, 1974, pp. 53–4).

The continued decline of Britain during the 1950s

Notwithstanding the relatively favourable conditions immediately after the war, the Labour government had not been able to prevent the British economy very quickly resuming the decline which had been temporarily suspended by the Depression and the war. This was clearly reflected in the development of industrial production during the 1950s, which was slower in Britain than in any other developed capitalist economy except for the United States (see Table 5.1).

Table 5.1 Indices of industrial production, 1950–8 (1953 = 100)

	FRG	FRA	ITA	NL	US	UK
1950	72	89	78	88	82	94
1951	85	99	89	91	89	98
1952	91	98	91	91	92	95
1953	100	100	100	100	100	100
1954	112	109	109	111	94	108
1955	129	117	119	119	106	114
1956	139	128	128	124	109	114
1957	147	139	138	127	110	116
1958	152	145	143	127	102	114

Source: Boyd, 1975, p. 20.

In the steel industry, developments during the 1950s were no better. The denationalization by the Conservatives after their electoral victory in 1951 proved that the situation for British steel was doubtful at best: many of the former owners of steel firms were not interested in buying back their interests, but instead had already shifted their activity to other, more promising, investments.

In the years 1952–8 investment in the UK steel industry was only one-third to half of that on the Continent, and investment per ton was lower in Britain than in the ECSC countries in all of these years but 1956 and 1958; productivity per man year reflected this (Burn, 1961, p. 454). Finally, steel prices in the UK also rose faster in this period than in the ECSC, while the recession of 1958 also had more serious effects in Britain than on the continent (Burn, 1961, p. 447). In short, during the 1950s the European steel industry performed much better than the British.

Developments in the steel industry were representative of developments in most British industrial sectors. Even though the growth rates achieved were extraordinary when compared to the preceding decades or even century, they lagged consistently behind growth rates on the European continent, not to speak of Japan, and continued to do so into the 1960s. From 1958 to 1967, industrial production rose by 70 per cent in the Common Market, and by 73 per cent in the United States. By contrast, in the UK the growth of industrial production over the same period was no more than 32 per cent (Boyd, 1975, p. 20). During the 1950s and 1960s, Britain also lagged behind as regards the rate of investment in relation to GDP, growth rates of GDP and industrial productivity, and international competitiveness. As a result, Britain's share in world industrial production declined from 8.6 per cent in 1950 to 5.4 per cent in 1970 (IPW, 1982, p. 28); its share in world exports of manufactured goods declined from 25.5 per cent in 1950 to 10.8 per cent in 1970 (Gamble, 1981, p. 21).

Concentration and centralization of capital

Under the influence of renewed British decline, there was a noticeably increased concentration and centralization of British capital, which is always one of the first reactions of capital to problems of decline in competitiveness and profit rates.

The concentration and centralization of capital, which had been tempered by the developments of the 1930s and 1940s (first by

123

the dominance of state-monopolist cartellization, then by the effects of the wartime controls and their retention by the Labour government), first regained momentum when the Conservatives returned to power. Between 1952 and 1973, 420 firms disappeared annually through mergers and takeovers, representing an average total value of £375 million (Aaronovitch and Sawyer, 1975, p. 124).

The merger movement was also more intense in the UK than in the Common Market: between 1958 and 1962 there were 3,384 mergers in the UK against 1,000 in the EEC (Jalée, 1970, p. 116). But the difference became especially striking in the wake of the 1966–7 recession: in 1967 there were 1,068 mergers in the UK, as against 12 in the Federal Republic, 8 in France, 5 in the Netherlands, and 5 in Switzerland (Stanworth and Giddens, 1975, p. 26n). As a result of this process of monopolization, during 1967 and 1968 10 per cent of all industrial, commercial and financial assets in the UK changed hands, while a quarter of all companies worth more than £10 million were taken over (Spiegelberg, 1973, p. 167). The government played an active part in some of these mergers (notably in the aircraft, shipping and cotton industries, as in the 1930s), while in most other cases it remained uninvolved. Of the approximately 1,000 mergers between 1965 and 1975 qualifying for scrutiny by the Monopolies Commission, only 33 were actually investigated (Van Iersel, 1976, p. 143ff.).

The result of this high mobility of capital was that the network of interlocking directorships between financial institutions and the top fifty industrial companies grew rapidly tighter: the total number of ties between financial companies and the top fifty industrials increased from 69 in 1946 to 88 in 1960 and further to 94 in 1970. The merchant banks were responsible for a disproportionate share of these ties (Stanworth and Giddens, 1975, pp. 19–23). During the 1950s and 1960s the merchant banks indeed became more and more central to the operation of British capitalism, not just to its international commercial activities, but also to the operation of the market in shares and bonds of British industry (cf. Brown, 1973). In 1966 merchant banks were represented on the boards of almost all big firms.

> Ultimately the boards of [those] investment trust companies are responsible for the decisions taken. In practice, virtually all the investment decisions emanate from the investment directors and, further down the line, from the ranks of the bank [that is, the merchant bank]. (Spiegelberg, 1973, p. 30)

The proportion of total share capital held by institutional investors increased sharply. From one-sixth in 1957, it rose to nearly 30 per cent in 1967 (Ferris, 1970, p. 153), and to 32 per cent in 1971 (Spiegelberg, 1973, p. 47). This enormous shareholding by institutional investors was precisely the form which finance capital assumed in Great Britain during this period (cf. Overbeek, 1980): it achieved the increasingly intimate integration of the circuits of money capital and of productive capital, although still on the (primitive) basis of relations between separate, 'autonomous', units of capital.

Labour relations in the postwar decades

The worsening international decline of the British economy, and the increased pressure (in terms of wage restraint primarily) on the workers resulting from this, led to a surge of strike activity in the course of the 1960s that was much stronger than elsewhere in Europe (see Table 5.2).

Table 5.2 Days Lost Through Industrial Disputes per 1,000 Employed, 1963–72 (annual averages)

	1963–7	1968–72
France	364	277
Germany (FRG)	34	74
Italy	1,050	1,912
Japan	200	226
Netherlands	16	56
United Kingdom	184	968
United States	930	1,534

Source: Boyd, 1975, p. 22.

Although strike activity was not negligible during the early 1960s, and increased sharply around the turn of the decade, it can hardly be maintained that labour unrest during the 1960s was responsible for the growing economic problems. On the contrary, these clearly predated the upsurge of industrial disputes.

Consideration of the incidence of strikes raises another question. Fordism was first of all a new way of organizing the labour process, and a new way of organizing labour both on the shopfloor and in society at large. In most European countries this restructuring of capital has led in an early stage (in Scandinavia before the war, in Germany and Holland immediately after the war) to the

125

restructuring of the trade union movement as well. But in Britain the union structure retained a very specific character until well into the 1970s.

In her comparison of British and other West European trade union movements, Gardiner arrives at three main distinctive features of Britain's union movement: the significant union presence in the workplace and workplace bargaining, the relative independence of unions from the state, and the lack of political and ideological divisions. The first feature refers to what (seen from the point of view of the development of modern capitalism) is the archaic organization of the trade unions, heavily centred around particular crafts and directed at workplace negotiations over wage and other work conditions (Gardiner, 1980, pp. 322–30). As Gardiner relates, the 1970s saw attempts in several West European countries by trade union activists to increase union influence at the level of the workplace. A reverse development has taken place in Britain: throughout the 1970s the bargaining level slowly shifted to the company, and even to the national, level. But taking the whole period from the end of the war to the early 1980s, 'the United Kingdom is unique ... for the importance of the shop, plant, or company bargaining role of shop stewards.' (Flanagan, Soskice and Ulman, 1983, p. 364).

The specificity of the organizational structure of British trade unions (crafts unions, industrial unions and general unions) reflects their genesis and, owing to its complexity, tends to be rigid (Barou, 1978, p. 94). In the period between the wars, as we have seen, this state of affairs was reproduced, and the participation by Labour and the unions in the national conduct of the war, and in the postwar government, established the existing trade unions (with their archaic structure) as reliable partners in postwar neo-corporatism. As a result, the Donovan Commission, appointed by the Wilson government to investigate some of the factors underlying Britain's economic decline, found in 1968 that 'the craft system is deeply rooted in much of British industry'. There is thus certainly a degree of truth in the thesis that the unions have made it impossible to shift the labour force flexibly to where it is most needed within firms, but it cannot explain the continued decline of Britain. In fact most of these difficulties have been overcome since the 1960s when during more general negotiations the privileges inherited from the past were abandoned in exchange for material advantages (Barou, 1978, p. 96).

A second 'accusation' often voiced regards the practice of the 'closed shop'. Barou estimates the total number of workers employed in closed shops at 750,000, mostly dockers, seamen and printers. However, in the course of the 1970s most closed shops have been abandoned (and those remaining have been all but eliminated by the labour laws enacted by the Thatcher government). One could therefore not seriously maintain, except perhaps for certain very limited cases, that the practice of the closed shop has had a negative effect on overall British economic development (Barou, 1978, p. 96).

Resistance to new technology on the part of the unions is a third accusation regularly heard (see, for example, Kilpatrick and Lawson, 1980). According to Barou, this has diminished since the 1960s. Quite often trade unions have negotiated the introduction of change precisely in order not to be left out in the end and in order to be able to obtain material compensation for the concessions in the sphere of employment and protection of crafts. In general one can say that restrictive union practices have been minimized since the 1970s, and possible remnants have been wiped out by the union policies of the Thatcher government.

Another characteristic of the British situation, related to development of labour relations and the composition of the working class, helps to explain some of the differences with developments on the continent: the relative absence of cheap and legally insecure immigrant labour (Barou, 1978, p. 97; see also Glyn and Harrison, 1980), which performs a particularly important function during periods of fundamental industrial restructuring.

Immigrant labour arguably serves a number of 'functions', broadly speaking directly economic (cheap labour, low reproduction costs, and so on) and social and ideological (division of the working class, ethnic segmentation of the labour force, and so on). Without analysing the debates of the last fifteen years about migrant labour, it is useful at this point to look briefly at one of its functions. There is a structural need in capitalism, and particularly in highly developed industrial capitalism, for a certain amount of cheap and mobile labour, either to facilitate temporary processes of restructuring (cf. Sassen-Koob, 1981), or to answer to the demand for such labour by firms that lack the means to take advantage locally of the cheap labour in the peripheral areas of core capitalism (cf. Portes, 1978). In order for migrants to be able to perform this function, it is essential that they be kept in an insecure legal position (a point stressed by Castells, 1975; Portes, 1978; Carchedi, 1979; Lever-Tracy, 1983) and it is also clear that such a weak position is made even weaker when the migrants concerned are 'racialized' (Miles, 1982) – collectively defined as a 'racial' or 'ethnic' group.

In Britain, immigration has not on the whole served these functions to the same degree as, for instance, in Germany or France (Barou, 1978, pp. 96–7). One aspect of the recent history of immigration in the UK that underlines this thesis is the numerical one. When compared to other West European countries, the number of immigrants into Britain has been rather low, while at the same time the number of 'internal migrants' (people moving from agriculture into industry) has also been much lower than in countries such as Italy, France, Germany and the Netherlands.[9]

Perhaps more important is the second aspect: although new immigration was made increasingly difficult by the racist anti-immigration campaigns, the legal position of immigrants once they had gained entrance to the UK was (at least until the Immigration Act of 1971) much better than that of the Turks in Germany.

Thirdly, the process of family reunion (secondary migration of 'dependants') probably started earlier in Britain than in other European countries (again because of better legal status), whereby the direct economic effects of employing migrant labour (to the extent that these positive effects did exist) disappeared.[10]

Modernization offensives in the 1960s

The rise of the Conservative corporate liberals

After 1945 the Conservatives strongly opposed the Labour government almost every step of the way, as could only be expected given the two-party electoral system. However, there was a widely shared consciousness that many of the policies pursued by Labour were necessary by any standard, and that only the supposed socialist inspiration was what made the Labour project unacceptable for the Tories.

In order to develop and articulate a new alternative to Labour's socialism, the Conservative Party in October 1946 set up an Industrial Policy Committee, prompted behind the scenes by the FBI (Middlemas, 1979, pp. 417–18). In this committee many of the well known 'Right Progressives' or 'One Nation Tories' (after Disraeli's expression) who had already made a name for themselves in the 1930s gathered under the chairmanship of R. A. Butler. Harold Macmillan, Oliver Lyttelton, Oliver Stanley, David Maxwell Fyfe, David Eccles, Derick Heathcoat Amory, Sir Peter Bennett and J. R. H. Hutchison were the members of this select committee, which presented its report, *The Industrial Charter*, to the party conference in 1947. It was defended by Peter Thorneycroft and Anthony Eden (Beer, 1969, pp. 314–15).

The most important long-term significance of the charter was that it accepted the basis of Labour's socio-economic policies: the level of state spending, the establishment of the welfare state, the extension of the state sector in the economy including most of the nationalizations. The charter was a manifesto of the corporate-liberal tendency in the Conservative Party. The opposition to its ideas came from what was known as the old Whig tendency in the party, the remnants of the maritime liberal fraction of the British bourgeoisie, as expressed in Beaverbrook's *Daily Express* (Gamble, 1974, pp. 44–5).

It has been suggested that the *étatiste* tendency expressed by the charter was rolled back by a resurgence of 'neo-liberalism', and that the charter closes rather than opens an era (see Harris, 1972, p. 77). This view must be rejected or at least qualified on two accounts.

First, we must recall that during the 1930s there were not one but two tendencies that could be called *étatiste*, the (then dominant) state monopoly tendency and the (then subordinate) corporate-liberal tendency. The state-monopoly tendency in fact came to an end, as far as Britain was concerned, with the Atlantic Charter of 1942, when the protectionism inherent in state monopoly capitalism was sacrificed on the altar of Atlantic unity. Corporate liberalism became the dominant trend, and *The Industrial Charter* is the clear expression of that new-found predominance (cf. Douglas, 1983, pp. 59–60).

Secondly, it was certainly true that the electoral programme of the Tories, *The Right Road for Britain* (1949), was less outspoken in its support for some of the elements of the welfare state (Middlemas, 1979, p. 419), but it did not renounce the charter. The same holds for the booklet *One Nation. A Tory Approach to Social Problems* which was written by a group of new young MPs, including Enoch Powell and Edward Heath (cf. Macleod and Maude, 1950). Rather, because the leaders of the party, Churchill and Eden, kept aloof from the new policies, the rhetoric of the election campaign and of the first years of the new Conservative government contained a rejection of Labour policies, without however in practice turning back on them (the denationalization of steel being the most important exception). This is not to say that the shift in party rhetoric in the course of 1947 was meaningless. The temporary setback for the corporate liberals (immediately after their great success with the charter) conforms to a general shift in 1947, also reflected in the economic policies of the Labour government and in its foreign policy orientation; indeed, 1947 was the watershed for the immediate postwar history of the whole Western world. This confirms our thesis that developments in Britain must be considered in their international context to be properly understood.

The Conservative government that came to power in 1951 reflected a balance of forces between the corporate liberals and the classical liberals. The position of the old liberal forces had temporarily been reinforced by the 'neo-liberal backlash' which the monopolization policies of the Labour governments had provoked among small and medium capital. The political representatives of this fraction of the bourgeoisie struck an accord with 'pro-City interests' in order to counter the weight of social democratic and corporate-liberal forces (Ingham, 1984, pp. 209–10).

In the new government, 77-year-old Winston Churchill again became Prime Minister. His right hand man, Anthony Eden, went to the Foreign Office, and his 'left' hand, 'Rab' Butler, became Chancellor of the Exchequer. Harold Macmillan, one of the earliest exponents of the corporate-liberal tendency, became Minister of Housing. The structure of the welfare state was kept intact by the Tories, but no new initiatives were taken, and there were no attempts at anything resembling planning. No industrial relations legislation was undertaken, there was no incomes policy to speak of (Flanagan, Soskice and Ulman, 1983, p. 369).

The wartime practice of the 'sponsoring' of departments (cf. Jessop, 1980) was retained, and most nationalizations were left untouched (steel and transport being the important exceptions). In fact, the line of subordinating basic industries to 'downstream' consumer industries was continued with the newest of the basic industries, that of nuclear energy.[11]

The period of the Churchill–Eden administrations was, then, a passive one as regards the further development of the Keynesian welfare state; it was a period in which the old liberal generation of the British bourgeoisie, although economically in decline, dominated the political scene for the last time, and in which it was able to impose its orthodox economic and monetary policies to a degree which was to prove exceptional for the 1945–79 era.

The Macmillan era

Perhaps the most significant exception to the general picture of inactivity was the area of housing: under Macmillan's inspiring leadership the annual production rose to more than 300,000 units. Macmillan's success strengthened his position in the party establishment considerably, and partly on that basis he became, against most expectations (which favoured Butler instead), the successor to Eden when he had to resign (weakened by both the Suez fiasco and his waning health) in January 1957. That it was Macmillan and not Butler who became the new Prime Minister might be explained by the fact that in spite of his corporate-liberal persuasion he was closely connected to the old families of the ruling class, a circumstance which might have made him more acceptable and trustworthy than R. A. Butler (the more obvious candidate) in the eyes of the old party establishment. Macmillan in fact recruited many of his relations in the Cavendish family into government service: of the eighty-five members of his new government, thirty-five were relatives; seven of the nineteen new ministers belonged to Macmillan's (extended) family (cf. Childs, 1979, p. 95). Further, several 'young' and promising MPs, mostly of the corporate-liberal persuasion, gained important positions: among them were Edward Heath, Reginald Maudling, and Christopher Soames (Enoch Powell being the exception).

Macmillan's government brought a rapid expansion of state welfare expenditure, first financed by a reduction of defence expenditures in the wake of the Suez affair, later by an increase in overall spending. The annual increase in government spending had been 0.26 per cent in the years 1953–7, and rose to 4.18 per cent in the years 1957–64 (Jessop, 1980, pp. 66, 92). At several points, Macmillan had to overcome opposition within the Cabinet against this expansionary line: in 1957, the chancellor Peter Thorneycroft and his junior ministers Enoch Powell and Nigel Birch resigned after a conflict over the desirability of deflationary policies intended to stem the slowly rising inflation and the threat of devaluation of the pound (Middlemas, 1979, p. 408). Almost at the same time, the government collided with the Engineering Employers' Federation (EEF) over the same issue: the EEF warned that real wages were rising faster than productivity and that this was eating into profits and deteriorating competitiveness (see Flanagan, Soskice and Ulman, 1983, pp. 374, 385). The EEF was 'coerced into submission' by Macmillan and Iain Macleod, who also played an important role in defusing potentially divisive issues such as decolonization and immigration (Middlemas, 1979, pp. 400, 420).

In 1959, the expansionist tendency in the Cabinet was strengthened by the report of the Radcliffe Committee on the Working of the Monetary System, whose conclusions pleaded against monetary regulation of the economy in general and of demand and employment in particular. In 1961 the chancellor, Selwyn

Lloyd, was removed from his post for his resistance to continued expansion of government expenditure, and replaced by Reginald Maudling, whose expansionist views were more in tune with those of Macmillan (Blake, 1985, p. 288).

At the persistent request of the FBI, the government took an important initiative with respect to the planning of economic development with the formation, in 1962, of the tripartite National Economic Development Council (NEDC). However, the whole planning apparatus was 'set aside from the central axis', the combination of Treasury and Bank of England, which remained in control of short-term government policy and was able to impose its priorities of balance of payments and reserve position (Middlemas, 1979; Jessop, 1980, pp. 39–40). From 1960 onwards an intense struggle developed between the City and its supporters on the one hand and the representatives of productive capital on the other. This struggle became apparent in the 1961–2 Plowden Report, for example, which recommended a thorough reorganization of the City, and a relaxation of Treasury control over departmental budgeting (Sampson, 1965, pp. 296–305; also Ingham, 1984, p. 212). The struggle continued for several years, and would reach a new climax under the Labour government of 1964–70.

The role of Macmillan, however, in extending the scope of the Keynesian welfare state and thus of the Fordist regime of accumulation was played out. Increasing balance of payments problems, General de Gaulle's rebuttal of Britain's application for EEC membership, and scandals such as the Profumo affair, were the factors responsible for making the final years of Macmillan's term in office (and the short interlude of Sir Alec Douglas-Home) rather ineffectual when compared to the years 1957–61. It would be up to the new Labour government of 1964 to take new initiatives to broaden the scope of the British welfare state.

Labour back in power

The period of the second postwar Labour government (led by Harold Wilson, in 1964–70) can be divided into two parts.

The first part (1964–7) is characterized by a dynamic and offensive policy posture. Overall government spending in the years 1964–7 grew by an annual 6.7 per cent, financed by a growing government debt. In fact, Labour's monetary policies were practically the same as those of the preceding Tory governments. Faced with the inevitable balance of payments crises, Labour's response was no different from earlier policy, and the stop–go cycle continued unabated. As the former Chancellor Mr

Maudling remarked with regard to the policy of his successor in 1964: 'It is true the Labour Government have inherited our [balance of payments] problems. They seem also to have inherited our solutions' (quoted by Miliband, 1972, p. 363). It is therefore no wonder that the economic policies of the period 1945–67 are often referred to as 'Butskellism', referring to the bipartisan originators of Keynesian policy in Britain, Hugh Gaitskell and R. A. Butler.

The second part of the Wilson government (1967–70) is characterized by the onset of crisis, in the world economy (the 1966–7 recession was the first generalized recession experienced synchronically by all Western countries), and *a fortiori* in Britain.

The Wilson government consisted of a large number of new faces, of people representing a new tendency in the Labour Party: a tendency which had little affinity with the socialism of the prewar period. The most influential source of inspiration for this new tendency had been Anthony Crosland's *The Future of Socialism* (1956). Crosland in turn was inspired by his meetings with the American Daniel Bell, who made a name for himself by preaching 'the end of ideology'. Gaitskell and another prominent Labour MP, Richard Crossman, were among those participating in the Milan conference of September 1955 on 'The Future of Freedom', in which such people as Friedrich Hayek, Seymour Lipset, Raymond Aron and Bertrand de Jouvenel took part (see Lipset, 1960, pp. 403–5; also Ingham, 1984, p. 213). People such as Hugh Gaitskell, Denis Healey and Roy Jenkins[12] were in the front rows when, after the election defeat in 1959, an intense debate over the future course of Labour raged through the party. The reformist social democratic tendency (so close to the corporate-liberal Tories) within the Labour Party eventually prevailed and came to dominate the government formed after Labour's victory in 1964. During its first years in office, the Wilson government attempted to deal with the country's growing economic difficulties by initiating a truly corporatist and dirigist offensive, aiming at a thorough overhaul of the structure of the British economy in accord with the needs of modern mass production industry.

In the area of wage determination, a new drive at voluntary wage restraint aiming to increase productivity in industry was launched, culminating in the publication in 1965 of the White Paper *Prices and Incomes Policy* and the establishment of a tripartite administrative agency, the National Board for Prices and Incomes, to which the unions agreed in exchange for access to the political decision-making process (Fallick and Elliott, 1981, pp. 264–80). The drive for wage restraint was intensified in 1966. The Sterling crisis of July of that year led to 'pressures from international bankers' for a wage freeze, and other deflationary measures (including a freeze of prices and dividends); these were regulated by the Prices and Incomes Act, which remained in force until November 1967 (Flanagan, Soskice and Ulman, 1983, pp. 388–90).

As well as overhauling the structure of the British economy, the Wilson government also wanted to set up a proper apparatus for economic planning, in addition to the framework already provided by the NEDC. In 1964 two new ministries were created, the Department of Economic Affairs (under George Brown) and the Ministry of Technology, or Mintech; in addition the Industrial Reorganization Corporation was created to assist and direct the restructuring of British industry. These innovations in the organization of state apparatuses show that there was an awareness of the need for radical changes which was quite unusual in the British context. Bacon and Eltis (1978) claim that the years 1964–5 represented a decisive turning point: purposeful action entailing the strengthening of the DEA and a sizeable devaluation might have broken through the vicious circle of industrial decline. Nevertheless, that did not happen, and we must ask why. The answer is that the interventionist industrial policy of the Wilson government, guided by a productive-capital concept, continued to suffer from two essential and mutually connected weaknesses.

The first fundamental problem was the fact that the central axis of Treasury–Bank–City was not incorporated into the overall structure. Thus, the City was not represented in the NEDC, and this corporatist body consequently 'had no legitimate authority' (Ingham, 1984, p. 211). The second promising institution, the DEA, failed because of increasing deflationary pressure from the Treasury, and was formally abolished in 1968, signalling the fact that the government had given up its attempt to restructure British industry actively (Ingham, 1984, pp. 214–17). Thus, the institutional embodiments of the money-capital concept were able to maintain their hold over overall state policy and to maintain final control over such advances as the corporate liberals were able to secure temporarily.

The second source of weakness in Labour's policy consisted in the fact that planning was indicative and voluntary, and required the active participation of the 'social partners'. These however were traditionally weak. The TUC was characterized by a weak central structure, made impotent by the multitude of unions at industry and company level and by the power of the shop stewards. The employers' organizations were even weaker on the national level. It was only in 1965, at the insistence of the Labour government, that the Confederation of British Industries (CBI) was formed out of the FBI, the British Employers' Confederation (BEC) and the National Association of British Manufacturers (NABM); George Brown had made it clear that he was willing to discuss and negotiate only with one 'social partner' on either side. Even now, not all relevant fractions of capital were organized in the CBI. Both the financial world and the retail industry stayed outside the CBI, so that in effect the CBI only represented industrial capital. The government, in a further attempt to resolve this problem of the inadequate representation of capital inside Britain, also played an active role in establishing the Retail Consortium and the City Liaison Committee (Grant and Marsh, 1977, p. 21). In this way, the disarticulation between money capital and productive capital in Britain was in fact reproduced at the level of political representation.

In 1965, the Monopolies and Mergers Act was passed, giving increased powers to the Monopolies Commission instituted by the first postwar Labour government in 1948. In 1966, the Industrial Reorganization Corporation was added to the apparatus at the disposal of the state for intervening in the development of the economy and of the industrial structure. The IRC was particularly involved in the restructuring of the nuclear, electrical and motor industries, resulting *inter alia* in the formation of the General Electric Company (the merger of General Electric, Associated Electrical Industries, and English Electric) and of the British Leyland Motor Corporation (BLMC) out of Leyland and the British Motor Corporation. Again however this instrument of public intervention was *de facto* subordinated to the money-capital concept: the first president of the IRC was Ronald Grierson of merchant bank S. G. Warburg, and his successor in 1968 was Charles Villiers (of merchant bank Schroder Wagg).

Despite some successes, the overall record of the Labour government in the area of industrial policy was a poor one: time and again attempts to give the government a strong hand in the investment policies of industry foundered on the consequences of the two fundamental problems: the continued dominance of the central axis Treasury–Bank [of England]–City dictating deflation whenever the pound came under pressure, and the inherent weakness of the organizations representing the backbone of corporate liberalism, the trade union movement and the industrial employers. Corporatism therefore remained confined to the top leaders, and never succeeded in trickling down to the rank and file (Jessop, 1980, p. 52). It was therefore unsuccessful as a strategy against the defensive power of the working class at shopfloor level.

135

The turning point for Wilson's government came in the final months of 1967. It had been increasingly hampered by the fundamental contradiction in its economic policies – the effort to restructure and increase industrial production and exports (requiring inflation and devaluation of the pound), and the acquiescence of the financial community through the defence of Sterling (requiring equilibrium in the balance of payments and deflation) (Mandel, 1974, p. 33). A new crisis of Sterling in November 1967 finally convinced the government of the need to devalue the pound and try and increase exports. It is generally felt that the devaluation came far too late, and was too small, to have any real effect, but even so it was strongly opposed by the City (Westergaard and Ressler, 1974, p. 240). After November 1967, wage restraint was coupled to drastic spending cuts of £300–400 million (made more acceptable by the government announcing simultaneously the withdrawal of British forces from Singapore, Malaysia and the Persian Gulf by 1971) (Miliband, 1972, p. 368). However, the government this time tried to go further in its attempts to break what it saw as the principal obstacle to progress: the 'veto power' of the unions at shopfloor level, and the rising number of unofficial strikes over which the national TUC leadership had no control. In 1968 the White Paper *In Place of Strife* (written by Barbara Castle) heralded a first attempt to tame the unions. The Bill following the White Paper in 1969 was somewhat more limited in scope, and was directed primarily at unofficial strikes (Flanagan, Soskice and Ulman, 1983, p. 394; also Middlemas, 1979, pp. 440–2).

The immediate government policies of the years 1968–70 were not realized. In 1969–70 there was an explosion of wage rises running up to 12–14 per cent, and the number of (un)official strikes rose from 2.8 million days lost in 1967 to 6.8 million in 1969, and 11 million in 1970, while pressure on the pound continued. The Wilson government did not succeed in securing the transformation of Britain into either a corporatist or a Fordist country. In fact, the 'foremost example of corporatism's instability is that of Britain' (Panitch, 1979, p. 140).

For some, all the Labour government did was to serve the interests of capital, by introducing unemployment as a deliberate policy (unemployment in 1969 had risen to almost 3 per cent), and generally by making capitalism 'run more efficiently and more humanely' (Glyn and Sutcliffe, 1972, pp. 177–80, 213).[13]

For others, the role of the Labour government was more complex. It had tried but failed to 'define, codify, and back by state sanctions the obligations of unions to employers and the state in a way consistent with securing a stable corporatism' (Panitch, 1979, p. 143).

The failure of Fordism

'You never had it so good' (Harold Macmillan, 1959)

The foregoing pages have shown that in the case of Great Britain the conditions for the successful introduction of corporatism after 1945 were particularly 'unstable because of international decline, due largely to irresistible external forces but aggravated by internal forces' (Jessop, 1980, p. 30). These external forces were in fact no different in principle from the internal factors: the difference is accounted for by the time factor. The constraints imposed by the maintenance of the pound as an international reserve currency and by the political and military obligations of Britain in the postwar world system were in fact the contemporary manifestations of factors which had been operating in British history for over a century, and which in turn had in earlier days fixated the roots of the 'internal factors' of the 1950s and 1960s, namely the nature of the organization and activities of the trade union movement (to which must be added the organization and activities of British capitalists) and the hegemony of financial over industrial capital. Because of these constraints, the postwar Labour Party can be said to have successfully introduced a fair degree of 'social democracy' – meaning the transformation of the wage-earning class into a 'supporting class' of the bourgeoisie – but to have failed to transform the working class into a true coalition partner in the management of the welfare state and the spread of Fordism. This failure of British Fordism finds expression in a number of 'specificities' of the British political economy (cf. Barou, 1978, p. 94):

- the heterogeneity of the productive apparatus leading to an accumulation of problems in the essential sector of the production of means of production;
- the separation between banking capital and industrial capital;
- the inefficacy and paralysis of the state;
- the originality of industrial relations and of the trade union practices of the British 'salariat' (wage earners).

These specificities responsible for the failure of Fordism in Britain are in fact the concrete manifestation in the 1960s of the specificities of the British case which were analysed in Chapter 2. However, they were *reproduced* in the 1930s and 1940s, and cannot

137

be seen as the simple extensions in time of the specificities of the era of classical imperialism. The concrete relations and phenomena responsible for the failure of Fordism were reproduced through the dialectical interplay between external and internal forces. Externally, the struggle with the US for leadership in the capitalist world shaped the contours of Britain's position in the postwar world economy and provided the constraints which were to operate upon Britain's domestic political economy and the formation of its foreign policy. Internally, the struggle between adherents of two different proto-concepts of control, (the money-capital concept and the productive-capital concept) shaped the course of British economic policy. The outcome of this struggle was determined on the one hand by the pre-given balance of class forces, on the other hand by the way in which the external constraints reinforced the position of the representatives of the money-capital concept. The restructuring of Britain's place in the world after 1945 took place under the conditions determined by the newly established hegemony of American imperialism. In that context I have argued that there was a relative failure to introduce the intensive mode of accumulation with its corresponding regulatory practices and structures in Britain. *Relative*, because in an absolute sense many of the characteristic practices of Fordism were in fact introduced. However, after an initial lag Fordism was introduced into continental Western Europe to a much fuller degree than in Britain.

In our account of the failure of Fordism in Britain we have used a broad definition, understanding Fordism as a mode of regulating essential economic, social and state activities and relations. If we return by way of conclusion to a narrower, 'economistic' meaning of the term Fordism we can see whether our thesis is also borne out by strictly defined empirical indicators.

The quintessential characteristics and correlations implied by the concept 'Fordism' can be summarized as follows.

In terms of 'mode of accumulation' Fordism denotes that the increase in labour productivity equals the increase in per capita fixed capital (the technical composition of labour) so that the organic composition does not rise, which would result (*ceteris paribus*) in a fall in the rate of profit; and with respect to the continuous adjustment of mass consumption to rising output, Fordism supposes that nominal wages are coupled to the cost of living *and* to the rise in labour productivity (see Lipietz, 1982).

The basic variables thus are labour productivity, purchasing power, and per capita fixed capital. In order for the virtuous circle of Fordism to have effect these variables should all increase more or less at the same rate for a prolonged period of time. We might expect to find that in much of the postwar period growth rates of the key variables were lower in Britain than elsewhere and, more importantly, that there were structural imbalances between these factors.

From a comparative perspective, Britain indeed shows a picture which is significantly different from that of its major competitors.[14]

Throughout the 1960s and 1970s productivity in Britain has grown much more slowly than elsewhere apart from the United States (which was to be expected because Fordism was consummated in the USA in the years 1920–58, after which it lost most of its dynamism).

As for investment in fixed capital, the 1960s show Britain lagging behind, but during the 1970s, when capital formation slows down everywhere, the British performance is in line with that of other large capitalist economies.

Real wages have again lagged behind in Britain: in other comparable countries real wages (and thus mass consumption) increased much more rapidly, which also implied that the potential for expansion for the industries producing mass consumer durables was much greater in Europe and Japan than in the UK (and the USA).

In Britain, productivity (although lagging behind that in other countries) grew more rapidly during the 1960s than real wages, which was the consequence of the stop–go cycle and the extreme openness to world market influences of the British economy. There was, therefore, a constant threat of over-production, and a constant pressure for larger exports. Conversely, industrial capital producing for the home market was confronted with a stagnant mass market, and was forced to turn to export markets or to foreign direct investments for its further expansion.

Capital formation in Britain was also slower than elsewhere, but even so the growth rate of fixed capital was still higher than the growth rate of labour productivity: the 'marginal efficiency of capital' was very low in international comparative perspective.

The restructuring of the pattern of consumption in Britain also lagged behind. Expenditure on food continued to take up a very large proportion of income, while the shift to consumer durables was much less pronounced (Barou, 1978, p. 106).

Finally, we may view Fordism in its aspect of the corporatist regulation of labour relations. The archaic character of working-class organizations and labour relations in postwar Britain, the outcome of the *logic of priority*, was essentially left untouched after 1945 because of the extraversion of British capital, thus explaining the relatively high degree of unionization in Britain as well as the high number of working days lost through strikes. All through the late 1940s, the 1950s and 1960s, and the early 1970s, the density of union membership in Britain moved between 42 and 47 per cent, and rose to over 50 per cent in the mid-1970s (Gardiner, 1980, p. 331). In 1980 union membership in the UK stood at 54 per cent, against 22 per cent in France, 33 per cent in West Germany, 37 per cent in Italy, 32 per cent in Japan, 38 per cent in the Netherlands, and 25 per cent in the USA (Therborn, 1984, p. 11). Strike intensity too was higher in Britain than in its most important competitor nations, even though being significantly lower than in the Mediterranean countries.

Our conclusion must be that Fordism, conceptualized in the way the notion is used by the French regulation theorists, did not develop fully in Britain in the postwar decades. As a result, the growth of productivity, the ratio of fixed capital per person employed and the growth of real wages have all lagged behind developments in comparable economies. Strike-proneness in Britain, although not nearly as high as is sometimes suggested, was clearly higher than in Germany or Japan. British Fordism, it seems justified to conclude, failed in comparative terms.

When by the late 1960s the downturn in the capitalist world economy announced itself through the 1966–7 recession in Germany, the impact on the British economy was serious and lasting. British capital had in the previous decades been unable or unwilling to modernize and rationalize to the same degree as European and Japanese competitors had done. The last chance for the corporate-liberal bourgeoisie to impose its concept of control on the historic power bloc dominated by the City was frustrated when Britain failed to secure entry into the EEC in 1963. From then on, the corporate liberals in Britain in fact fought a losing battle.

CHAPTER 6

Global crisis and the rise of neo-liberalism

The crisis of the 1970s

Capitalism and crisis

Our analysis of the decline of Britain has shown how long-term processes originating in the era of Britain's ascendancy in the world system have determined in large measure how structural transformations of that system have worked out in Britain. In particular, we have shown that the century-old characteristics of the British political economy and of Britain's class structure combined with the specific conditions of the global system pertaining in the decades after 1945 to result in a continuation of the decline of Britain from a central to a secondary role in the capitalist world. The Fordist regime of accumulation, which was responsible for the unprecedented growth of the world economy in this period, was only partially adopted in Britain, and its relative failure was responsible for the severe economic problems with which the 1964–70 Labour government struggled. The notion of economic crisis, absent from academic discussions for decades, could no longer be ignored. Economists were taken by surprise when economic policy quite suddenly appeared to have lost the effectiveness which had been ascribed to it in the period of fast growth and insignificant conjunctural oscillations after the Second World War. Now, the debate over the causes of crisis (or 'serious disturbances') came to be conducted with new ardour.

The basic view of the economic liberals, the neo-classical economists, is that the state cannot foresee economic crises, nor can it prevent them. The state, by letting the market forces do their work, can only hasten the crisis process. Social security, workers' rights, collective bargaining, are – in the eyes of the true liberal – just so many impediments to the free operation of the market which alone can quickly restore economic equilibrium. Postwar capitalism has run into serious trouble not because of the nature of capitalist development as such, but because the manifold interventions by the state have disrupted the operation of the market.

In the eyes of Keynesians, the causes of the crisis lie else-where. The crisis of the 1970s in their view does not represent the failure of state intervention as such, but is due to such internal and external excesses as overaccumulation, speculation, oil price rises, and the general increase in the price of materi-als. The solution is not less but rather *more* state intervention.

The two schools thus have both different diagnoses and differ-ent remedies. What both approaches have in common, and what distinguishes them from Marxist approaches, is their view of the essential nature of state intervention. State intervention is seen as the interference by a political institution (that is, from the outside) with the economy, and this intervention is, further, a matter of free choice: the state can choose to intervene or not to intervene. To put it another way, Keynesians hold the state responsible for the suc-cesses of state intervention, but not for the failures, while liberals do exactly the opposite. In fact, both views are not simply academic constructs, but, as we have seen, they are linked to competing gen-eral concepts of control supported by different class coalitions.

Both approaches also analyse economic crisis by reference to a supposedly 'normal' equilibrium. This implies that eco-nomic crisis is not inherent to capitalism, but the result of faulty state intervention (the liberal view) or of the lack of state inter-vention (the Keynesian view) (cf. Poulantzas, 1976b, pp. 20–1).

The view that crisis (at least as a tendency) *and* state intervention are inherent in capitalism (are integral aspects of the mode of existence of capitalism) is to be found – not exclusively but most importantly – among Marxists of different persuasions. Traditionally, Marxists have looked for causes of crisis that would explain all crises in the history of capitalism. They have either looked at tendencies towards underconsumption (Sweezy, [1942] 1968; Luxemburg, [1912] 1970), or at the tendency of the rate of profit to fall (Gillman, 1969; Mandel, 1975), or at combinations of these two (Bukharin, [1917] 1972; Lenin, [1917] 1978). In the course of the late 1960s and the 1970s, new explanations of crisis came to the fore, which tried to account for the new manifestations of crisis then becoming apparent. The best known of these have become the 'profit squeeze' approach (Glyn and Sutcliffe, 1972; Glyn and Harrison, 1980), and the French 'regulation school' approach (cf. Aglietta, 1979, 1982; Lipietz, 1982, 1985; De Vroey, 1984).[1]

It would be wrong to go along with the view that both the occur-rence and the resolution of capitalist crises are somehow predeter-mined or guaranteed. This view is particularly popular in vulgar versions of long-wave analysis, but it is not completely alien to some of the other explanations either. To counter this tendency, we should stress that the form which crisis assumes is dependent upon the balance of class forces, not on any single 'final' law of motion. The different sorts of crisis are the shapes that crisis can assume in different historical settings, manifestations of the underlying impossibility, inherent in the capitalist mode of production, of letting the process of accumulation proceed evenly and smoothly.

The crisis of the 1930s, it is generally agreed, appeared as a typical crisis of underconsumption. The American and even more so the European working classes were unable to defend their interests adequately because of the severe defeats suffered in the preceding years (the failure of the revolutionary movements in Germany and Italy, the rise of fascism, and the failure of the British General Strike are some of the important examples).

The crisis of the 1970s, on the other hand, took the form of a crisis of falling profits due to the combined effects of a rising organic composition of capital and a falling rate of surplus value. Working-class organizations have been so strong that in general they have successfully averted attempts to shift the burden of falling profitability from capital onto labour, and even by the late 1980s the essentials of the welfare state and the late capitalist mode of regulation are still intact in practically all Western countries. It was only through the reactions by capital (capital exports and relocation of production, for example) and the state (such as cuts in unemployment and welfare benefits) that the present crisis in the second instance has also acquired some traits of underconsumption.

Still, the dominant character of the present crisis is that of a valorization crisis and not of a realization crisis. For capital, this means that any real restoration of long-term profitability must necessarily be preceded by a radical restructuring of social relations, the position of the working class, and the wage relation. After an initial reaction of capital directed at reducing the general level of wages, the emphasis has more and more shifted to a perceived need to increase wage differentials and differentials between wages and social security benefits. The objective here is not in the first place to reduce the financing deficit of the state (benefits are largely financed out of withheld wages anyway) but rather to 'improve the operation of the labour market'. The thinly disguised objective is a fundamental shift in the balance of power between social forces, between capital and labour, in order to promote a class compromise that helps to reduce the overall social wage through a far-reaching redistribution of income in favour of the 'propertied classes'.

The present crisis is more than a temporary disturbance: it is a structural crisis (in Gramscian terms, a crisis of hegemony), a

143

crisis of the fundamental relations underlying the postwar social formation, the Fordist mode of accumulation. When we speak of a structural crisis, a crisis of hegemony, this means that existing social relations must be radically restructured in order to safeguard the continuance of the capitalist system. Bourgeois hegemony over the working class must be *re*-established on all levels, from the immediate process of production to the state, the organization of political power and the ruling ideology. It is precisely because crisis is a disruption of the 'normal' relationship between classes that the resolution of crisis is brought about (that is, *if it is*) through the active and conscious intervention of class forces. On the other hand, we must not see the economic crisis as simply a capitalist strategy: the emphasis on the aspect of bourgeois control over the economy would then become too strong, it might even lead to a voluntaristic view which overestimates the degree to which capital really controls the process of capitalist development (De Brunhoff, 1976, p. 141).

The conjunctural development of a structural crisis is determined by the interplay between structural developments in the capitalist world economy and the strategic action of class forces. A more detailed analysis of this conjuncture of crisis will take us to the third layer of the historical process, the short-term layer of *histoire événementielle*.

The international context

The first signs of a breach in the postwar expansion of Western capitalism came with the recession of 1966–7, which was strongest in West Germany but was felt more or less simultaneously in most capitalist countries (Gamble and Walton, 1976, p. 165). The onset of crisis was indicated by the 'seismograph' of capitalism – that is, by falling profits, both as percentage of national income and as percentage of output (Aaronovitch and Smith, 1981, p. 180).

The fall in profit rates in Japan and Europe was due to a combination of falling profit shares (as approximation of the rate of surplus value) and a falling output/capital ratio (an approximation of the organic composition of capital). In the USA the stagnation had set in earlier (in about 1957), and in combination with the weak position of the trade unions in the USA this explains why profit shares and profit rates actually increased in the years leading up to 1975.

The basic development underlying these trends was the slowing down of the growth of labour productivity from the 1960s, leading to a disruption of the delicate web of regulatory mechanisms and institutions making up the postwar 'social structure of accumulation'. The productivity slowdown led to falling profits but also to inflation and structural unemployment, and eventually to the 'fiscal crisis of the state' (cf. O'Connor, 1973, who first coined the phrase).

Overall productivity growth slowed down after 1968; in manufacturing, productivity continued to grow at the same pace, but the rapidly increasing capital/labour ratio there should have led to higher productivity gains (Armstrong, Glyn and Harrison, 1984, pp. 248–50). The ratio of new investment to output in the period 1968–73 was highest in Britain, and the gap between Britain and the other major capitalist countries increased dramatically after 1973: the differential with the US increased from 0.9 to 7.6; with Germany, from 1.0 to 4.8; and with Japan, from 2.1 to 5.1 (NEDC, 1982, table 11). This means that the amount of investment needed to achieve a given increase in production (other things being equal) was considerably higher in Britain than in its competitor countries, which in turn indicates the low productivity of labour in Britain.

The comparatively slow rate of growth of productivity in Britain and the United States in the 1960s and 1970s led to a continued deterioration of the shares of world production and world exports for American and British capital, which was intensified by the overvaluation of the pound and the US dollar. In the US this process started after 1950, while for Britain the deterioration had set in during the last quarter of the nineteenth century, but had been temporarily reversed in the years 1931–50.

The most important, and most conspicuous, aspect of the development of the crisis was of course the decline of the supremacy of American capital in the world market.[2] The first clear indication of the crisis of American hegemony was the 'fall' of the dollar. It was the expression of the diminished capability of US imperialism to gain automatic acceptance of its own interests as if they were the general interests of the 'Free World'. The United States of course remained the dominant power of the capitalist world, and was able to impose its will upon Western Europe through superior economic and military power, but the element of coercion became much stronger in these years. Thus the consensual character of American leadership weakened considerably.

The predominance of American corporations in terms of sheer size and market power, still so important for supporters of the thesis of American super-imperialism during the late 1960s, was progressively undermined in the years 1967–75.

In the economic field, then, the uneven development of world capitalism led, during the late 1960s and the 1970s, to increasing equality and growing economic rivalry between the most important capitalist economies. In the ongoing debate in Marxist theory regarding the 'unity–rivalry' problem, those adhering to the thesis of inter-imperialist rivalry once again appeared to gain the upper hand (for a survey of this debate see Willoughby, 1979).

Against the view that American supremacy had come to an end, Petras and Rhodes argued that imperialism is no technical and strictly economic concept, but rather a global class structure, supremacy over which cannot be expressed solely in economic terms, but must first of all be conceived of in political and military terms (Petras and Rhodes, 1976). As confirmation of their view they pointed to the American offensives of the years 1973 (Kissinger's 'Year of Europe') and 1974 (the year of the 'oil crisis' and the Washington Energy Conference). In retrospect, however, this episode did not signal a lasting reimposition of American leadership in the West. On the contrary, relations with the European Community remained strained, and Nixon's trip to China was a major factor in the deterioration of US–Japanese relations. The period of the Carter administration again confirmed that the decade of the 1970s was the decade of continued decline of US hegemony. The shortlived attempt to reimpose hegemony over the West must be seen against the background of a general crisis in imperialist control over the world economy, which erupted when Third World demands for a New International Economic Order (NIEO) were reinforced by the sudden success of OPEC and a general increase in commodity prices. These developments briefly threatened the security of American and European control over the Third World, and the conflict between the two blocs was primarily one over the course of action to be taken *vis-à-vis* the NIEO demands (cf. Cox, 1983, p. 171; Van der Pijl, 1988). Whereas Nixon's policies towards Europe and Japan were aggressive, asserting the global interests of the US in opposition to the 'regional interests' (Kissinger) of Europe and Japan, the United States under Presidents Ford and Carter returned to a position of concerted Western action, complemented by a programme of international Keynesianism meant to 'resolve' the economic crisis (cf. Parboni, 1986).

A final aspect of the development of the world crisis which needs to be mentioned briefly here (because it forms one of the essential features of later developments in Britain as well) is the important role of money capital in the restructuring processes set in motion or intensified by the crisis: as capital is withdrawn from spheres of production where valorization conditions are worse than average and is reinvested in spheres where profits are higher, money capital more prominently performs the function of 'organizing' capital.

As Keynes had also noticed, at the level of the firm this takes the form of a strong preference for liquidity which even led in some instances to accusations of unlicensed banking by industrial corporations during the late 1970s.

At the level of the national economy, the rise to prominence of money capital and its specific solutions is reflected in the adoption of monetary targets for state policy, and in the imposition of 'cash limits' on nationalized industry.

At the level of the world economy, the renewed control of money capital over the overall accumulation process is reflected in the 'revenge of the *rentier*' and the predominance of internationally operating banks and financial groups, who succeeded in increasing their share of total surplus value (the mass of profits) in these years (Fennema and Van der Pijl, 1986). The subordination of dependent economies in the world economy during the 1950s and 1960s, increasingly taking place in the form of the operation of multinational corporations through direct foreign investment, now assumed a different nature: the direct control over production was tendentially relinquished, left to local capital, and replaced by indirect control through the internationalization of credit and the engagement of the national state bureaucracy as the most important relay and local ally (cf. Frieden, 1981; also Palloix, 1982).

This, then, is an outline of the international context in which the crisis evolved in Britain: a general slackening of productivity growth and accumulation, a fall in profits, the decline of American hegemony (forcing the US to actively apply its political and military power to secure its interests), and severe unrest in the international monetary sphere. We must now see how this international crisis interacted with specific factors operating in the British political economy to result in the very serious organic crisis of British capitalism manifesting itself from the late 1960s onwards.

Britain and the crisis

General theories of crisis cannot, Hodgson rightfully states, 'explain the acute nature of the *British* crisis relative to other capitalist countries, even if they may (or may not) provide a general explanation of capitalist decline' (Hodgson, 1981, p. 142). It is therefore essential to determine empirically which explanation of crisis best fits the actual deterioration of the competitive position of British capital from 1967 onwards, which expressed itself in the continuous erosion of profitability and the steady rise of unemployment. However, in their interpretation of what took place authors diverge widely. We shall look first at some aspects which can, at least in theory, easily be expressed in figures. Other, more

147

'political' interpretations will be considered later. The following subjects will be briefly addressed: investment (rate of investment, foreign investments), cost of capital, the labour share of national income, the level of government spending, the level of military expenditure, and finally spending on research and development.

A central point in discussions about the origins of the British crisis of the 1970s has been the rate of investment: was the British rate of investment really so low, and, if so, was low investment a cause or rather an expression of the deplorable state of the economy? When we look at the share of gross fixed investment in the national income, we see that in Britain this share was approximately 18 per cent over the whole period 1960–87, while it varied from around 22 per cent in West Germany to 30 per cent in Japan (*European Economy*, July 1986, p. 147). Indeed, Britain did have a lower overall rate of investment, but Smith is right to point out that this lower investment rate must itself be explained, and cannot be considered as the root cause of the problem (Smith, 1984, p. 197).

The sluggish development of British industry has sometimes been partially ascribed to *high interest rates* which pushed up the cost of external finance for industrial corporations (cf. Brett, 1985). One way of looking at this matter is shown in Figure 6.1. As an indicator of real capital costs, I have taken the (long-term) lending rates, corrected for the rise in wholesale prices for the period 1952–70:

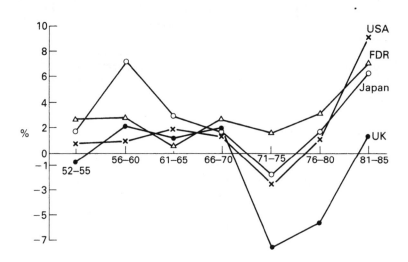

Source: calculated from IMF *Financial Statistics*.
Figure 6.1   Interest rates in selected countries, 1952–85 (real rates, 5-year averages).

also long-term money market interest rates and consumer prices for Germany, Italy and the Netherlands for 1971–7. It is quite clear that, for the period surveyed, the cost of capital in Britain has not been higher than in other countries.[3] Due to the very high rate of inflation real interest rates during most of the 1970s have been negative, and from 1979 on they have been barely above zero. Therefore, it would seem that low investment cannot be attributed to high capital costs. However, low capital costs are no independent variable: they may well be connected to low profitability and resulting low demand for capital (cf. Aaronovitch, 1981, pp. 290–1). This might also be indicated by a comparison of the indebtedness of industrial capital which shows that business borrowing as a percentage of fixed investment between 1968 and 1972 amounted to 27.2 per cent in the USA, 29.4 in Japan, 31.8 in France, and 33.8 in West Germany, against no more than 5.2 per cent in the UK (Armstrong, Glyn and Harrison, 1984, p. 265).

A further matter for discussion has been the share of labour in the national product: high wages supposedly ate up profits thus causing low investment and growth rates. However, the share of labour income in GDP has certainly not been higher in Britain than elsewhere in the developed capitalist world, nor has it risen significantly either between 1961 and 1987 (*European Economy*, July 1986). It is therefore difficult to agree with one of the central theses of Glyn and Sutcliffe, who have maintained that profits were squeezed out by international competition on the one hand and rising wages on the other.

Government expenditure is often thought (cf. Bacon and Eltis, 1978) to crowd out the private sector, thus causing a slowing down of the growth of the economy. Were British government expenditures generally higher than those of its competitors? In all cases government expenditure continued to grow until the early 1980s. The years in which the highest percentage was reached (and after which a fairly rapid decline set in) were 1982 for Germany (58.1 per cent), 1984 for France (52.8), 1985 for Italy (58.4), 1984 for the Netherlands (62.5), and 1984 for Britain (46.2) (*European Economy*, July 1986). Government expenditure in Britain has consistently been lower, in fact, than in comparable countries.

One area in which the effects of the former hegemonic status of Britain have continued to weigh heavily long after the country had lost that status is defence expenditure. In Chapter 4 we saw that Britain has long clung to the illusion of still being a great power; even after the Suez disaster had made the illusory character of this belief clear to almost everyone, Britain maintained a semi-independent nuclear deterrent, and in the late 1980s the Labour

Party is still being accused of unpatriotic behaviour for wanting to dispense with the British *force de frappe*. Many have maintained that the result has been that Britain has spent comparatively more than her main competitors on defence, and further that this has represented an important drain on resources which could have been put to civilian use. During the 1970s and 1980s, Britain indeed spent a greater part of GDP on defence than any other major Western country except for the United States, namely between 5 and 6 per cent, against about 4 per cent in France, 3.5 per cent in West Germany, and 1 per cent in Japan (*SIPRI Yearbook*, 1986).

It has recently been argued from several directions that Britain's industrial decline is to be explained first of all by the abysmal state of research and development spending, either in general terms (Smith, 1984, pp. 87–94), or specifically because of the negative effects of heavy spending on military R and D (Kaldor, Sharp and Walker, 1986). On the basis of his findings Smith advocates an industrial policy aimed at 'overcoming the R & D problems and investment deficiencies which have been identified as the core of Britain's problems' (Smith, 1984, p. 236), while Kaldor, Sharp and Walker state that 'if Britain is to break the vicious circle of decline, an important precondition must be a reduction in the relative size of the defence sector and level of military R and D' (1986, p. 48). As a matter of fact, the UK does not spend less overall, but it spends more on military R and D than most countries: only the US spends more on military R and D, but there this high figure is not related to a low figure for private R and D, as in Britain. In Japan and Germany, military R and D is very low, government R and D is about the same as elsewhere, but private R and D spending (which may 'hide' a certain amount of defence-related R and D) is very high. In France private R and D is lower than in the UK, but there civil government R and D is much higher (*SIPRI Yearbook*, 1986, table 15.3).

An important qualification, however, throws doubt on the hypothesis that low civil R and D spending has been a major cause of the British industrial decline: during the 1960s, civil research and development in Britain was considerably higher than in Japan, West Germany and France, and only in the 1970s – when the crisis of British capital was already quite apparent – did British R and D fall behind compared to Japan and West Germany. The relative position *vis-à-vis* France and the US did not change significantly at all. We therefore cannot accept the view that R and D spending or rather the lack of it explains the decline of Britain: rather, the deterioration of Britain's relative position in R and D is itself a *symptom* of the disease, and not a cause.

A final explanation for the decline of Britain which is often offered is the role of multinational companies, or rather the tendency of (big) British capital to turn to foreign operations. Of course, the fact of the outward orientation of British capital is undisputed – apart from the years between 1932 (the Ottawa agreements) and 1949 (the devaluation of Sterling) British capital, both industrial and financial, has shown a high propensity to operate internationally. However, it does not seem warranted to conclude from this that domestic industry was 'starved' of finance: real interest rates in Britain were never particularly high, and during the 1970s they were exceptionally low. In Chapter 2, we argued that the relation between foreign investment and domestic investment is complex and cannot be grasped in one simple formula. Furthermore, the relative degree of internationalization of British capital has actually decreased during the 1970s. In 1971, the stock of British direct investment abroad approximately equalled the value of British exports, while the same ratio was 2:1 for the United States, 1:4 for the Netherlands, and 1:5 for Japan and West Germany. In 1979, these ratios were 1:1 for the US, 1:2.3 for the UK, 1:2.6 for the Netherlands, 1:3.2 for Japan, and 1:5 for West Germany (Overbeek, 1984, calculated on the basis of UN and OECD figures).

We are left with the inescapable impression that all attempts to isolate a single factor as 'the' cause of the decline of Britain fail when put to the test. For one, most of these 'causes' are either economic, or (less often) political. These explanations do not do justice to the fact that – certainly in the case of Britain – decline and crisis are at once political *and* economic (cf. Wright, 1987). Furthermore, some significant differences between Britain and other countries have shown up but, although they are still to be explained, they are a symptom of Britain's decline, and cannot explain *why* things went so wrong. For this purpose, more complex historical explanations must be looked for.

WEAK STATE, STRONG CITY

The first explanation involves the effects of the international character of British capital. British capital has in fact been much more international in orientation and activity than continental European and Japanese capital. This international orientation of British big capital was reinforced when the City of London regained a central place in the international financial circuits. The City was so successful that it came to resemble an 'offshore' island much like the Cayman islands or Curaçao, a development which became particularly prominent after the floating of the dollar.

151

The conditions prevailing during the nineteenth and early twentieth centuries, which had been considerably modified by the transformations of the 1930s and 1940s, were reproduced in contemporary form, adapted to and determined by the conditions of the new organization of world capitalism in the guise of the *Pax Americana*. First and foremost, these were the weakness of the British state, and, connected to this, the weakness of the British industrial bourgeoisie as a consciously organized class *für sich*, whose demands might otherwise have forced the state to engage more actively in the reconstruction of the British productive apparatus.

During the 1950s and 1960s, the City's hegemony over British monetary and economic policy forced the British economy (through the 'stop–go' cycle) into constant relative stagnation. This complex of factors is part of the explanation, perhaps the most important explanation, of the postwar decline of Britain, and is shared by Andrew Gamble (1981) and Sam Aaronovitch (1981), as well as by Bob Rowthorn. Rowthorn has argued that

> British big capital is still among the strongest in the world ... Yet the British *state* has not aggressively pursued the interests of a specifically British capitalism ... British big capital has always had a major international dimension and the conditions of the post-war world led to an *accentuation* rather than modification of this pattern.

British capitalists operating internationally have always chosen domestic stagnation: 'Thus leading sections of the British bourgeoisie have been effectively "denationalized", not through their own weakness but through the weakness of the British state and their own home base. The overseas strength of British big *capital* has compounded the debility of British *capitalism*' (Rowthorn, 1975, pp. 173–5).

THE PROBLEM OF UNION STRENGTH

A second explanation, of a different character, has gained adherence from both the Left and the Right of the political spectrum. Andrew Glyn and John Harrison are of the opinion that 'the fundamental problem was the slow increase in the technical composition of capital which meant that the demand for labour was too high and the rate of productivity growth too low' (Glyn and Harrison, 1980, p. 49). Because of the already low proportion of the labour force employed in the agricultural sector after the war, and the low rate of immigration, shortages of labour occurred very soon after 1945, leading to increasing participation of women in the British economy and to a strongly organized working class.

The UK working class's strong organization at factory level thwarted many of capital's attempts to increase productivity ... Successful resistance of this sort seems the principal explanation for productivity in the post-war UK growing less than three-quarters as fast as the technical composition, whereas the two grew at an approximately equal rate in other countries. (Glyn and Harrison, 1980, p. 50)

This line of reasoning maintains that in the long run labour militancy obstructs working-class prosperity. Exactly the same point, with neo-liberal rhetoric replacing Marxist jargon, was put forward by Friedrich Hayek (1986) and Sir Keith Joseph (1986), to mention only two of a number of monetarist and neo-liberal authors.[4]

In 1979 Sir Keith Joseph published a pamphlet entitled *Solving the Union Problem is the Key to Britain's Recovery*, and in 1984 the Institute for Economic Affairs published a text by Friedrich Hayek bearing the title *1980s Unemployment and the Unions*, in which the trade unions were accused of exploiting non-union workers, of 'hurting the working man', of being the chief cause of unemployment, and of being the British 'sacred cow' (reprinted in Coates and Hillard, 1986, pp. 98–114).

A well-argued Marxist contribution to this line of thought is that of Andrew Kilpatrick and Tony Lawson. Particularly relevant to the main theme of this book is their attempt to link the characteristics of present-day British trade unions to their history, and to the period in which and the circumstances under which they came into existence (Kilpatrick and Lawson, 1980, pp. 85–102). The early industrialization of Britain, and thus the early emergence of an industrial working class, also led to an early acceptance of trade unionism. In fact trade unions were well established before mechanized factory production became generalized. It is due to this fact that a significant trait of British trade unionism, persisting until at least the 1960s, was its craft-type organizational structure and mode of operation.

Kilpatrick and Lawson's second important observation is that British employers were less compelled than their colleagues in other countries to resist union advance every step of the way, because they had recourse to protected imperial markets. Fine and Harris (1985) argued against this line of reasoning, and attributed certain specificities of British working-class activity to its weakness instead of to its strength. For them, real strength would have been translated into higher real wages, and what has generally been considered as the strength of the British working class was in reality the only form of defence left.

Indeed, the British trade union movement in the postwar period did have a strong, albeit defensive, position within the firms. Even if this strength was not used, or was insufficient, to oppose techno-logical innovation with success, it did succeed, on the social level, in enforcing adherence to full employment until the latter half of the 1960s. This full employment priority contributed to the slow rate of the restructuring of British industry, and reinforced the propensity of British capitalists to invest abroad. The organized working class was too weak at the national level to induce the state (even in the exceptionally favourable circumstances of the late 1940s, and later during the years 1962–7) to adopt a conscious industrial policy to make up for the negligence of British capital-ists. The organizations of both the industrial working class and the industrial bourgeoisie were weak, decentralized, unaccustomed to dealing with each other constructively, and opposed by a state that was just as weak and just as unaccustomed to intervening in industrial relations and the industrial structure.

THREE OPTIONS

By the late 1960s, there were three options for dealing with the cri-sis. The *first* option, popular with the establishments in both major parties, was to ride out the storm, and hope that the crisis would be dissipated through the beneficial effects of EEC membership, for instance (the line taken by Heath in 1972–4), or because of renewed growth in the world economy (that taken by Wilson and Callaghan in 1974–9 . The *second* option, developed by the left wing of the Labour movement, acknowledged that there was a serious crisis and maintained that a combination of strong state involvement in industrial restructuring and a relative retreat from the world market would be able to set Britain back on the right road. The *third* option, developed by the right wing of the Conservative Party, acknowledged the fact of crisis but emphasized the strength of the working class and the growth of the state sector in the economy as the major causes. The remedy in this view entailed the restoration of the market: all obstacles to the free operation of the market should be removed, first of all the monopoly enjoyed by the trade unions, second the 'monopoly' of the state in the economy.

The changing alignment of class forces and political coalitions supporting these options is the subject of the two remaining sec-tions of this chapter.

The neo-liberal revolt in the Tory Party

The Heath years

The postwar period had been characterized by a fair degree of consensus regarding the main objectives of social and economic policy, notwithstanding the limits defined by dominant City interests. But as the British political economy became more and more crisis-ridden from 1964 on, an increasing number of people began to express doubts regarding the value of the 'Keynesian revolution'. The main content of that revolution had been the viewpoint that capitalism was not necessarily a 'zero-sum game': that it was possible, in other words, for both major social 'partners' to profit from growth. This view was in direct contrast both with classical liberal views *and* with orthodox socialist thought, which considered capitalism as a game in which the advantage of one party equals the loss of the other. Within the Tory Party this critique of the Keynesian compromise also came to be supported by industrial capital (in particular by the Engineering Employers' Federation, the EEF) which lobbied for radical changes in trade union practice on the shopfloor and for the restoration of a 'free labour market' (Aaronovitch, 1981, pp. 17–18).

Edward Heath himself, who had become Tory leader in 1964, remained true to his corporate-liberal leanings, which he had first exhibited in his maiden speech in the Commons in 1951. By 1969, however, he was no longer able to withstand mounting right-wing pressure, although his campaign manager Peter Walker thought along the same lines as Heath did. As Keith Middlemas has remarked, 'Heath attempted to reimpose the genial statism of the fifties but had to concede to his opponents the so-called 'Selsdon doctrine' in 1969 – at immense cost to the support of his subsequent government from both sides of industry' (Middlemas, 1979, p. 423). According to one commentator, William Keegan, the Heath Shadow Cabinet increasingly used the *rhetoric* of the 'laissez-faire radicals' without initially intending to translate this rhetoric into concrete policy. However, once in office, the Heath Cabinet indeed embarked on a course of confrontation with the trade unions. Keegan attributes this to Heath's relative lack of governmental experience and the sudden death, a month after the 1970 elections, of Iain Macleod, the prominent, charismatic and experienced One Nation Tory (Keegan, 1985, pp. 28, 85; see also Blake, 1985, pp. 311–12). Be that as it may, it is a fact that the Heath government embarked on a course characterized by rhetorical radicalism. As Heath had said to the party conference of October 1970, he set out 'to change the course and the history of

155

this nation, nothing less' (quoted by Blake, 1985, p. 309). The first objective of this 'quiet revolution' was the restoration of profitability for British capital. The strategy devised to achieve this was inspired by President Nixon's 'New Economic Policy' in the United States (Barnett, 1973, p. 19). Improving the competitive position of British capital would entail a sharp attack on what was perceived as the trade union problem (particularly the increase in unofficial strikes), as well as a 'strengthening of the market'. Thus, two important elements of the accumulation strategy which Heath pursued during the first two years of his government were the strengthening of competition and of the market through the elimination of state subsidies, and the restoration of free collective wage bargaining and curtailment of union action through the Industrial Relations Act of 1971.

EUROPE

Perhaps the most important element of the strategy was entry into the Common Market. The European policy was meant to work as a catalyst reconstituting ruling-class unity; it was 'the ruling class's way out of a hazardous political situation' (Nairn, 1973, pp. 37–8). In a way, it did indeed serve this purpose: the British ruling class became aware for the first time that it had 'no choice but to integrate and share the fate of European capitalism' (Yaffe, 1973, p. 53), and that it was necessary finally to terminate 'the attempt to sustain centre country status' (Brett, 1985, p. 159). In the end, the success of Britain's bid for EC membership, which became effective from 1 January 1973, was to be the most important lasting achievement of the Heath government, the import of which however would only fully become clear years later.

Two factors were responsible for the success of Heath in an area where both Macmillan (for whom Heath had negotiated with Brussels) and Wilson had failed earlier.

On the one hand, Valérie Giscard d'Estaing's accession to power in France, first as Minister of Finance, later as President, cleared the way on the French side: Giscard was a prominent representative of the fraction of the French bourgeoisie associated with Atlanticist corporate liberalism (Van der Pijl, 1984, pp. 190, 223–5), and as such he was not opposed to British membership of the EEC.

On the other hand, the changing attitudes in the City with regard to European integration removed an important domestic obstacle. The growth of the Eurodollar markets, primarily in the City of London, had already led to the decoupling of the fates of Sterling and of the City: the profits of City firms (particularly the banks) depended less and less on the exchange rate of Sterling.

The turning point must be located somewhere around 1971 and 1972. Notwithstanding the growing importance of the Euromoney markets, many in the City were still opposed to British accession to the Common Market early in 1971. But the dollar crisis which erupted in August of 1971 made it plain that the hegemony of the dollar had come to an end, or at least had undergone a fundamental transformation. And it was precisely in the context of the postwar economic and monetary *Pax Americana* that the City had been able to regain its predominance in Britain. The dollar crisis led City strategists to rethink London's place in the international financial world. Europe, they became convinced, would provide the direction for the City's flight forward: London would find a new role as the 'financial growth pole' for Europe (Nairn, 1973, pp. 24–8). This new outlook in the City combined very well with Heath's 'Europeanist' policies in response to Nixon's August measures. In September, important reforms of banking regulations were effected, among others enabling banks to own shares and thus obfuscating the hitherto sharp distinction between different financial institutions, and in particular propelling the clearing banks (owing to the enormous size of deposits at their disposal) into a much more prominent and activist role. In 1972, the new role of the City as an offshore banking centre was confirmed by the floating of the pound, thus putting an end to the last remains of the City's interest in a high value for the pound.

ECONOMIC MODERNIZATION

Entry into the EC would, in Heath's view, be one of the strongest stimuli to industrial modernization. That this was badly needed was underlined by the enormous flight of capital in the early 1970s. The export of private capital amounted to £500 million in 1970, and rose rapidly to £1,272 million in 1972, and to £2,073 million in 1973 (Brett, 1985, p. 160). Apart from low productivity, other important causes were the steady decline of manufacturing profitability (from 20 per cent in 1968 to 14.9 per cent in 1973, and to 6.3 per cent in 1974), the rise in nominal wages (which had risen by an annual average of 4.9 per cent in the years 1964–9, and were rising by 12.6 per cent a year in the years 1970–3), and the increase in strike activity (3.7 million days per year in 1964–9, 13.9 million days per year in 1970–3) (Brett, 1985, pp. 159–69). The deterioration of the competitive position of British industrial capital expressed itself in the rapidly increasing degree of import penetration which was not at all compensated for by a larger British share in world exports: in 1970 17 per cent of the sale of manufactured products in Britain

GLOBAL CAPITALISM AND NATIONAL DECLINE

concerned imported goods; in 1973 this figure had risen to 22 per cent (Glyn and Harrison, 1980, p. 83).

The strategy outlined by the Heath government was one of non-intervention and disengagement: non-intervention in wage-bargaining, and disengagement from the support of 'lame-duck' companies.[5] True to this strategy, the new government abandoned the Ministry of Technology and the Industrial Reorganization Corporation upon coming into office. In their place, the Department of Trade and Industry was created with a low-profile approach (Jessop, 1980, p. 44). In a similar vein, the Heath government proposed to follow a policy of 'hiving off' the nationalized industries and selling profitable parts to private owners, thus creating a precedent for the later 'privatization' by the Thatcher government.

In April 1971, however, the idea of 'hiving off' was abandoned after an inquiry into the effects of the proposed splitting of the British Steel Corporation. The policy of ending subsidies to loss-making private companies was also abandoned almost before it was put into practice. In January 1970 Nicholas Ridley had argued in a memorandum that subsidies to Upper Clyde Shipbuilders (UCS) should be stopped, and the remains of the company sold off. But in February 1971 the government decided to extend credit to UCS, and the workers achieved an important victory. In the same month another lame duck, Rolls Royce, was nationalized when it threatened to go bankrupt, thus completing the reversal of the initial government strategy. The 1972 Industry Act codified this policy reversal.

The third element of the government strategy to be abandoned halfway was the adherence to deflation. The government's strict credit controls came under increasing criticism during 1971, and in March 1972 both the CBI and the *Economist* called for an expansionary policy to increase demand and promote investment. These demands were met in the 1972 Budget, presented by Chancellor Barber the next month, which included tax cuts of £1,800 million. The expansion did not result in self-sustained growth, however: private investment took the form of stock-building and speculation (real investment in the finance sector increased by 42 per cent, but in the manufacturing sector fell by 9 per cent), and public investment took place in public works and services, not in the nationalized industries. What the expansionary boom did effect was an enormous expansion of credit, and a sharp rise in inflation. According to the *New York Times* of 7 September 1973 this led the IMF to express its anxiety 'about the possibility of new labor strikes that would further undermine the British balance of trade and payments' (quoted by Kolko, 1974, p. 112). It was not until December 1973, however, that the Bank of England tried to re-establish monetary restrictions, prompted by the effects of the oil crisis and the surge in labour unrest. The tightening of controls caused serious problems for the secondary banking system which was bailed out, through the Bank of England's 'lifeboat operation', by the clearing banks who thus further reinforced their position in the financial sector.

The willingness of the government to undertake its U-turns was influenced (just as its original neo-liberal inclination) by comparable developments in the United States: there the Nixon administration undertook a spectacular U-turn in 1970 which brought an end to expansionism (cf. Shanks, 1977, p. 64).

TACKLING THE UNION PROBLEM

The government's industrial relations policy rested on two pillars: the abolishment of a statutory wage policy, and the introduction of the Industrial Relations Act, designed to put an end to the problem of unofficial strikes. Both policies were to fail at the hands of the National Union of Mineworkers (NUM).

The new pay policy for the public sector resulted in a national strike in the mines, because the miners were determined to catch up with the wages being paid in other industrial sectors. The strike proved very successful, not least because of the effective picketing tactics employed (at Saltley Coke Depot, for example, where 15,000 pickets eventually forced the police to lock the depot).[6] The government's position was weakened by the beginnings of internal dissent, and by increasing criticism from the CBI and other leading sections of the ruling class (cf. Barnett, 1973). Heath was advised by his political friends abroad to return to established (corporate-liberal) policies, and Willy Brandt urged him to return to a policy of co-operation with the unions (Keegan, 1985, p. 31). However, the forces in the Cabinet pushing towards further confrontation held the upper hand.

The real hope of the government for breaking through working-class resistance lay in the Industrial Relations Act, which was fashioned after the American National Labor Relations Act (cf. Flanagan, Soskice and Ulman, 1983, p. 402). The Act's main provisions were:

- that the closed shop was illegal;
- that unions were required to register, giving specifications of the circumstances under which strikes could be called and of the powers and duties of the shop stewards;
- the removal of legal immunity for sympathy strikes;

- the introduction of a sixty-day 'cooling-off' period;
- a ballot before a strike if that threatened 'the life of the nation' (see Glyn and Harrison, 1980, p. 62).

In March 1971, after an intensive publicity campaign, the TUC urged its member unions to boycott the Act. The first confrontation in May 1972 involved the railway unions, and resulted in a defeat for the government, after the compulsory ballot had given a 6:1 majority in favour of strike action. The dockers were the next targets of the Act, in July 1972. When five dockers were imprisoned because of unlawful picketing, the TUC General Council was forced by its rank and file to call a one-day general strike for 31 July. The House of Lords intervened shortly before the strike by establishing as its interpretation of the Act that individuals could not be held responsible for illegal collective action, thus getting the government off the hook. *The Times* described the Act as a 'disordered slot-machine' (see Glyn and Harrison, 1980, pp. 61–4). It was a remarkable fact that private capital on the whole refused to invoke the Act (Flanagan, Soskice and Ulman, 1983, p. 404), and Campbell Adamson, President of the CBI, openly denounced the Act because it had destroyed good relations between employers and unions (Glyn and Harrison, 1980, p. 72; Coates, 1982, p. 149).

The final blow for the Heath government's union policy was administered by the miners, in the midst of the context of the international oil crisis. The conflict originated in NUM wage claims of 22–46 per cent. The government turned down these claims, and the NUM responded with an overtime ban and threats of further action. The confrontation escalated quickly and resulted, in December, in government preparations for a state of emergency, and in the calling of a three-day week. Conciliatory forces on both sides during January attempted to dampen the conflict: the TUC General Council stated on 9 January that the government would not be faced, as a result of concessions to the miners, with comparable demands elsewhere (Glyn and Harrison, 1980, p. 88), and from the other side, as Douglas Hurd recounts, a prominent industrialist 'renowned for the robustness of his right-wing views' offered to pay the miners what they asked for on a private basis (quoted by Grant, 1980, p. 145; see also Glyn and Harrison, 1980, p. 89). Both offers were rejected, and Heath called a general election for 28 February 1974, under the slogan 'Who governs Britain?'. Apparently, the electorate did not feel that the business of governing Britain could be left to Edward Heath and the Tories any longer; and when Campbell Adamson – not realizing that he was being recorded – remarked to a conference of managers that he (and the CBI) would like to see the next government repeal the Act, he did nothing to help the Conservative Party in this respect (quoted by Childs, 1979, p. 240). The miners brought down the Conservative government, but 'moderate Conservatives may well have been happy to see a Labour Government returned' (Middlemas, 1979, p. 445).

In an indirect way, the Heath years did modernize certain aspects of labour relations in Britain. During the years of recession and stagnation after 1968, certain work practices (such as job evaluation and measured-day work systems) were introduced on a wider basis than before, and single-employer and plant-wide bargaining started to replace industry-wide bargaining on the one hand and fragmented shopfloor bargaining on the other. This meant that a gradual power shift took place in favour of senior, full-time shop stewards (Flanagan, Soskice and Ulman, 1983, pp. 404–5). In this way, some of the intentions behind the Industrial Relations Act were indeed fulfilled, although not as a consequence of the application of that Act. However, unionization kept increasing (from 43 per cent in 1968 to 52 per cent in 1975: Flanagan, Soskice and Ulman, 1983, p. 371), and real wages increased faster than productivity (p. 406).

The neo-liberal revolt

The radicals in the Conservative Party held the view that Heath was responsible for this development, because he had gone back on the agreed strategy at every point except the last (when it was too late). There is much truth to this criticism, in the sense that it is questionable whether Heath was ever committed to the 'Selsdon' line in the first place (a doubt shared by Grant, 1980, p. 160). Edward Heath, as stressed earlier, made a career as a clear exponent of the corporate-liberal fraction of the British bourgeoisie, and placed himself in the Disraeli tradition of One Nation Tories (cf. Keegan, 1985, p. 27). One can come to no other conclusion about the economic policies of the Heath government than that they were 'still committed to the social-democratic goals of full employment and growth' (Gamble, 1983, p. 117), and 'still Keynesian in [their] general outlook' (Coates, 1982, p. 145). This continued commitment to the postwar consensus, expressing itself in the government's U-turns in 1971 and 1972, was precisely what angered the real Selsdon-radicals in the Conservative Party. These people (among them Margaret Thatcher and Keith Joseph) accused Heath of betrayal – and they were eventually to dominate the Thatcher Shadow Cabinet.

The new current, which at the beginning was rather heterogeneous, combined three elements in its political ideology: monetarism, classical liberalism, and ultra-conservatism. Monetarism essentially involves the belief that inflation (reaching the 25 per cent mark in 1975) is primarily caused by too great a supply of money. A remarkable characteristic of monetarism, which gives it a compelling logic in times of crisis, is that it allows the state to withdraw from the immediate involvement in power struggles and negotiations, and to sit back and let the logic of the market do its work. Monetarism appears as a technical and non-political solution, affecting all parties equally, to what are essentially political problems (cf. Aaronovitch, 1981, p. 24). Everyone wants inflation to be brought down, so a doctrine offering a quick and simple (though perhaps temporarily painful) solution can easily claim to represent 'the general interest', and thus become an essential component of a new comprehensive concept of control challenging corporate liberalism.

As a corollary of City dominance, monetarism has always enjoyed a certain popularity in Britain, not only in the 1920s and 1930s but even during the 'Keynesian' 1950s and 1960s. Intellectuals and private lobby groups have played a central role in disseminating monetarism, and the work of the Nobel Prize winner Milton Friedman has been introduced and popularized in Britain by the Institute of Economic Affairs, which was established in 1955. Approximately 70 per cent of its income (amounting to over £500,000 in 1984) is derived from corporate donations, from all sectors of business. The institute has produced more than 200 publications, including papers and books by such well known monetarists and right-wing economists, journalists and politicians as Milton Friedman, James Buchanan (who also sits on the advisory council of the IEA), F. A. Hayek, James E. Meade, Peter Jay (of *The Times*), William Rees-Mogg (of *The Times*), Samuel Brittan (of the *Financial Times*), Robert Bacon, Walter Eltis, and even J. Enoch Powell.

An internationally operating organization of monetarists and neo-liberals is the Mont Pelerin Society, which was established in 1947 on the initiative of Friedrich Hayek. Today this organization has more than 600 members, meeting annually in one of the home countries of its members (O'Brien and Roddick, 1983, pp. 56–7). According to O'Brien and Roddick, the Mont Pelerin Society played a leading role in the establishment in 1955 of the IEA, which set out to propagate the liberalism espoused by Hayek and Friedman.[7] Until the late 1960s, however, the views expressed in these publications attracted little serious consideration.

It was only in 1967–8 that monetarist targets were first adopted in government circles, and then because the chancellor, Roy Jenkins, had to appease the IMF. From there, the spreading of monetarist and neo-liberal ideas gained momentum, for the time being more in Britain than elsewhere in Europe. This rise of monetarism was partly the result of, and at the same time compounded, the failure of Fordism in Britain.

The crucial role in this respect, particularly in the popularization of monetarism among non-professional economists, was played by strategically placed journalists and their counterparts in the City: both stockbrokers such as Greenwell and economic commentators for the *Financial Times* and *The Times*, Samuel Brittan and Peter Jay respectively (Keegan, 1985, p. 41). On the academic front, monetarist ideas were imported from across the Atlantic first of all by Professor Harry Johnson, who simultaneously held chairs at the London School of Economics and at the University of Chicago, the home base of Friedman and the place where Friedrich Hayek had been a visiting professor in the 1950s (cf. Butler, 1983, pp. 5–6). Prominent roles were also played by David Laidler and Michael Parkin of Manchester University, and by Alan Walters of Birmingham University, who was later to become one of Premier Thatcher's chief economic advisers (Keegan, 1985, pp. 43–4).

Such was the situation at the beginning of the 1970s: journalists and economists were showing signs (of varying intensity) of disillusionment with Keynesian recipes, and were growing more and more receptive to the fragrance blowing over the Atlantic with the prevailing wind. The U-turns by the Heath government in 1972, and the subsequent failure of the 'Barber Boom', provided the decisive turning point. In 1972, Tom Nairn could still make fun of the monetarists: 'Enoch Powell, this trader in national resurrectionism and necrophilia, has been forced back into the margins of political life since 1970 ... There, he occupies his time with the now outmoded currency-crankery of Milton Friedman's Chicago School' (Nairn, 1973, p. 14). By 1974 this view was no longer defensible and would have been a dangerous underestimation of an ideological current which, in the face of the surge of inflation which apparently could not be stemmed, acquired a degree of conviction difficult to withstand even for strongly orthodox Keynesians.

The fall of the Tory government in 1974 also forced many Conservative politicians to reappraise their position. Sir Keith Joseph, in an interview with William Keegan, recounts how he was lectured by Alan Walters for having allowed, as Secretary of

State for Health and Social Security in the Heath government, the explosion of government spending and the enormous inflation that Walters had been predicting (Keegan, 1985, p. 46). The conversion of Sir Keith Joseph to monetarist views brought him into the same camp as that other big spender in the Heath government, Education Minister Margaret Thatcher, who proved very receptive to monetarist explanations as well, probably because of her 'right-wing instincts' and her grocer's daughter's attraction to 'household economics' (Keegan, 1985, p. 47). Together, Joseph and Thatcher founded the Centre for Policy Studies, the CPS (with permission from party leader Heath) in order to study the example of the West German 'social market economy'. As full-time director they appointed Alfred Sherman of the London School of Economics, known for his ultra-conservative columns in the *Daily Telegraph*. Sherman defined the centre's purpose as being 'to reshape the climate of opinion. The Centre proposes to fight vigorously on this front of the battle of ideas' (quoted in Keegan, 1985, p. 47). Heath's associates were soon eliminated from the leadership of the CPS, and the CPS presented itself as an alternative to the semi-official Conservative Research Department which has since had a languishing existence.

The CPS in fact did not stand alone in this fight: the rise of the neo-liberals in Britain occurred in the context of a worldwide advance of neo-liberal forces, especially in Latin America, to which continent the Mont Pelerin Society, involved in the establishment of the IEA earlier, had also spread its wings. In Argentina this had led to the establishment of a Centre for Studies in Liberty. The movement got another major boost when General Pinochet, who had seized power in Chile in 1973, turned to the neo-liberal Chicago boys for inspiration (O'Brien and Roddick, 1983, pp. 56–7).[8] In the years after the coup, such leading neo-liberals as Friedman, Hayek, and the Chicago professor Arnold Harberger visited Chile to lend their support to the experiment in the application of their ideas. In 1980, their Chilean counterparts established a Centro de Estudios Públicos, of which Hayek became honorary President. In 1981, finally, the triumph was complete: Pinochet gave his new constitution the name 'Constitución de la Libertad',[9] and the Mont Pelerin Society held its 1981 annual meeting in Chile (O'Brien and Roddick, 1983, p. 56).

There is another transatlantic bond linking the American extreme Right scene to the British. The American Heritage Foundation, so prominent in the ideological background of the Reagan administration, maintains close ties with the Adam Smith Institute in London, established in 1977; its academic advisory board is chaired by (who else) Professor Friedrich A. Hayek.

To sum up this section, we have seen that between 1972 (when the policy of U-turns began to alienate right-wingers in the party) and the leadership election of 1975, the ideological climate in the Conservative Party moved considerably to the Right. The immediate issues responsible were the alleged sell-out to the unions in 1974 and the sky-rocketing rate of inflation which were both threatening the position of small business and *rentier* elements in the British bourgeoisie, as well as millions of pensioners unable to defend their income against inflation as the working class could through the indexation of wages. The ideas put forward by the Right thus fell on fertile ground.

Britain was experiencing a serious crisis, in which measures to defend the *status quo* – and the Heath policies were very defensive after 1971 – were clearly inadequate. In the years following the defeat of Heath, the task of renewing the political programme of the Tories was entrusted to their Thatcherite wing. As Keegan shows, many 'ordinary' Conservatives did not vote *for* neo-liberalism or monetarism, they simply voted *against* Heath. However, by doing so they placed the leadership of the Conservative Party in the hands of a group that *knew precisely* where it wanted to go and used the time until the next general election to prepare for power. They would at all cost try to avoid the miscalculations that led to the abandonment of the Selsdon project in 1972–4. 'Thatcherism' was put on the rails, and would not be stopped for a long time.

The rise of the new realism in the Labour Party

The crisis of 1974

In the previous section we saw that the Conservative government coming to power in 1970 responded to increasing right-wing pressures by embarking on a course of monetarist austerity and an all-out attempt to curb the powers of the trade union movement. The Prime Minister, however, went along with this programme only reluctantly, and in 1972 deflation was exchanged for a classic attempt to restore growth by expansion of government expenditure. The clash with the unions was continued, however, and eventually resulted in almost total confrontation between the Tory regime and the 'vanguard' of the working class, the National Union of Mineworkers. This serious political crisis, taking place against the general background of the century-long decline of Britain, coincided with the deterioration of the British economy which had set in in 1966–7 with the crumbling of the Keynesian compromise underlying the extension of the welfare state in the postwar period, and with the oil crisis of 1973–4.

This *conjuncture of crises* constituted a truly organic crisis: the basic structures of bourgeois hegemony were being seriously challenged, and even a military solution was, at the time, no longer unthinkable. The military were not only used in attempts to break the strikes ravaging Britain by doing the work that strikers were refusing. This of course was no new phenomenon: in fact, the Heath government made use of troops only very sparingly, in contrast to the Labour government of the years 1974–9 (cf. Hain, 1986, ch. 6).

What was almost without precedent was the threat of the *political* use of troops – using troops to break picket lines, and even, veiled threats of the possibility of a military coup. On 29 February 1976, the *Sunday Times* disclosed that Sir William Armstrong (head of the Civil Service and regarded as 'Deputy Prime Minister') had at the time of the miners' strike 'compared Britain to the Phoenix rising from the ashes of a smash-up and began to define the conflict in military terms'. Confronted with this atmosphere, the Scottish miners' leader Mick McGahey warned in the same article that he would 'appeal [to the troops] to assist and aid the miners. Troops are not all anti-working class ... many of them are miners' sons' (quoted in Glyn and Harrison, 1980, p. 88). Although his remarks evoked cries of treason, the *Evening Standard* conceded that he had posed 'exceptionally delicate questions' (see Glyn and Harrison, 1980, p. 88). In the course of 1974, military forces were deployed for the protection of Heathrow Airport allegedly against possible terrorist attacks. The first time this happened was in January, in the midst of the longest-lasting state of emergency since the General Strike of 1926. The exercise was repeated several times, and on 5 August 1974 (when the political situation was still far from stable) *The Times* carried an article asking whether the armoured cars that had been spotted at Heathrow Airport in July of that year had represented 'A rehearsal for a coup?' The possibility of a military coup was also contemplated, indeed expected, by none other than Oswald Mosley (Frank, 1980, p. 165). As it turned out, things never went quite so far, but these episodes illustrate the degree of seriousness of the crisis.

The 1974–9 Labour government

This was the situation in which Labour returned to power. Its primary task consisted in restoring some degree of social peace. The chief imperative at this point was to pacify the unions.

This task was taken up by postponing any unpleasant decisions which would have to be made eventually, and lasted until after the referendum on the terms of the renegotiation of British EC membership in June 1975. No truly revolutionary measures were to be expected anyway: the leadership of the Labour Party which came to power in 1974 was hardly different from the leadership which had led party and government in the years 1967–9 and which in that period had been responsible for attempts to curb union rights and to abolish full employment as the foremost policy imperative. From the very start the government was aware of earlier conflicts with the Governor of the Bank of England, who had impressed upon Wilson in 1964 that difficult external circumstances required 'Tory measures', 'whatever the opinion of the electorate' (quoted by Brett, 1985, pp. 152, 162). After his second electoral victory in October 1974, Wilson was quoted as saying: 'It is vital that we do not imperil this improvement of our balance of payments ... fighting inflation is a matter of national survival' (in the *Financial Times* of 15 October 1974, quoted by Frank, 1980, p. 115).

Notwithstanding these pressures, the government began by borrowing its way out of the acute impasse: total borrowing increased from £3 billion in 1973 to almost £9 billion in 1975 (Brett, 1985, p. 162). The claims of the miners were met: they received a wage increase even larger than they originally demanded (Flanagan, Soskice and Ulman, 1983, pp. 416–7). General wage increases amounted to 28 per cent between July 1974 and July 1975, inflation rose to 25 per cent, and the balance of payments in 1974 showed a deficit of £3.6 billion. Profits in manufacturing collapsed: from 14.9 per cent in 1973, they fell to 6.3 per cent in 1974 (Brett, 1985, p. 162; see also Coates, 1980, p. 63).

The answer of the Labour government to the mounting problems in 1974–5 was the 'social contract', which included numerous concessions to the trade unions in return for the prevention of total collapse, and which was in fact 'more far-reaching than any since the late 1940s' (Middlemas, 1979, p. 446).

The radical election manifesto of the Labour Party (*Labour's Programme 1973*) appeared for a time to be effectively put into practice with the establishment of price and dividend controls, the promise of planning agreements, and the announcement of forms of industrial democracy (Leys, 1985, p. 16). The years 1974 and 1975 also saw attempts to integrate government money directly into the circuit of productive capital, principally through the operation of the National Enterprise Board (NEB) (Jessop, 1980, p. 45).[10] All in all, the package represented a significant if temporary expansion of trade union rights, expressing the strong conjunctural position of the unions.[11]

Conjunctures, however, have a tendency to be unstable and susceptible to change. Internationally, the hopes which the Left entertained over the promises of a New International Economic Order crumbled in 1975. Kissinger's Year of Europe brought the Europeans back in line, and the north–south dialogue dragged on in Paris without leading to any real results. That same year also saw the turning point *inside* Britain.

The test of strength for the Left in the party and in Cabinet (where Tony Benn headed the important Department of Industry) came with the referendum over the results of the 'renegotiation' of the terms of entry into the Common Market. The Left in the Labour Party, joined in an unholy coalition by the extreme Right, vehemently opposed British membership and favoured leaving the EC. The party establishment, led in this case by Healey and Jenkins, campaigned for acceptance of the terms, and was supported by the Liberal Party, the Conservative leadership, and Britain's multinationals who financed the Britain in Europe campaign (cf. Butler and Kitzinger, 1976). Two years later the *Economist* surveyed the results of the first years of British membership. Its broad conclusions were that

> the impact of membership has been generally less than expected. The farm policy has pushed up food prices by only about 3% and Britain's payments into the EEC budget have been way below those forecast. The industrial benefits have been slow to appear, but are now beginning to show up. Britain's trade deficit with the EEC is still large, but improving fast. And the country is still run by the British. (*Economist*, 11 June 1977)

For some big firms such as the General Electric Company and Imperial Chemical Industries membership was an outright success. As regards British Leyland, 'but for EEC membership, the company might have been pushed right out of the mass car market' (*Economist*, 11 June 1977).

Among the general public, the verdict concerning British membership was rather more ambivalent: a poll conducted in July 1977 showed that 40 per cent of the British people thought that membership was 'a bad thing', with 35 per cent feeling it was 'a good thing' (*Economist*, 9 July 1977).

The successful conclusion of the referendum – successful in the sense that two-thirds of the votes were in favour of membership – provided the signal for a turn to the right. The budget presented in

November 1974 had already foreshadowed the move to the right, urged upon the Labour leadership by interventions from the Bank of England and the CBI. Now the rightward shift was put into a higher gear. Within a week of the referendum, Tony Benn was removed from the Department of Industry and in protest his deputy Eric Heffer resigned. Thus an opening was created for a closer relationship between the DoI and the Treasury (Shanks, 1977, p. 76).

Secondly, the 'social contract' was now adapted to function as the framework for a restrictive incomes policy, which followed the generous concessions to union demands of the previous year (Coates, 1980, pp. 53–67).

Important for the change in climate which enabled the government to enforce its incomes policy in the face of trade union opposition was the familiar recurrence of yet another Sterling crisis. The fall of the pound from $2.00 in March 1975 to $1.60 in October, and the ensuing policy of austerity, 'effectively destroyed the Labour government's social programme' (Coates, 1982, p. 143). Thus, when deficit financing was finally tried for the first time in Britain in 1975, it was almost immediately blocked by the reactions of the City and the Treasury demanding the return to financial orthodoxy (Radice, 1984, p. 126).

In March 1976, Prime Minister Harold Wilson suddenly resigned and was succeeded by James Callaghan. Wilson himself has always maintained that he had planned to leave office at about mid-term in 1974, and that there were no political reasons for his move (Wilson, 1979, pp. 227–8). He is supported in this interpretation by close associates of the time (cf. Castle, 1980, p. 671). However, speculation has surfaced time and again that there were additional reasons for his sudden resignation.[12]

International capitalist discipline

Wilson's resignation and the changes in governmental policy resulting from it occurred in the international context of the years 1975–7 – that is, in a general offensive against the New International Economic Order and against those Western forces willing to serve as 'relays' for a policy of compromise with radical forces in the Third World (cf. Cox, 1983; Krasner, 1985; Van der Pijl, 1988). The concept of control that gained initial prominence in these years was that of trilateralism, named after the Trilateral Commission.

The essence of trilateralism was the attempt to unify the capitalist world in the face of perceived external and internal threats

169

(such as Eurocommunism)[13] to the existing order and in the wake of the US defeat in Vietnam. This consisted of concerted action by the important capitalist countries, with a distinctly corporate liberal undertone as regards the management of the capitalist world economy (cf. Parboni, 1986). In more theoretical terms, trilateralism attempted to place capitalist co-operation once more on a consensual basis, replacing the coercive posture of the Nixon years which had proved ineffective in suppressing Third World radicalism and Eurocommunism.

Prominent corporate liberals came to the fore in Western Europe, such as Helmut Schmidt in West Germany (replacing Willy Brandt after a scandal), and Giscard d'Estaing in France, who succeeded President Pompidou. The replacement of the Portuguese, Greek and Spanish dictatorships by (social) democratic regimes, and Callaghan's succession of Wilson, fitted the same pattern, which was confirmed and reinforced by the election of Jimmy Carter (whose connections with the Trilateral Commission are well known) in November 1976 (Van der Pijl, 1984, pp. 272–6; also Frieden, 1977).

British involvement in the Trilateral Commission was extensive, from both major parties. The Labour Party was not directly represented during its years in office (no publicly elected officials were allowed to keep their seats on the commission) but relations between the right wing of the party (particularly Denis Healey and David Owen) and the commission were nevertheless close.

Although the Trilateral Commission bore the hallmark of international corporate liberalism, it would be misleading to think that it was populated exclusively by corporate liberals. To some degree, other currents were also represented by such figures as Peter Jay.

Throughout 1976, the balance of payments deficit steadily increased, and the pound continued to fall against the dollar. In such a situation, an appeal to the International Monetary Fund (IMF) is the usual if not very popular recourse for capitalist governments. The first approach to the IMF by the British government had already been made in November 1975, when Britain applied for credit from the so-called 'oil facility' (Keegan and Pennant-Rea, 1979, p. 159). In the course of 1976, the situation deteriorated for the Labour government. Monetarism was gaining adherence in the City and the financial press, but also with certain high Bank and Treasury officials; the publicity activities of Milton Friedman at this time focused on Britain and on the way Keynesianism and socialism were causing the decline of the British economy (cf. Keegan, 1985, p. 88). This mood was seized upon by the American Secretary of the Treasury William Simon and the president of the Federal Reserve System Arthur Burns, who 'wanted to use the fall in the sterling balances to ensnare the British Government"', and by the British Treasury which used the plight of Sterling to impose even sterner wage restrictions on the unions (Keegan and Pennant-Rea, 1979, p. 163).[14] The pressure was kept up by the visit of an IMF team in May, and renewed US Treasury steps in June.

The final surrender of the Labour government came in September, and decided in the week of 27 September 1976, the same week as the annual Labour Party conference. At that conference, Callaghan made the speech in which he told his audience that he considered it impossible to 'spend his way out of the recession'. 'The Speech' served as a sign to all parties concerned that the Labour government had definitively abandoned Keynesianism: at home it was an omen of what was to happen to the relationship between the government and the trade union movement, and it was also taken up by such Tory monetarists as Sir Keith Joseph and Nigel Lawson as confirmation of their point of view, a fact to which they would refer back years later. Externally, the speech also served to strengthen those in the American administration willing to bail Britain out. Callaghan's stance at the time was strongly influenced by the monetarist views of his son-in-law, Peter Jay, who filled his columns in *The Times* with regular exhortations to control the money supply and freeze government spending. In fact, it was Peter Jay who actually wrote Callaghan's speech (Keegan, 1985, p. 91; this is confirmed by Callaghan himself in his 1987 memoirs). The message was welcomed in Washington, where the decision to save the British government was made by the White House itself (Keegan and Pennant-Rea, 1979, p. 165). Henry Kissinger and other advisers of President Ford were afraid that a failure to help now might eventually lead to a new government dominated by the Labour Left, and it was therefore decided to support Callaghan and Healey against the Left, presumably still led by Tony Benn.[15]

The IMF loan was requested on 29 September, and on 1 November the IMF team arrived in London to start the negotiations over the terms of the agreement. The German Chancellor Helmut Schmidt at the eleventh hour also intervened and convinced the British that the terms already offered could not be improved, and that it would be wise to accept them without delay: this occurred in the first week of December (Keegan and Pennant-Rea, 1979, pp. 165–8; also Sampson, 1983, pp. 329–30).

The most important conditions of the $3.5 billion IMF loan,

which also gave access to private banking facilities, were the maintenance of a high interest rate (to attract foreign funds), sizeable cuts in public spending, stern wage restraints, and the sale of £500 million worth of government-held shares in British Petroleum (Brett, 1985, p. 164). In general, the conclusion is justified that the essentials of the Thatcher government's later monetary strategy were already 'contained in the Letter of Intent sent by Denis Healey as Chancellor of the Exchequer to the International Monetary Fund in December 1976' (Riddell, 1983, pp. 58–9).

The episode of the request for and granting of the IMF loan was of great symbolic significance, because it represented the terminal stage of corporate liberalism as the hegemonic concept of control. International capitalist discipline had been reimposed upon the British Labour government, which would henceforth recognize the 'realities' of capitalism. In fact, the Labour government had already, as emphasized earlier, given up its attempt to implement its left-wing programme by 1975. But symbolically, and partly also in real terms, the IMF prescriptions implied the final demise of the basic principles of Keynesianism and the replacement of a productive-capital concept by a money-capital concept. It was remarkable that it should be the Labour Party – the historic bearer of the productive-capital concept since the 1940s – which carried Keynesianism to its grave.

The policies prescribed by the IMF were very successful in terms of their objectives. The holders of Sterling who had caused the downfall of the pound by withdrawing their funds a year earlier soon moved their funds back into Sterling when they saw that their holdings were guaranteed by the IMF and the US government. In combination with the revenues flowing from North Sea oil, which were just beginning to flow in this period, this restoration of confidence soon prompted the appreciation of the pound against the dollar. The chancellor's decision to let the pound float freely was another milestone on the road towards monetarism (Keegan, 1985, p. 94). It made Healey 'much fêted in Washington', where, just a year after Britain's most serious balance of payments crisis since the late 1940s, he was chosen to chair the IMF's 'Interim Committee', its central policy steering organ (Keegan, 1985, p. 108).

By this time, the balance of payments was back in order. Nevertheless Healey found it convenient to prolong Britain's obligations under the terms of the IMF loan in order to force unwilling ministers and trade unions to accept his cuts and wage restraints (cf. Keegan and Pennant-Rea, 1979, pp. 147, 169). By the middle of 1977 the acute crisis which had faced the Labour government when it came to power in 1974 had been brought under control.

In that sense, indeed, 'Labour's "integrative function" looked uncommonly secure' (Middlemas, 1979, p. 456; also Winkler, 1977, p. 83). The trade unions hardly opposed the stringent measures imposed by Healey. The Callaghan government was extensively praised in the international business press for eliminating all thought of a Left alternative economic strategy, and for having abandoned Keynesianism. Callaghan had successfully defused 'muddle-headed left-wing proposals' (*Business Week*, 17 April 1978). His government's economic strategy represented 'a significant break with the neo-Keynesian "demand management" ', and he was instead pushing in the right direction with its 'more monetarist strategy' (*Business Week*, 30 October 1978).

The real economy

But, however successful the government strategy was in restoring international financial confidence and the balance of payments, and in subduing the unions, hardly any progress was made at all in the 'real' economy.[16] Between 1970 and 1979, employment in Britain's manufacturing industries declined by 17 per cent (Aaronovitch, 1981, p. 9),[17] leading to debates over the 'de-industrialization' of Britain. By 1979, industrial production (excluding oil) was still 4 per cent lower than it had been at its peak in 1973 (Brett, 1985, p. 166). Unemployment, which had amounted to 500,000 in 1972, had by 1977 increased to over 1.5 million, while investment stagnated (Pollard, 1982, p. 59).

Overall the development of productivity in the manufacturing sector lagged far behind that in other countries, and in combination with the high exchange rate of the pound this meant a steady deterioration of Britain's competitive position (see Table 6.1).

Table 6.1 Competitive Position in Industry 1975–80 (1975 = 100)

	FRG	FRA	ITA	NL	UK	USA	JAP
Productivity	117.7	125.1	133.1	129.2	105.4	108.9	148.0
Relative unit labour cost*	108.7	100.9	88.1	93.7	135.8	97.1	82.0

* Unit labour costs in a common currency by reference to the weighted average for nineteen main competing countries.
Source: European Economy, March 1984, pp. 112–24.

The conclusion of the social contract and the concessions made to the unions in 1974–5 had also contributed to the stagnation of the modernization of labour relations in Britain: British Leyland, haunted during the 1970s by numerous strikes, still concluded 200 separate contracts annually, a situation protracted by the structure of trade unions and by the strength of local shop stewards. The main answer to British Leyland's problems had to be sought in Britain itself, although the company did expand its foreign operations. Truly transnational corporations (such as Ford) could instead rely on their operations elsewhere to supply the British market: indeed by February 1978, Ford had become Britain's largest car *importer* (*Economist*, 11 February 1978).

Not only were trade union structures on the national and company level still rather archaic, but at the plant level the old problems of deficient management control also still persisted (Barou, 1978, pp. 112–14). The main consequences were that corporate planning of investment was made more difficult, and that the technical division of labour in the firms was only slowly adapted to new technological developments.

The limits of Labour's success came into view in the course of 1978. The underlying crisis of hegemony, which Labour had successfully repressed for a number of years, was triggered again by Callaghan's attempt to emulate the 'Modell Deutschland' by setting the limit for wage increases at 5 per cent (while inflation was still not below 10 per cent) (Keegan, 1985, p. 109). However, the social consensus which had been the basis of post-war 'Butskellism' had been eroded by the developments of the past ten or twelve years. From the attempt by the Wilson government to introduce legislation restricting trade union rights in the late 1960s, through the Heath episode, up to the application of the IMF solution after December 1976, the welfare consensus had gradually disintegrated. The strategy which Labour pursued in its attempt to restructure and modernize British society and economy not only failed in its own terms but also alienated its mass base. For, the intermezzo of 1974–5 notwithstanding, it involved a far-reaching attack on the established positions of the trade unions (Jacques, 1983, p. 54).

Labour's strategy in the 1970s was complex and ineffectual: Labour did indeed introduce monetarism, but only in the area of monetary and financial policy. This was combined with strong state interventionist policies in wage determination and industrial policy – though not as strong as the Labour Left advocated nor as strong as would have been necessary to overcome the antagonistic world market forces. Finally, monetarism was used by Labour as if it were indeed a class-neutral, objective policy, and it was not recognized that for monetarism to 'work' it would necessarily have to be embedded in a wider *political strategy*, in a truly global concept of control. The *need* for a *political* framework within which monetarism could work was put into words in 1977 by one of the most influential monetarist journalists, Samuel Brittan: 'we need not another revolution in economic theory, but a revolution in constitutional and political ideas, which will save us from the snare of unlimited democracy, before we find ourselves with no democracy – and very little freedom – left' (Brittan, 1977, p. 49). The elections of June 1979 provided the *possibility* to create such a framework, and gave the Tories 398 seats with which to carry their revolution forward.

CHAPTER 7

Thatcherism in power

The Thatcherite concept of control

The year 1979 was a year of crisis, or rather a year of a conjuncture of crises. Internationally, the crisis of Fordism, of the Keynesian welfare state and of American hegemony was compounded by the effects of the second oil crisis and the Soviet invasion of Afghanistan. In Britain, these crises were superimposed on the long-term decline of Britain. The concrete manifestation of this conjuncture of crises in the Winter of Discontent brought out once more the archaic capital–labour relationship in Britain, and the acute crisis of the political system reflected the 'unfinished' bourgeois revolution and the incomplete 'nationalization' of the British state. Ruling circles in Britain had gradually become aware in the course of the 1970s that the problems which Britain was facing were of a structural character and that their solution required a fundamentally different political approach. 'Thatcherism' represented an attempt to provide a radically new answer to this 'triple crisis' of the British social formation. It of course did not drop out of a clear blue sky, but was constructed over a number of years and out of elements which predated their integration into this single framework. The formative period of what has eventually become 'Thatcherism' was the period from the 1973–4 crisis to the 1979 election campaign. During these years isolated ideas and partial programmes gradually acquired some degree of coherence as the previously hegemonic corporate-liberal coalition of class interests disintegrated under the impact of the unfolding structural crisis in the world economy. 'Currency-crankery' became respectable monetary policy, racism became a respectable expression of 'Britishness', anti-socialist free market ideology[1] replaced Keynesianism as the norm defining the role of the state in the economy, and the call for law and order replaced the 'permissive tolerance' of the 1960s.

One strand in the analysis of Thatcherism has concentrated on its ideological dimension (cf. Hall and Jacques, 1983). It identified Thatcherism as an authoritarian populist project which was successful (thanks in no small measure to the failures of social

176

democracy) in shifting the terrain of political debate decisively
to the right: the crisis 'has begun to be "lived" in its terms', and
Thatcherism 'operated directly on the real and manifestly contradictory experience of the popular classes under social-democratic
corporatism' (Hall, 1983, pp. 30, 31). Hall has pointed out that
the structural crisis of world capitalism, compounded in Britain
by the long-term process of decline, undermined the Keynesian
compromise, and showed that Keynesianism (social democracy)
was unable to formulate an adequate response to the crisis. In
fact, because Keynesianism is based on the premise that crisis
is not a necessary phenomenon, it has never really been able to
accept that indeed there was a structural crisis which required
a structural solution. The disintegration of hegemonic social
democracy created the space for a new battle of ideas from which
'Thatcherism' emerged victoriously, because it gave expression to
the 'real experience of the masses', to reactionary common sense.

The problem with this analysis is threefold: first, it tends
to blame (the leadership of) social democracy for the rise
of Thatcherism (which goes much further than saying that
social democracy was unable to formulate a credible socialist
response to the crisis); secondly, it tends to analyse Thatcherism
exclusively in political and ideological terms (as an -*ism*), and
to ignore the identification of the class forces whose interests
are represented in the new project; and, finally, it tends to
view Thatcherism as primarily reactionary and destructive.

These problems have been recognized by many. Thatcherism
would not have lasted as long as it has (and perhaps will do) if it
was true that its project is 'to force-march the society, vigorously,
into the past' (Hall and Jacques, 1983, p. 11). Thatcherism is not
reactionary in the sense that its aim is to return to the nineteenth
century. It is so successful because (among other reasons) it aims
in a real sense to take Britain into the twenty-first century. Social
democracy is failing (not just in Britain but in most other north-
west European countries as well) because fundamentally speaking
it now is a reactionary ideology, which has no other promise than
to take us back to the 1960s, when the threads of the Fordist
accumulation regime had not begun to come apart. The point
that Thatcherism does provide a perspective on the future, and
does establish a new regime of accumulation, has been put forward by Fiona Atkins (1986) who points out that when seen in its
global context the Thatcherite de-industrializing strategy is quite
viable. Bob Jessop *et al.* (1984, 1985, 1987) argue that Thatcherism
is the hegemonic project for the post-Fordist era. Jessop has also
been one of those authors pointing out that Thatcherism is not

177

only an ideology, but is at the same time based on the 'decisive function exercised by the leading group in the decisive nucleus of economic activity' (Gramsci, 1971, p. 161)–that is, concretely identifiable capitalist interests are grouped behind the Thatcher regime and form the core of a new power bloc being constructed in the 1980s. In particular, Jessop *et al.* have analysed the emerging socio-economic structure resulting from Thatcher's introduction of a post-Fordist accumulation regime in Britain. However, because of the essentially voluntarist conception underlying his notion of a hegemonic project (see Clarke, 1983), Jessop does not actually succeed in theorizing the link between these structural developments and the level of strategic action – the identification of the concrete interests involved and the precise ways in which the dialectical interaction between structure and strategy is expressed in the articulation of the Thatcherite project.

It is precisely here that an approach in terms of comprehensive concepts of control can enhance our understanding. Every comprehensive concept of control contains at least four central elements. These four core propositions of every concept of control concern:

(1) the relationship with the outside world and the aspired position of the national bourgeoisie in the world class structure;
(2) the balance of forces between the social classes within the country;
(3) the role of the state in the accumulation process and the overall relation between state and civil society;
(4) the relations between the different fractions of the ruling class and the way in which these can be induced to subscribe to the dominant concept of control.

It is my thesis in this book that 'Thatcherism' is a reasonably coherent[2] and comprehensive concept of control for the restoration of bourgeois rule and bourgeois hegemony in the new circumstances of the 1980s – that is, in the context of the transformation of world capitalism now taking place.

As I have argued in Chapter 6, the rise of Thatcherism is the specific British manifestation of a global phenomenon: the rise of *neo-liberalism*. The precise meaning of this term must be clarified, because it can easily lead to misunderstanding. An earlier meaning of the term (which we encountered in Chapter 5) was actually quite similar to the notion of corporate liberalism (cf. Harris, 1972). Here, neo-liberalism is taken to be a radical alternative for corporate liberalism, not the same thing by a different name. A second cause for misunderstanding may be the recent popularity

of the term in the USA where 'liberalism' had the same con-
notations as corporatism in Europe, and where 'neo-liberalism'
designates those political forces which try to revive the liberalism
of the Kennedy era, but pragmatically incorporate many of the
conservative criticisms of traditional American liberalism (cf.
Rothenberg, 1984).[3]

In the context of this book, neo-liberalism has been chosen as
the label to be affixed to the overall project, which is variously
known as 'the New Right', 'neo-conservatism', 'Thatcherism',
'authoritarian populism' (Hall and Jacques, 1983) or the 'Two Nation project' (Jessop *et al.*) in Britain. In an enlightening attempt to
unravel the different strands of thought involved, Andrew Belsey
has described ideal-typical 'neo-liberalism' as the politics constructed from the individual, freedom of choice, the market society, *laissez-faire*, and minimal government. Ideal-typical neo-con-
servative politics is constructed from strong government, social
authoritarianism, a disciplined society, hierarchy and subordination, and the nation (Belsey, 1986, p. 173). Belsey is absolutely
right when he states that in political practice the two sides inter-
mingle to such a degree that it becomes impossible to make a clear
separation. In so far as it is possible to make an analytical distinction between the political and the economic, neo-liberalism is situated in the sphere of economic ideas, whereas neo-conservatism
is located in the political sphere. Therefore a combination of the
two is not nearly as contradictory as it sometimes seems.

If we take a closer look at the nature of the contradiction, we
also gain an understanding of the class basis of Thatcherism.
Neo-liberalism combines a strong moral reaction against the
social consequences of advanced capitalism with exuberant praise
of the forces of the market. These two elements of neo-liberalism
form a dialectical unity, a fact which was (*mutatis mutandis*) already
grasped by Gramsci in his analysis of the European reactions to
Fordism and 'Americanism' (Gramsci, 1971, p. 317).

In the concrete case of Thatcherism in the 1980s, we see that
the two elements are responsible for two distinct segments of its
popular electoral basis.

The first is the moral reaction against modern society with
its extreme individualism on the level of personal life, its
tendential destruction of the traditional nuclear family, its
internationalization which is seen to 'undermine the nation',
but also its collectivist tendencies in the shape of the monopolistic organization of both capital and labour; this reaction is
primarily aroused in the petty bourgeoisie and the (white, male)
skilled workers who feel threatened or restrained by 'socialism'.

179

The second is the praise, and the belief in the beneficial effects, of the free market which is particularly strong among small to medium capitalists and among the 'new middle class' in the commercial service sectors.

There is, however, another layer of reality involved. As a concept of control, Thatcherism is not only an 'authoritarian populist' ideology, it is also the formulation of an identifiable fractional interest in terms of the 'national' or 'general' interest. Thatcherism, it will be argued in the course of this chapter, is the fundamental expression of the outlook of *circulating capital* and *transnational capital* inside Britain, while expressing a 'general interest' through its reactionary-populist elements which make it attractive for small capital and for large segments of the middle and working classes.

The precise mix of the two elements (free market ideology and neo-conservatism) may vary from country to country, and also from one phase to another depending on the political conjuncture. A final element which can enhance our understanding of neo-liberalism in general and of Thatcherism in particular therefore concerns the phasing of its practice. We have said that Thatcherism represents an effort to resolve the crisis of British capitalism and to reverse Britain's decline. As Stuart Hall has said,

> If the crisis is deep – 'organic' – these efforts cannot be merely defensive. They will be *formative*: aiming at a new balance of forces, the emergence of new elements, the attempt to put together a new 'historic bloc', new political configurations and 'philosophies', a profound restructuring of the state and the ideological discourses which construct the crisis and represent it as it is 'lived' as a practical reality: new programmes and policies, pointing to a new result, a new sort of 'settlement' – 'within certain limits'. These new elements do not 'emerge': they have to be constructed. Political and ideological work is required to disarticulate old formations, and to rework their elements into new ones. (Hall, 1983, p. 23)

Neo-liberalism is at once directed towards disarticulating the old formation which is in crisis, that is, towards *deconstructing corporatism and the Keynesian welfare state*, and towards the formation of a new configuration, the *construction of a post-Fordist accumulation regime*. In almost every concrete neo-liberal policy, both the deconstructive and the constructive elements can be discerned. Yet, during the first phase of a neo-liberal regime, the deconstructive element will necessarily dominate: the first priority then is to dislodge the power structure of the previous era, and not much thought is given to the precise shape of the alternative to be built. As the disarticulation of the old formation progresses, the need for a constructive programme grows.

Such a constructive programme is not based on a blueprint which can readily be pulled out of a drawer, but is instead articulated as the regime struggles along, on a trial and error basis (Jacobs 1988), reacting to the internal political conjuncture and to changing conditions in the global political economy. The general direction into which the project evolves is however still determined by the underlying configuration of class forces of which the neo-liberal concept of control is the expression.

The basis for this underlying configuration is to be found in the dynamic conditions of capital accumulation. Indeed, the distinction between circulating and productive capital is related to the basic contradiction of capitalist accumulation between developing the forces of production without limit and the need to confine accumulation to the limits of capitalist ownership – that is, to the contradiction between the socialization of production and the private appropriation of surplus value (Clarke, 1988). But this contradiction is not overcome automatically, as if by nature. It requires the strategic intervention of consciously operating social forces. The essence of the approach in this book – an approach in terms of *concepts of control* – is precisely to attempt to bridge the conceptual gap in Marxism between these two levels of analysis, between a 'voluntarist' and a 'fundamentalist' approach.

In order to do that, we shall look at four main areas of policy-making and struggle under Thatcherism:

(1) the global context in which Thatcherism arose and played an important part;
(2) the assault on the working class;
(3) the nature of the Thatcher government's accumulation strategy;
(4) the analysis of the concrete material interests behind Thatcherism.

The transatlantic context of neo-liberalism: the evolution of British foreign policy under Thatcher

From Atlantic partnership to unilateralism

After the lessons of Suez were internalized, British foreign policy was guided by the concept which President Kennedy labelled

'Atlantic partnership': a strong alliance between the United States and a united Western Europe, of which Britain strove to become a member after 1961. The remains of the British Empire were decolonized on the basis of an almost complete national consensus: by the end of the 1970s, only a few spots of British presence remained (Rhodesia, Hong Kong and the Falklands, for example), while of course South Africa was still an unresolved problem.

The Thatcher government broke with this consensus and fundamentally reoriented Britain's foreign policy in response to the crisis in the postwar international order and the changes taking place in American foreign policy from 1979. American foreign policy under President Reagan was, certainly during his first term in office, 'unilateralist': its main traits were a very aggressive policy towards the Soviet Union (the Empire of Evil) and towards signs of independence in the Third World, and a relative indifference towards Europe, in line with the shift of America's economic interests from the Atlantic to the Pacific Ocean.

The strategic choice of the Thatcher government was to follow America's lead: the term 'Iron Lady' was first given to Margaret Thatcher in the Soviet Union because of her strong anti-Soviet stance. In fact, Britain was the first developed capitalist country (even before ·Reagan came to power in January 1981) to take an active role in shaping a new, neo-liberal, international economic order (later followed by the US, Germany, France, Holland, Belgium, and so forth). But it also set out to transform the international political landscape, and in this field the other European neo-liberal regimes moved far more cautiously.

The new Thatcherite foreign policy was very clearly reminiscent of earlier phases of British 'grandeur' politics, especially Churchill's foreign policy. 'Churchillism', when taken to its ultimate consequence, meant opposition to any European co-operation in the area of defence in which the United States was not directly involved. Unilateralists regard any such co-operation as potentially anti-American (cf. McGeehan, 1985).[4]

One important difference between Thatcherism and the Churchill option is the role of the Commonwealth in British foreign policy. In the 1940s and 1950s, Britain's ties with the Commonwealth formed the basis of the three-circle theory and of the claim to a world role of its own. The Conservative governments of Churchill and Eden refrained from taking part in the Messina Conference preparing the foundation of the Common Market in 1955, ostensibly because the ties with the Commonwealth took priority over any bond with Western Europe. By 1986, however, the Commonwealth had become a nuisance deflecting Britain from its 'real interests', for instance by insisting on sanctions against South Africa (Chalfont, 1986, p. 10).

The admiration of Mrs Thatcher for Winston Churchill became especially apparent during the Falklands crisis. The events in 1982 have been interpreted in two ways. From one point of view, the way the conflict was handled by Thatcher and by all relevant political forces in Britain constituted a revival of 'Churchillism', and a reaffirmation of a constant in Britain's foreign policy. Barnett's view (1982) is that Margaret Thatcher must be taken seriously in her boastful utterances about Britain's grandeur: 'The lesson of the Falklands is that Britain has not changed and that this nation still has those sterling qualities which shine through our history' (Margaret Thatcher, Cheltenham, 3 July 1982).

The opposite view seems more probable: it is that the Falklands crisis represented another spasm in the ongoing process of the decline of Britain.[5] The shining (though somewhat 'lucky') victory and the considerable American support masked the fact that British sovereignty over the Falkland Islands is an imperialist atavism which cannot be supported indefinitely, not even by granting the US landing rights for the new airbase at Mount Pleasant (*Financial Times*, 26 February 1987). The liaison with the United States was quite remarkable: American support for Britain cost the US a considerable amount in terms of its position in Latin America, the more so as the latter was very important.[6]

Nevertheless, the most important effects of the Falklands crisis have probably been of a domestic nature (Hobsbawm, 1983), through its effects in 'saving' Thatcherism electorally, and in providing an opportunity to remove 'wets' from important positions.[7] In this context the episode of the sinking of the *General Belgrano* was significant. Doubts as to the wisdom of the war were still being expressed in certain influential circles,[8] and these doubts were shared by the Foreign Secretary Francis Pym, who was involved in delicate negotiations through the Peruvian President Belaunde Terry. The *Belgrano* was sunk precisely at the moment when these negotiations entered a critical phase (*NRC Handelsblad*, 6 June 1983), and on express orders from the Prime Minister herself (Riddell, 1983, p. 217). Negotiations were broken off, a military 'solution' was achieved, and Britain's 'unilateralism' was clearly established.

The European Community

Indeed, the Falkland stance of the Thatcher government has been the clearest expression of the 'new nationalism', of which the second major expression was Britain's guerrilla tactics over the EC budget (Gray, 1983). For four and a half years, Mrs Thatcher haunted the EC with her demands for a 'rebate', which she eventually secured at the Fontainebleu Summit of June 1984: Britain would get a rebate of £850 million on average for three years. Domestically, the Labour Party was outmanoeuvred and could not cash in on its anti-EC stance. Britain's European policy amounted effectively to reducing the EC, or at least Britain's membership in it, to a free trade area. It frustrated all attempts to increase the political and economic role of Europe, and in fact reduced it to the sort of inter-governmental organization that Britain (or Churchill) had always envisioned.

Since 1984, little progress has been made in the EC, or in Britain, in solving the basic causes of the problem. On the one hand, Britain trades less with her EC partners, and more with countries outside the EC, than the other European countries, and thus pays more into the Community's 'own resources' than other European partners. On the other hand, the fundamental problem of the Common Agricultural Policy, which is a problem for the whole Community and not just for Britain, is still there. Britain's strategy of making progress in other areas (such as technology policy) dependent upon a restructuring of the agricultural policies proved counterproductive for several years by blocking progress in *all* areas of co-operation (see Riddell, 1983, pp. 211–15). The British government also refused to join the European Monetary System (EMS), although joining would partially stabilize the fluctuations in the exchange rate, and would thus allow lower interest rates (see Keegan, 1986). For these reasons the CBI, as the mouthpiece of British industrial capital producing for the domestic market and for export, has long been in favour of Britain's joining the EMS (*NRC Handelsblad*, 11 November 1986), but the Thatcher government remained unresponsive to pleas for a more active role in the process of further European integration. It clung to its reformulation of Churchill's vision of Britain as a power with its own role to play in alliance with the United States, and it has maintained the 'independence' of Sterling.

This view of Britain's place in the world has also dominated British defence policies during the first half of the 1980s. The voices raised against strong identification with the USA were few and politically weak. On the extreme right and on the far left, isolationist views were sometimes heard, calling for a move out of the Common Market and a looser relationship with the USA (and on the left there were complementary calls for unilateral nuclear disarmament). On the right, Britain's own Gaullist, Enoch Powell, has said that 'successive British governments down the last 30 years have *Finlandized* the United Kingdom in relation to the USA' (Powell, 1983, my emphasis).

In the centre of the political spectrum (which is now quite crowded) most people agree with some version of what the 1986 SDP–Liberal Alliance report on defence and disarmament proposed. In the words of David Owen: 'If there could be a tripod of Franco–German–Anglo understanding, the so-called European pillar within NATO would be immensely strengthened ... The US dominance within NATO must end' (quoted by Ian Davidson in the *Financial Times*, 20 January 1986).

The Westland Affair

The ideological contradictions in Thatcherism came forcefully to the political surface in the upheaval over the Westland Affair.[9] The events surrounding this affair and the resignation of Michael Heseltine in January 1986 have been interpreted by many against the background of an alleged struggle between an Atlantic fraction led by the 'pro-American' Prime Minister and a European fraction led by the 'pro-European' Heseltine. This view seemed to be supported by the fact that both direct opponents, Leon Brittan and Michael Heseltine, implicated relations with the United States in their position. In his notorious conversation with Sir Raymond Lygo of British Aerospace, Brittan expressed his concern that the proponents of the 'European' solution for Westland were evoking an anti-American sentiment in the country. In his turn, Heseltine warned time and again of a rising tide of anti-Americanism that would result from a complete domination of the European defence industries by American companies. In fact, this argument occupied almost half of the space of Heseltine's five-column apology in the *Observer* of 12 January 1986, which indicates that he felt vulnerable on this point.

The view that what was involved was a struggle between pro-American forces and anti-American/pro-European forces must however be questioned. Much of the confusion around these terms is caused by the fact that their precise meaning is usually left in the dark. In the Westland Affair, the case for European co-operation rested on the Independent European Programme Group (IEPG), which had been reactivated by Michael Heseltine and the Dutch Secretary for Defence Jan van Houwelingen in 1983. Initially, Heseltine had trouble convincing his government that European defence co-operation was desirable: 'the overall posture [of the British government] throughout 1983 and the first half of 1984 appeared to be one of scepticism'.[10]

In fact, the IEPG, in the area of defence co-operation, came to perform the role of rallying point for the remaining trilateralist forces in the face of increasing unilateralist pressures from the USA. Michael Heseltine played a prominent role in the attempts to rationalize the European defence industries in order to make them into more attractive partners for American arms manufacturers.[11]

> Alliance equipment procurement cannot be based on US domination of the high technology end of the market. There has to be a genuine two-way street across the spectrum of defence equipment or the Europeans will have no choice but to rationalize amongst themselves and buy from each other. I do not underestimate the difficulties in evolving an effective transatlantic partnership; but the prize is worth the effort. (Heseltine, 1984, p. 3)

Heseltine lost the gamble: he was defeated by Mrs Thatcher. The unilateralist line pursued by the Thatcher government was reconfirmed, and Heseltine's attempt to further the case of West European co-operation in arms procurement received a serious setback, even though this setback may only have been temporary (cf. Freedman, 1987, p. 18).

In the light of this, it was only logical that Great Britain should have been the first European power to show willingness to participate without restrictions in the American Strategic Defense Initiative (SDI).

When President Reagan announced his initiative in March 1983, it came as a complete surprise to the British government. Britain's initial reactions, given by the MoD and the Foreign Office, were critical and reserved, and these doubts persisted for more than a year (Taylor, 1986, pp. 217–19). It was 'apparently on the personal insistence of the PM' that Great Britain eventually agreed to participate in the SDI on 6 December 1985 (Taylor, 1986, p. 219). During the negotiations over the final agreement, Heseltine demanded that it would contain a guarantee for $1.5 billion worth of orders for British companies. The demand was rejected, but continued to play a role in the public discussion.

One of the arguments put forward in favour of British participation by Thatcher was the chance for British companies to acquire new knowledge and to gain access to the most advanced American technology. Many of the companies in the British military-industrial complex actively sought to win orders from the Pentagon, among them Rolls-Royce, British Aerospace, Dunlop, GEC, Pilkington, Westland, Plessey, ICI, ICL and Ferranti (*Financial Times*, 26 February 1986). However, their great expectations have not been rewarded: as of March 1987, the orders for British companies in the context of the SDI programme have amounted to only $34 million (out of a total spending of $7 billion): the lucky ones were GEC, Plessey, BAe, Ferranti, Thorn-EMI, and Racal (*Financial Times*, 25 March 1987).

In the meantime, concern has grown that the flow of advantages might be reversed: 'British involvement in SDI might actually serve to increase the brain drain as Americans were better informed of what Britain had to offer' (Taylor, 1986, p. 222). There is also concern about the question of the patent rights of findings by British companies and their possible application in civil industry: normally, the Pentagon claims all rights of research and development it pays for. As Taylor concludes, 'prudence suggests that UK enterprises participating in the SDI should have good lawyers as well as scientists on their staff' (Taylor, 1986, p. 224).

December 1986 witnessed another instance of the British government sacrificing the interests of a British company in favour of an American deal: the case of Nimrod, the airborne radar system developed for the MoD by General Electric, but abandoned in sight of the harbour in favour of the Boeing-built AWACS system. Although there was broad agreement among commentators that the Nimrod project failed to meet the quality standards that might be required of it, this was vehemently denied by GEC's James Prior, the former 'wet' Employment Secretary, and the government refused to publicize the test results on which it based its appraisal, leaving room for doubt.

Other instances of Thatcher's uncritical support of Reagan's policies include the decision to leave UNESCO, and Britain's involvement in the US bombing of Libya in April 1986.[12] This last instance was a rather delicate matter, not only because of the danger in which it put British subjects in Libya, but also because the issue of the sovereignty over the US bases on British soil was revived. As the former Foreign Secretary, Dr David Owen, pointed out in an article in *The Times* on 16 April 1986, President Truman and Prime Minister Churchill had stated in 1952 that the use of these bases was a matter for 'joint decision' (see also Baylis, 1986), and therefore Mrs Thatcher was fully accountable for the operation, which once more confirmed the nature of the US–UK alliance in the early 1980s.

The assault on the working class

The second core thesis of the Thatcherite project was the alleged need to 'solve the union problem', the view that an all-out attack on the strongholds of the organized working class was a prerequisite for a real capitalist recovery. True to the neo-liberal creed, the Thatcher government directed its offensive at the 'monopolistic' characteristics of the labour market, which prohibited a decisive shift in the balance of class forces in favour of capital and to the detriment of labour. By 1979, the prospects for the success of such an enterprise looked much better.

The deepening of the economic crisis since the early 1970s and particularly the enormous rise in unemployment (which doubled between 1979 and 1981) had weakened the unity and resolve of the trade unions (cf. Ravier, 1984; Gregory, 1985).[13] The crisis also led to a noticeable hardening in the posture of many employers (Flanagan, Soskice and Ulman, 1983, pp. 445–6). Increasingly, radical neo-liberal organizations such as the Institute of Directors urged the Thatcher government to make haste with 'closing down the unions', while traditional corporatist voices grew weaker and weaker (cf. Moore, 1982, p. 312).

Secondly, the failure of the Heath government in the early 1970s had led the Thatcher Shadow Cabinet in the years 1975–9 to prepare carefully for the task ahead. In this preparation, special attention was given to the National Union of Mineworkers, with its radical tradition and the special role it had played in serious confrontations between capital and labour in Britain in 1926 and 1973–4.

In 1977, the right-wing MP Nicholas Ridley was asked to write a report suggesting a new Tory policy for the nationalized industries and its unions. Part of this report was leaked to the *Economist* in May 1978. The report concluded that it would be unwise to take on the whole union movement at the same time (as the 1971 Industrial Relations Act had effectively done). Instead, Ridley advocated a cautious 'salami' approach – one thin slice at a time, but by the end the whole lot has still gone (CIS Report, 1984, pp. 3–4). The Ridley Report was followed almost to the letter once Thatcherism gained power in 1979. Early conflicts were fought out when the government felt confident of winning (as in 1980 with the steel industry, in 1981 with the Civil Service, and in 1982 with the Health Service workers and British Rail). However, the government backed away from conflicts which it felt it could not yet win: in 1981 50,000 striking miners prevented the closure of pits in Wales. As Ridley had said, when workers 'have the nation by the jugular vein, the only feasible option is to pay up' (CIS Report, 1984, pp. 4–5). In the meantime, legislation would have to improve the position of the government for future confrontations. It aimed at gradually eroding the unity and strength of the trade union movement by making illegal all those tactics that had proved successful in earlier times (for good surveys, see Kahn *et al.* 1983, and

Mitchell, 1987). The Employment Acts of 1980 and 1982 limited the right to strike and to picket, outlawed most sympathy strikes, and attacked the 'closed shop', making it dependent on a vote giving an 80 per cent majority. Trade unions were further subjected to far-reaching judicial influence: the courts were given the instruments of 'injunction', of fining (up to £250,000) for contempt of court, and of 'sequestration' of union assets in case of a refusal to pay the fines (CIS Report, 1984, pp. 12–15; Hain, 1986, pp. 122–4).

The years leading up to 1984 were also used by the government to follow up some of the other recommendations in the Ridley report: stocks of coal at the power stations were increased, power stations were converted to dual firing, and small sea ports were reconstructed to be able to handle the import of large quantities of foreign coal.

After the elections of 1983, which were a great victory for Thatcher (or rather a terrible defeat for the Labour Party), the government apparently felt that the time had come to tackle the most powerful union, the NUM. Eventual victory over the NUM 'was always bound to be the seminal test of Mrs Thatcher's economic policy: the test of whether her Tory radicalism could restructure British industry, shaking out the restrictive practices and protectionism which encased it, ending its subsidies, cartels and closed shops' (*Economist*, 6 October 1984).

The coming confrontation was in fact announced by the appointment in August of 1983 of Ian MacGregor to the top job at the National Coal Board (NCB). This successful Scottish-Canadian banker (a partner in Lazard Bros of New York) was brought to Britain in 1980 on the advice of Sir Keith Joseph to take over at British Steel. After breaking the steel strike of 1980, MacGregor 'shook out' enough workers to make British Steel a profitable firm again: in three years time the workforce was reduced from 168,000 to 78,000.

So, when it was announced that 70-year-old MacGregor had been appointed president of the NCB, it was clear from the start that his main job would be to break the resistance of the NUM to large-scale closures, and perhaps to break the NUM itself.

The miners' strike

In 1983 Anthony Sampson wrote: 'The ability of the government to undermine Scargill's militant leadership and face down the miners remains the most critical question in the future of the trade union movement' (Sampson, 1983, p. 71). The importance of the miners' strike can indeed hardly be exaggerated, because it represented the culmination of many elements of the Thatcherite strategy, both as regards its policy *vis-à-vis* the unions and as regards industrial policy.

The choice was whether to let 'the market' decide the future of Britain's coal mines, or whether to consider the place of the mines in the context of a comprehensive plan for energy production and consumption in the medium and long term. After the 1985 defeat of the NUM, the road ahead seems fairly clear. It will involve the decentralization of British Coal, and the transfer of authority to local and regional management; privatization is then the logical end of the road, with an eventual loss of jobs of between 50,000 and 130,000, depending on one's particular definition of 'profitability'.

Decentralization was also pursued because it stimulated dissent within the NUM. The Coal Board actively supported the 'working miners' in Nottinghamshire, who started the legal proceedings against the NUM that led to the sequestration of the union's assets, and who eventually established the breakaway Union of Democratic Mineworkers (cf. G. Taylor, 1985; Crick, 1985).

In the press, particularly the popular tabloids, the government was strongly supported in its confrontation with the miners. That this ideological support was in many cases reinforced by colliding material interests received little attention. However, the owners of practically all major British newspapers have important interests in energy production: Associated Newspapers (*Daily Mail*) has interests in North Sea oil and gas; Fleet Holdings (Trafalgar House), owners of the Express group, also have interests in oil and gas production and in offshore industries; News International (Rupert Murdoch, owner of the *Sun* and *The Times*) has oil and gas interests in Australia; Pearson & Son (*Financial Times*) has interests in oil, gas, and nuclear energy; and Lonrho (*Observer*) has extensive interests in coalmining in Southern Africa.

The defeat of the NUM cannot be blamed exclusively on the Thatcher government. In many left-wing comments on the strike, it has been pointed out that Arthur Scargill himself was one of the most important assets to the government in the struggle to win public opinion. These comments usually refer to the tactics which were applied (both internally and externally) by Scargill, and which contributed towards consolidating the split among the miners. It might however also be argued that these tactics (even if indeed they were counterproductive) were inevitably forced upon the NUM leadership. The strategy which had been followed by the Coal Board and the government in the previous years had been very effective in creating (through strategic investments and so on) the material basis for these regionally based splits.

A more fundamental criticism is that the NUM (and I would add the Labour Party) should have spent much more energy on producing a new plan for coal. Such a plan would have had to be developed in the context of an overall energy strategy (as argued by O'Donnell, 1985), taking account of the long-term development of relative production costs of alternative sources of energy and possible secondary costs (pollution, nuclear waste, 'national' self-sufficiency, strategic industries, and so on). The plan adopted by the NUM Conference in 1982 might have served as the basis for such a new energy policy. This plan envisages a doubling of production by the year 2000, the use of coal instead of oil in power stations, no privatizations, no further development of nuclear energy, and the introduction of 'technology agreements' by which the miners can share in improvements of productivity in the form of shorter working hours, early pensions, and better health and safety regulations in the pits, for example (Fine, 1984, p. 81).

But, true as it is that the NUM did not succeed in presenting its struggle as one for a long-term national energy policy, its chances of success would anyway have been very slim, because the Thatcher government was absolutely not interested in reaching a compromise. The conflict was meant to show the government's toughness *vis-à-vis* the unions, and more particularly it had to prove Thatcher's ability to defeat and humiliate the NUM. 'The conflict was a summation of Conservatism's desire to restructure radically production relations: the free economy can only be created by the strong state' (A. J. Taylor, 1985, p. 9).

The demise of the NUM is (although *in extremo*) symptomatic of the intended fate of trade unionism under Thatcherism more generally.

The decline of the unions

British labour relations and production conditions are archaic. It was not so much the alleged power of the unions but rather the organizational weakness of British capital and labour alike which led to the situation described in a study of forty-five British and German firms: in factories with similar machinery installed and producing similar products, average labour productivity in Germany is 63 per cent higher than in Britain (*Financial Times*, 22 February 1985). The principal causes are the quality of management in Britain, and the barriers between skilled and unskilled labour, and between different skilled trades. This represents the inheritance of the failure of British Fordism. In Britain the labour process was not restructured along the lines of ideal-typical Fordism, and many elements of the craft nature of industrial production in Britain survived until the early 1980s. These British peculiarities were superimposed on the impact of the general capitalist crisis, which has been a serious one in *all* capitalist countries.

The Thatcher government's anti-union policies, ranging from the banning of unions from the intelligence-gathering centre (GCHQ) in Cheltenham to the miners' strike and from the 1980 Employment Act to the 1984 Trade Union Act, aimed to remedy this situation by undermining the unions' ability to hold on to their members and to achieve any positive results for them. Union membership has consequently declined.

However, the decline of the unions in Britain is not only the result of Thatcher's policies. Rather, these policies have reinforced and intensified tendencies common to all highly developed capitalist economies. Many of the workers on 'flexible' contracts do not bother to join a union at all, perhaps because 'work' is no longer synonymous with 'life', but rather life begins exactly where work ends. In other cases (such as the Lowestoft plant of Sanyo) the unions (in this case the EETPU) have signed 'single union no strike' deals with the employers (usually Japanese firms).

As a result of these two developments, trade union density, while still significantly higher than in comparable countries, has fallen sharply from its 1981 record level of 54 per cent to below the 37 per cent mark (*Financial Times*, 5 September 1987).

The 1984 Trade Union Act has gone a step further: it 'breaks with the tradition of non-interference in unions' self-government and also moves to a more restrictive position on their political activities' (McBride, 1986, p. 335). The new Act lays down rules according to which leadership elections in trade unions should take place, and outlaws lifelong appointments such as that of Arthur Scargill. These rules, although they indeed represent government interference with the internal functioning of the unions (another instance of the fact that the ideal of the neo-liberals, freedom from regulation and interference, does not apply equally to every sort of organization), have not met with strong opposition from the unions, probably because these rules are designed to affect the position of 'militant elements' and to play into the hands of 'moderate and responsible' trade union leaders. Although it can be doubted that 'handing the unions back to the members' will in all circumstances lead to moderation (McBride, 1986, p. 338), the past years have shown that open opposition to government interference has been virtually absent.

The all-out offensive to eliminate all 'monopolistic' characteristics of the organization of the labour market, and to shift the balance of class forces decisively in favour of capital, has definitely been a success. The Employment and Trade Union Acts have outlined a new course which, though sharing the ultimate objectives, has successfully bypassed the factors responsible for the failure of the Heath government's attempt to restructure capital–labour relations. The culmination of the strategy came with the miners' strike of 1984–5. For the miners, the stakes in this struggle may have been narrowly 'non-political', but the strike was a political struggle nonetheless: the Tories had planned the confrontation carefully, and the elimination of the NUM as a serious political force was certainly one of the most important aims of the government. The defeat of the miners has enabled the government to scare most other unions into acquiescence, or at least to tilt the balance in favour of the moderate forces in the union movement.

However, it is too soon to toll the funeral bell for the unions. Trade union density is still high by international standards, and the union movement still has the capacity to mobilize its members, if only the organizational structures are adapted to the new circumstances of the 1980s and 1990s. Mrs Thatcher's union policy has three severe internal weaknesses (McBride, 1986, p. 338):

(1) her approach is predicated on a *total* victory over the unions as organizations;
(2) the policy of handing the unions back to their members does not guarantee moderation;
(3) Thatcher's policy clearly depends on the disciplining effects of recession and unemployment to ensure union compliance: there is no certainty that economic recovery will not also show the recovery of union militancy.

In Chapter 8, we will consider the likelihood of these weaknesses developing into real political problems for Thatcherism.

The neo-liberal accumulation strategy

The economic liberalism of the 1830s was the product of the rise of the manufacturing class; the rise of neo-liberalism in the 1970s is the product of the demise of this same manufacturing class. The classical liberal campaign against the Poor Law aimed at creating a 'free labour market'; the neo-liberal offensive of the 1980s aims to *re*-create a free labour market. Ricardo provided the academic underpinnings for the classical campaign; Hayek and Friedman did so for the neo-liberal offensive. But the labour market was not the only target zone of liberalism:

> A similar keying up of economic liberalism from academic interest to boundless activism occurred in the two other fields of industrial organization: currency and trade. In respect to both of these *laissez-faire* waxed into a fervently held creed when the uselessness of any other but extreme solutions became apparent. (Polanyi, 1957, p. 137)

Indeed, Polanyi was referring to the 1830s, but his words are once again fully applicable to the 1980s: Friedman's 'currency-crankery' (Tom Nairn) became the dominant monetary dogma, and liberalization of trade its companion. The analogy is limited of course: in the 1830s liberalism was a historically progressive and constructive force, setting capital free from the remaining pre-capitalist restraints on its global operations. In the 1980s, neo-liberalism reacts against the results of the development of the very mode of production it wants to restore to health. In the early phases of the present neo-liberal era, the *de-constructive* aspects have been dominant.

In the following account (which does not attempt to present an overall analysis) I shall concentrate on three elements of the neo-liberal accumulation strategy of the Thatcher government, elements that were, and still are, central to it, and that are complemented by the framework provided by the wider political and ideological offensives undertaken. These three elements are: industrial policy; liberalization and internationalization; and the effort to push back the state.

Industrial policy

A fundamental trait of Thatcherism is its preference for non-industrial, even anti-industrial, policies and and its total dedication to the exchange value aspect of capitalism. This preference for liquidity and safe *rentier* income, however, cannot last without endangering the productive source of all this surplus value, which must be produced, extracted and realized before it can be appropriated through its redistribution in the circulation sphere. By 1982–3, when Thatcherism seemed, for a while, on its way to a speedy demise, this was clearly illustrated by the complaints of the great banks that major industrial companies were on the verge of collapse (Grant, 1983, p. 175). Internationally, the same phenomenon was expressed in the international debt crisis (cf. Furtado, 1987).

Industrial production declined sharply after Thatcher came to power. This recession occurred within the context of a general capitalist recession, but the pro-cyclical policies pursued in Britain reinforced the recession enormously. The industries that were the principal victims of this acceleration of de-industrialization were precisely the core industries of Fordism, the industries that had come to life during the Depression Boom of the 1930s (Livingstone, 1983, p. 72). The Thatcher government has done very little to counter this rundown of the Fordist industries in Britain. It has relied fully on the operation of market forces to improve the conditions for the valorization of capital. This policy initially led to considerable productivity increases, but by 1984 productivity growth rates were in line again with those in the major OECD countries. The initial gains must therefore be the result of other factors than 'intrinsic' improvements in production practices. One such explanation is that the severe recession of 1979–81 put a disproportionate number of inefficient firms and production facilities out of business, thereby statistically raising overall labour productivity without any improvement whatsoever in the productivity in remaining units (cf. Beynon, 1983; Hodgson, 1984). A related explanation is that the Thatcher policies made possible the 'shakeout' of superfluous labour through mass redundancies or through a systematic policy of not filling vacancies, thereby raising average productivity within existing firms through a better organization of production. Although these productivity gains are much more real than the statistical gains mentioned above, the trick can only be performed once.[14]

As a result of the insufficient growth of productivity in industry, the balance of trade in manufactures, which had traditionally been positive until 1981, fell dramatically to a deficit of £8.5 billion in 1986 (*Financial Times*, 30 March 1987). There is, however, one export sector which is doing very well: Britain in 1986 overtook France and even the Soviet Union on the list of arms exporters. The United Kingdom became the second largest arms exporter in the world in 1986, with overall sales amounting to $5.8 billion, and that position may well be maintained in the coming years (*Economist*, 4 July 1987).

According to some, the great weight of the defence sector is partly responsible for the delapidated state of civilian manufacturing in Britain. In the year 1984/5 defence equipment expenditure surpassed total fixed investment in the manufacturing industry: £7.8 billion against £7.1 billion (Kaldor, Sharp and Walker, 1986, p. 34). Defence R and D absorbs a large proportion of available skilled manpower. There is, however, contrary to what Kaldor, Sharp and Walker suggest, no compelling reason to assume that if it were not for the defence sector, civilian manufacturing industry would put these resources to better use. As a matter of fact, this would only happen if the prospects for civil manufacturing industry were to be structurally improved. Such an improvement requires more than a reduction of the military budget.

Liberalizing the City

The first act of the Thatcher government that made clear its dedication to the 'free market' was to lift all exchange controls. This led to an enormous export of capital from Britain. The stock of British direct investment abroad shot up and reached £110 billion at the end of 1986 (up from £80 billion in 1985), amounting to a postwar record 28 per cent of GDP (*Financial Times*, 18 March 1987). British takeovers in the United States reached the level of $5.2 billion in 1985, up 33 per cent from 1984 (*Financial Times*, 20 February 1986).[15] A combined result of the extremely liberal policy towards foreign capital and the great weakness of British capital has been the large-scale sale of British industrial assets to foreign companies.

The multinationalization of the British economy did not stop at the gates of the City. The first steps on the road to the full liberalization of the City were announced in 1983 and the Budget of 1984 mapped out the road to the Big Bang of 1986. The principal motive behind the deregulation of the City was the realization that the London Stock Exchange was in danger of losing its traditional position: even shares in British companies were now being traded in New York (cf. Plender, 1987). The Big Bang, of which the four main elements were the deregulation of the financial markets, the equal treatment of banks and building societies, the overhaul of the clearing system, and a revision of the tax system for financial institutions, opened up the Stock Exchange for the clearing banks who all bought up one or more of the traditional Stock Exchange firms, as did many of the American banks that also got access to the trading floor of the London Stock Exchange.

Conversely, the big British clearing banks continued their internationalization strategy begun in the 1970s. In doing so they joined the Americans in demanding more business opportunities in Japan (*Economist*, 27 October 1984), to compensate for the fact that by 1983 Japanese banks had a share of 27 per cent in international bank lending from Britain, more than the share of UK banks (21.4 per cent) and also more than the share of US banks (20.5 per cent) (Coakley, 1984, p. 115).

Numerous pleas have appeared for continuation of the liberalization process, particularly by the big clearing banks which can exploit their massive resources far better than the traditional smaller City firms such as merchant banks and brokers (cf. Rybczynski, 1985; White and Vittas, 1986).

The expansion of business in the City of London and the conscious aim of the Thatcher government to recoup a central role for London in the global financial networks is part of the wider strategy which aims to remake Britain into a 'service economy'. In the context of that strategy Britain has been pushing for the liberalization of international trade in services within GATT, and the Foreign Secretary Sir Geoffrey Howe has even taken the crusade for liberalization into Eastern Europe: when visiting Hungary, he urged his hosts to 'let the market loose' (*Independent*, 11 March 1987).

In 1986 the invisibles surplus reached a level of over £10 billion, half of it in the shape of earnings on foreign investments, the other half in the form of earnings from services. Britain was successfully being transformed into a *rentier* economy, making up for its growing deficit in the trade in manufactures by its rising income from foreign investments.

Pushing back the state

The most important element of Thatcherite strategy towards the state is the reduction (through spending cuts and privatization) of the public sector. The state sector is seen by the neo-liberals as a burden weighing on the private sector which, if only left alone, would tend to a 'natural' equilibrium. Other elements of the restructuring of the state were the abolition of the metropolitan councils and the gradual erosion of the significance of such corporatist para-statal organs as the NEDC.

In the area of privatization, the Thatcher programme progressed according to plan, or rather the plan (which hardly existed in 1979) developed along with the practice, as Thatcher was edged on by the constant pressure for more privatization by such neo-liberal pressure groups as the Adam Smith Institute (ASI).[16] The concept of privatization had hardly taken shape when the Thatcher government took office in 1979. At that time 10 per cent of Britain's GDP was produced in nationalized and state-owned firms, and 15 per cent of total British investment was in the state sector, where 1.5 million people were employed; it was one of the largest of any developed capitalist country.

In general, privatization entails two principal forms of reduction of state control over the economy: the sale of state-owned companies (whether to the employees and/or management, a private firm, or the public at large), and the contracting out of services previously performed by the state itself (Young, 1986). Whereas the latter form of privatization is often the result of the simple drive to reduce costs, the former can, almost by definition, take place only in the case of (potentially) profitable state firms: if not, what private investor would be interested? (see Young, 1987).

In Britain, the aims of the privatization programme which was developed after 1979 were the promotion of competition and efficiency on the one hand, and the creation of a 'people's capitalism' on the other. However, the programme was never elaborated into a coherent *plan* for restructuring the state sector in order to achieve these goals and, further, what was done was seldom done consistently (Abromeit, 1986). By early 1987, the proceeds from sales amounted to almost £10 billion (*Financial Times*, 25 March 1987). The money thus earned, however, has not been used to finance structural improvements in the British economy, but has been employed mainly for a 'cosmetic' reduction of the 'public sector borrowing requirement' (PSBR). The absence of any coherent industrial policy has made itself strongly felt here.

Privatization has at best been a mixed blessing for Britain. In the first place, the *costs* of privatization have been underestimated. The fact that only (potentially) profitable activities can be privatized means that the fiscal crisis of the state is reinforced in the long term, because income-earning capacity is sold off (Young, 1987). Further, the direct costs in terms of fees for merchant banks and so forth involved in the large-scale sale of state assets is considerable.[17] Thirdly, rationalizations in the privatized firms lead to higher costs in terms of unemployment benefits, for instance, while the internationalization of privatized firms can lead to tax evasion and thus again to an aggravation of the fiscal crisis of the state (Young, 1987).

In the second place, the objectives of privatization were contradictory. In several cases (British Telecom, for instance) the government has had to grant the privatized firm a quasi-monopoly in order to make it attractive to private investors; yet the original purpose of the programme was to introduce or increase competition. On the other hand, the enforcement of 'competition' in an industry dominated by a monopoly (such as the electricity industry) would require massive state intervention and would thus counter the second purpose of privatization, that of reducing the 'reach' of the state.

The second important consideration underpinning privatization is that of creating a 'people's capitalism' by qualitatively enlarging property-owning by ordinary citizens: the Tories' 'property-owning democracy'. One important avenue has been the sale of council houses to tenants: in the first six years of Thatcherism this programme reached a total sum of over £6 billion, and still continues. The second pillar of people's capitalism is supposed to be the extension of shareholding. Privatization is intended to increase the proportion of the British populace enjoying the satisfaction of being a capitalist. Of course the laws of the market will cause the number of shareholders to drop very quickly: the number of shareholders in British Aerospace decreased within ten months after privatization from 158,000 to 27,000 because people cashed in on the profits the government had offered them by selling BAe (too) cheaply (*Economist*, 23 February 1985).

The same objective is served by deregulation: setting up a business has been made more attractive. This has resulted in the rise of 'management buy-outs' (600 since 1982) and it has resulted (or so the Tories claim) in the total number of British businesses increasing from 1.29 million in 1979 to 1.43 million in 1984 (*Economist*, 25 October 1985). This increase can perhaps also be explained by the increase in the number of people who are forced by unemployment to start some sort of business to keep their heads above water.

The emphasis on stimulating people to become 'self-employed' or 'property owners' serves the purpose of constructing a social and electoral base for Thatcherism. The lasting success of this undertaking is intimately bound up with the attempts to construct a new neo-liberal bourgeois power bloc.

Towards a neo-liberal power bloc

In the debate about the nature of Thatcherism which was conducted in the columns of the *New Left Review* in 1984–5 (Jessop *et al.*, 1984; Leys, 1985; Hall, 1985; Jessop *et al.*, 1985) one important theme was the question as to what degree Thatcherism expressed concretely identifiable economic interests. Jessop *et al.* named four rather obvious 'interests': the City, the US Federal Reserve and the IMF, the Treasury, and the CBI. Leys placed his analysis of Thatcherism in the context of the opposition between industrial capital and financial capital in Britain. In an interesting and promising book, John Ross attempted to identify in detail the industrial sectors that profited from the policies pursued by Thatcher (Ross, 1983). In this section I shall try to bring several of these threads together and consider how far such a combination can take us towards identification of the building blocks of the emerging Thatcherite power base.

Capital fractions and the redistribution of surplus value

As in earlier crises, the 1970s have seen the rise of money capital to renewed dominance: multinationally operating banks in particular increasingly played a central role in the global reorganization of capitalist production and trade (cf. Andreff, 1984; Fennema and Van der Pijl, 1987). This new hegemony of banking capital found its expression in the distribution of profits among fractions of capital and in the resurgence of *rentier* income (cf. Van der Pijl, 1984), and also in the divergence of the effective rates of taxation for financial and non-financial companies.

Looking at taxation first, we see that in the cases of the Netherlands, France, Japan, and most spectacularly the UK, financial companies have seen their tax rate diminish during the latter 1970s, while the effective tax rate for non-financial companies has moved upward.[18] For Britain, these figures were confirmed in a report by the Institute of Fiscal Studies (commissioned by the Midland Bank) which found 'a strong *prima facie* case indicating that banks have earned higher rates of return ... and that their payments of mainstream corporation tax have been absolutely and relatively small' (quoted in *The Banker*, May 1983, pp. 15–19). The divergence of the tax rates in the case of Britain is very clearly brought out in Figure 7.1.

The same increase in prominence for financial capital *vis-à-vis* industrial capital is reflected in the relation between operating surplus and property income payable, which gives us an approximation of the indebtedness of industrial capital. The figures for the major capitalist countries indicate that there is a clear cyclical pattern, in most cases combined with an underlying upward secular trend (especially in the cases of France, West Germany and the United States). During the recession years the burden of property income payable (interest payments and so on) increased greatly for non-financial companies. The grip of the banks tightened during these years, and in France, West Germany and the US industry did not recover completely after the recession.

The rise of money capital is expressed not only through the dominance of banks over industry, but also through the 'monetization' of industrial capital. Thus, the highest authority in industrial corporations has shifted from the entrepreneurial and technical experts to the financial experts (cf. Franko, 1976). Industrial corporations also increasingly undertake financial activities, such

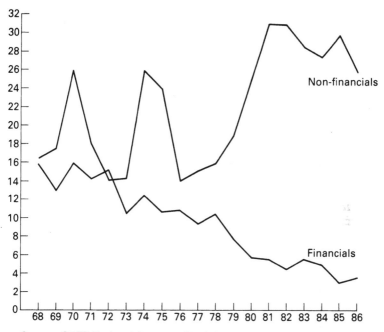

Source: OECD National Accounts Statistics.

Figure 7.1 Direct taxes as percentage of current receipts, UK, 1968–86.

as credit, short-term deposits and foreign exchange deals. Taking these factors together, we can speak of a tendency in the 1970s and early 1980s for industrial companies to downgrade their specific function of producing and marketing concrete products, use values and products of concrete labour, and instead to concentrate on the profit criterion and the exchange value of its activities and 'products'. Speaking about finance capital, Ticktin correctly remarks that 'It is precisely as abstract capital, capital without specific commitments to concrete production, that it is able to shift itself rapidly on an organized basis ... the role of finance capital is not to organize *production* but *capital*' (Ticktin, 1983, p. 36)

The fact that only productive capital creates surplus value sets limits to the freedom of finance capital to detach itself from concrete production. A trend towards 'monetization' is therefore necessarily conjunctural in character. The structure of earnings of corporations indeed confirms this. There was a clear tendency for the ratio of property income to operating surplus to rise in the course of the 1970s. This indicates the increased importance of

201

income and profits from non-productive activities by industrial corporations. Japan provides the only exception, a fact which expresses the unusually strong position of Japanese industry on the world market.[19]

These statistics confirm that the rise of neo-liberalism is correlated with the resurgence of money capital domination. Indeed, in the late 1970s and early 1980s financial companies appropriated an increasing share of surplus value: they paid lower taxes and exacted larger interest sums from industry, and even within industry financial activities gained the upper hand and became a more important source of profit in many cases than the production and sale of actual products. The rise of Thatcherism, as the British version of neo-liberalism, has coincided with these developments in Britain.

Business organizations and the Thatcher government

We have seen (in Chapters 5 and 6) that British capital has traditionally been weakly organized at the social and political level. British capital was also fragmented: in particular there were major divisions between industrial, financial and commercial capital (cf. Sargent, 1983, p. 22). The most important organization of capitalists in the postwar period was the (Con)Federation of British Industries (FBI, later CBI), which mainly organized industrial capital. The period of the 1960s and early 1970s was characterized by a co-operative attitude on the part of the CBI vis-à-vis the working class and the trade union movement. The CBI was the mouthpiece of corporate liberalism in which 'tripartite' firms set the tone, and its relations with the government (whether Labour or Tory) were generally good (Grant, 1983; see also Grant and Marsh, 1977). The advent of the new Tory government in 1979 caused a relatively far-reaching turnabout in these relations. The CBI was increasingly critical of the government's economic policies as the number of bankruptcies skyrocketed (Riddell, 1983, p. 16; Grant, 1983, p. 173). The culmination of the CBI's criticism came with the announcement of a 'bare-knuckle fight' against the monetarist policies of the government by CBI Director-General Beckett (Keegan, 1985, p. 155).

These criticisms caused several important members of the CBI to renounce their membership and turn to the Institute of Directors (IoD). At about the same time, this organization's public profile was revolutionized by its Director-General Walter Goldsmith, who was eager 'to elbow out the CBI' (*Observer*, 25 March 1984). The IoD established close links with the Thatcherite hierarchy and 'has become an active lobbyist for private enterprise and against the public sector' (Riddell, 1983, p. 54). After 1983, the links between the IoD and the Thatcher inner circle were intensified through the appointment of Sir John Hoskyns, a personal adviser to Mrs Thatcher during her first years in office, as its new Director-General.

The government's attitude towards the corporatist strongholds in the CBI, the TUC and the NEDC varied from indifference to outright hostility. Mrs Thatcher 'deliberately demoted Neddy', and made this clear by appointing top Thatcherites to its council: Nigel Lawson became Chairman, and he was flanked by Patrick Jenkin, Sir Keith Joseph, Cecil Parkinson, and Norman Tebbit (Sampson, 1983, pp. 216–17). The Thatcher government isolated itself almost completely both from national industrial capital and from the trade unions (Coates, 1982, p. 158): 'In terms of its ability to disregard major interests, [the Thatcher government was] the most politically autonomous government of the postwar period' (Grant, 1983, p. 175).

The Thatcher government has made considerable progress, we may conclude, with the deconstruction of the structures and institutions of corporatism. At the same time, it is actively organizing a new social base, by freeing small capital from the 'strangulation of labour', by 'handing the unions back to the members', by creating a broad layer of small stockholders and home owners, and by creating new organizations representing the newly dominant sections of capital. It has even collided with certain sections of the City over its monetary policies and the liberalization of the City itself, which exposes all City firms to enormously intensified international competition even on Britain's domestic financial markets. This extreme liberal strategy might perhaps be characterized as a comprador strategy.[20] Since 1979 British capital has increasingly been 'denationalized', and this process of denationalization finds expression in the fact that the network of interlocking directorships among the largest British industrial and financial firms has become less tightly knit, thus breaking with the trend of the years prior to the Thatcher reign (cf. Overbeek, 1988, appendix I).

The question which remains is this: can any concrete capitalist interests be identified inside Britain which have clearly and unambiguously profited directly from Thatcher's policies? According to John Ross, particular sectors such as oil, agriculture, communications, finance, and electronics have benefited from Thatcherism and considerably improved their profitability. When his data are compared to the average rates of return during the pre-Thatcher 1970s, however, it transpires that most sectors in 1980 showed rates of return

Table 7.1   Rates of Return on Capital Employed in % (Historical Cost)

Branch	Average 1970s	1980	1984
Capital goods	16.1	12.0	15.8
Contracting and construction	17.2	14.6	13.5
Electricals	17.6	14.3	18.0
Electronics	21.5	23.7	23.4
Mechanical engineering	15.8	11.9	13.4
Motors	12.0	2.6	9.8
Consumer Group	17.0	15.3	17.7
Brewers and distillers	14.7	12.8	13.9
Food retailing	22.9	21.5	23.4
Health and household	24.3	19.9	26.1
Leisure	17.6	15.2	13.5
Newspapers and publishing	20.8	14.3	17.7
Packaging and paper	15.1	13.8	16.9
Stores	19.0	15.2	18.3
Textiles	14.6	10.4	17.3
Tobacco	17.6	18.2	20.5
Chemicals	15.1	9.9	16.4
Shipping and transport	9.3	11.4	11.0
All Industrial Groups	16.3	13.7	17.0
Oil	27.6	26.6	18.7
Industrials and oil	18.3	16.7	17.4

Source: calculated from *Bank of England Quarterly Bulletin*, vol. 25, no. 3 (September 1985).

which were lower than during the 1970s, with the exception of electronics, tobacco, and shipping and transport (see Table 7.1).

By 1984 profits had recovered from their low point in 1980 (except for oil, where the exceptionally profitable conditions of the 1970s were eroded as the real price of oil fell during the 1980s). For all industrial groups, profits during 1984 were slightly higher than during the 1970s, but there were no sectors that did exceptionally well in comparison with the 1970s.

If we are to make any progress in this area, we will have to look at the relationship between Thatcherism and individual firms. A good indication can be gained from an analysis of the donations to the Tory Party by private firms.

Before 1967 political donations by business were completely free. In that year, the Labour government of Harold Wilson adopted a Companies Act, which determined that all annual contributions of over £50 by companies to political parties would have to be declared in the company accounts, so that some information is now publicly available.[21]

The level of political donations fluctuates fairly strongly from year to year: in election years more companies contribute a greater sum than in other years. In absolute terms the contributions increased strongly during the 1970s (from £1 million in 1973 to £3.3 million in the election year 1983), but corrected for inflation they decreased in real terms. According to *Labour Research*, the Tories experienced a real 'funding crisis' in 1983, with 40 per cent of the manufacturing firms reducing or withholding their contributions. A large number of traditional supporters of the Tory Party have thus backed away since Margaret Thatcher came to power and with her government's strongly pro-cyclical policies put the tip of the knife on manufacturing industry's throat, which was also hit hard by the sharper foreign competition accompanying the liberalization of Britain's external economic relations. GKN, for example, a traditional corporate-liberal manufacturing firm, has all but stopped its contributions, having consistently been among the top three donors in the years up to 1978.

But Thatcher has been able to attract new support from other sectors of British capital. Within these sectors, a small number of firms have developed over the past few years into very important financiers of the Thatcherite Conservative Party: while manufacturing industry was pushed out, big building contractors and developers such as Newarthill, Trafalgar House, London and Northern, Taylor Woodrow, Tarmac, George Wimpey (with their interest in the speculative strain in neo-liberalism), food and drink firms such as Allied Lyons and United Biscuits, electronics firms (Racal, AGB Research, Plessey), and speculative conglomerates (Hanson, BCS) have stepped in (see Table 7.2).

It might be that with many of these generous donors other motives than the general interest have played a role. Lord Cayzer (of BCS) is the brother-in-law of Sir Brian Wyldebore-Smith, who shares responsibility for the Tory Party finances with Alaistair McAlpine, the son of Lord McAlpine of Newarthill (*Labour Research*, June 1983).

Further, a comparison of the table with the list of people who have received peerages or honours in the past few years gives rise to amazement: this list includes Lord Cayzer (BCS, 1982), Lord Hanson (Hanson Trust, 1983), Sir Ernest Harrison (Racal, 1981),

Table 7.2   The Ten Top Donors to the Tory Party, 1982–5

Firm	Total contributions
British and Commonwealth Shipping	373,466
Allied Lyons	293,500
Taylor Woodrow	256,370
Hanson Trust	237,000
Guardian Royal Exchange	213,459
Racal	205,000
Plessey	185,000
United Biscuits	175,000
Northern Engineering	175,000
Trafalgar House	170,000

Source: calculated from *Labour Research*, 1982–6.

Sir Nigel Broackes (Trafalgar House, 1984), Lord Matthews (Trafalgar House, 1980), Sir Patrick Meaney (Rank Organization, 1981), Lord Taylor (Taylor Woodrow, 1982), Lord Forte (Trusthouse Forte, 1982), and Lord McAlpine (Newarthill, 1980) (*Labour Research*, June 1983; *Economist*, 6 October 1984, p. 25).

The Honours Act of 1925 abolished the sale of titles; it would seem that Mrs Thatcher has reinstated this medieval practice.

The contours of a new neo-liberal power bloc are becoming clear. In this chapter, we have analysed some of the most central policies of the Thatcher government, and shown their general direction. Thatcherism is a comprehensive concept of control, which is structured by the money-capital perspective, and which is supported by a diversity of societal interests in Britain. What are the prospects for the concept of Thatcherism to become hegemonic? This question is addressed in the final chapter.

CHAPTER 8

Perspectives for Thatcherism

The decline of Britain reversed?

When the Thatcher government came to power in 1979, it promised to eradicate the roots of the 'British disease'. Unlike many other governments which start out with a radical programme, Thatcherism has been remarkably consistent. This is not to say that it has not been plagued by its own internal contradictions, and that the Thatcher government has not had to develop its strategy as it went along. However, the general thrust of its policies has remained the same, and this is an exceptional quality, not only in the context of postwar British history, but also by international comparison. Mrs Thatcher's position has even been strengthened by her unprecedented third election victory of June 1987. Indeed, it is hard to see from where the alternative to Thatcherism should arise.

According to the neo-liberals, Thatcherism has succeeded in reversing the process of the decline of Britain. However, we have seen that at least some signs of success (rising productivity, higher growth rates, lower budget deficits) are optical illusions, and may well revert to their usual pattern.

More fundamentally, the success of Thatcherism is not without its contradictions. First, the basis for the Thatcherite coalition was the fact that in 1979 the rule of capital itself was at stake (in the eyes of most of the British bourgeoisie). However, the rule of capital no longer seems at stake, which means that the fractional compromise which brought Thatcher to power becomes potentially unstable. Continued support for Thatcher in many cases is caused not so much by positive attraction to the policies of the Thatcher government, but more by the nature of the British political system, which still lacks the flexibility that characterizes proportional representation. Secondly, monetarism and free market liberalism have been successful in restoring profitability for capital, but their continued application offers no hope of a successful reconstruction of the industrial base of the country. To achieve this an interventionist industrial policy would be called for, but the very nature of free market liberalism almost excludes this option. Finally, Thatcherism has found no solution for the problems of unemployment and social decay, which can erupt again (as they have before) any day and which represent a constant (if submerged) threat to the stability of British society.

The resolution of crises in capitalism has never taken place through the wholesale replacement of one regime of accumulation by another, but rather through a new combination of elements of the old order with certain new elements, resulting in a new regime of accumulation. It is, however, necessary that the essential nexus of the old order is destroyed before the building of a new one can take effect. Turning to the crisis of the years since the late 1960s, the crisis of Fordism, one could argue that Thatcherism has come a long way (even if the process is not nearly completed) towards destroying some of the essential structures of Fordism (particularly those pertaining to the national level, the mode of regulation), thus clearing part of the way for a new, post-Fordist regime of accumulation. In other respects, however, a resolution of the crisis still seems far off. (Cf. Gamble, 1988; also Jessop *et al.*, 1987.)

Let us briefly review the main areas in which the Thatcher government has attempted to construct a new reality – in foreign policy, labour relations, the accumulation strategy, and the political and state system.

The global context

The disagreements over the orientation of British foreign policy, which became particularly clear in the course of the Westland Affair and around Britain's participation in Star Wars, were not a struggle between 'Europeanist' and 'Atlanticist' forces, but between those forces clinging to an 'Atlantic partnership' and those forces wanting to hitch on to Reagan's 'unilateralism'. These latter forces have until now held the upper hand, but their position might in the future become less naturally obvious.

The Reagan policies which aimed at the reimposition of American leadership over the West were relatively successful in the early 1980s, but were increasingly plagued by internal contradiction and dissension. In the USA, the period since 1984, roughly coinciding with Reagan's second term, was one of struggle between the unilateral faction on the one hand, and a 'triadic' faction on the other.

The unilateral tendency favoured the continuation of a tough stand against the Soviet Union ('dealing from a position of strength', which meant not dealing at all), against the Third World (with regard to the debt crisis, for instance), and also against the European (and Japanese) allies. This line, however, carried with it risks that some factions in the Reagan entourage were not prepared to take. In particular, the chances that further unilateral steps by the United States (such as the attacks on Libya in 1986) would contribute in the end to the emergence of a feasible 'Europeanist' alternative were by no means imaginary.

Inside the USA, this has led to the emergence of a 'triadic' tendency which aims at some sort of accommodation with Europe and Japan to ensure that neo-protectionist tendencies[1] will be held in check and will not seriously obstruct transnational capital in its global expansion and reorganization. Apart from attempts to solve the debt crisis on the basis of concerted action by the great capitalist powers (the Baker plan), the triadic conception is concerned first and foremost with the management of rivalry between Europe, Japan and the USA.

The result of these factional battles behind the scenes is that in fact the USA pursues a 'mixed strategy' consisting of unilateral, bilateral and multilateral elements (Gill, 1986b). This mixed strategy contributes to the emergence and consolidation of a 'transnational historic bloc': foreign-based transnational corporations are becoming much more dependent upon the US market at the same time as US manufacturing capital has shifted to high profit sectors, such as energy reserves, financial services, defence equipment, and new technology (cf. Davis, 1984; 1985). This has the effect of 'generally strengthening a transnational historic bloc and the power of internationally mobile (finance) capital *vis-à-vis* labour and some states' (Gill, 1986b, p. 328).

Externally, the effects of Reagan's foreign policies also give reason for doubt about the lasting success of the attempt to reimpose American supremacy over the capitalist world. The cost in economic terms of the Reaganite project was enormous. For the first time in decades the United States is now a debtor nation (in fact it has in the course of two years accumulated more foreign debt than the two biggest debtor nations of Latin America, Brazil and Mexico, taken together). Its present foreign debt (over $300 billion in 1987) is expected by Morgan Guaranty Trust to increase twofold by 1990. (Morgan Guaranty Trust, *World Financial Markets*, March 1986, p.9, as quoted by Parboni, 1986, p. 16). It is far from certain that the Bush administration will be able to resolve these problems without eventually resorting to a period of very strong isolationism and protectionism, if only because internal pressures will become so strong that they may no longer be ignored.

Every sign of American 'withdrawal' forces the European bourgeoisie to reconsider its options. The 1986 Reykjavik summit between Reagan and Gorbachev and the subsequent developments in the field of arms reduction agreements have made this particularly clear. The agreement in principle between the two superpowers to remove middle-range nuclear weapons from Europe has caused great confusion and unrest in ruling European circles. Quite suddenly, talk of European defence co-operation has assumed a markedly different quality than only a short while ago, and most remarkably even the Thatcher government seems to be moving into the direction of closer European co-operation and independence in this area. Increased willingness to discuss West European defence co-operation also expressed itself in the enlargement of the West European Union in December 1988, when Spain and Portugal acceded.

For Mrs Thatcher, however, this is a road to be taken only reluctantly, because 'there is no alternative'. She made this quite explicit in her speech of 20 September 1988 in the Europa College in Bruges. In this speech she acknowledged that Britain's future was irrevocably tied in with that of the other EC countries.[2] But she added two qualifications which have everything to do with her ambition for Britain to remain (or once more become) a power with global responsibilities. Thatcher pointed out that Europe extends beyond the boundaries of the present EC, and made it clear that Britain's European policy will also be concerned with Eastern Europe; and, striking a familiar chord, she expressed her conviction that the EEC is still part of 'that Atlantic Community – that Europe on both sides of the Atlantic – which is our greatest inheritance and our greatest strength' (quoted in the *Economist*, 24 September 1988). The Bruges speech, obviously prepared with much care, serves as a reaffirmation of the basic orientation of Thatcherite foreign policy, from which the Thatcher government will only be deflected when and in so far as global political developments force such policy changes upon it.

Otherwise, it is to be expected that Britain's European policy will develop into a major subject of political debate within the Conservative Party. Bearing the episode of the Westland Affair in mind, we may safely expect Michael Heseltine to play a leading role in the 'pro-Europe' faction.

Nevertheless, Mrs Thatcher's reluctance *vis-à-vis* further European integration has served to temper some of the immoderate expectations surrounding '1992'. Abolishing the internal boundaries in the EC will certainly create new opportunities for enterprises which have until now been unable to operate on a European scale, and this will possibly have a positive effect on economic growth rates. However, these advantages accrue not only to European firms, but also to American and Japanese firms in Europe. The history of the EEC in the 1950s and 1960s has shown that American capital was able to gain much more from the establishment of the Common Market than European capital. The events in the financial world after Big Bang showed much the same pattern. Why this should be any different in 1992 has not yet been satisfactorily explained.

Is the class war over?

In 1987 opinion polls showed that only 1 per cent of the electorate considered trade unions to be an important issue facing the country, whereas in 1979 this percentage had been 73 (*Financial Times*, 6 April 1987). Yet the radicals in the Thatcher government were not content at all. The 'unsatisfactory results' of the anti-union drive led the Tories to design new and tougher legislation to replace the 1984 Act. The new Act, amongst other provisions, prohibits unions from disciplining members who do not take part in industrial action, even after a lawful ballot. This new provision caused moderate Tories to question the wisdom of the new Bill (*Financial Times*, 28 October 1987), but it was pushed through anyway. One major reason for the radicals, led by Norman Tebbit, to push for tougher legislation had been the failure of the attempt, based on the 1984 Trade Union Act (part 3), to eliminate the trade union political funds providing 80 per cent of the Labour Party's income. The Trade Union Act of 1913 established the right of trade unions automatically to deduct a portion of membership dues and transfer this to the Labour Party. Individual trade union members could only avoid this by explicitly forbidding the union officials to use their dues for this purpose (the 'contracting-out' system). In the aftermath of the defeat of the General Strike, the Conservative government changed the system into a contracting-in system (1927): individual trade unionists now had to declare explicitly their wish to contribute to the Labour Party funds before the union could use a portion of the dues for the 'political funds'. The postwar Labour government reversed the law again, and in 1946 reintroduced the 'contracting-out' system, which became a thorn in the side of the neo-liberals. By 1984, the Tories imagined that conditions were favourable for yet another reversal of the regulations regarding political funds: union membership had fallen considerably since 1979, and in the 1983 elections only 39 per cent of the union members voted Labour (against 73 per cent in 1964). It was expected that rank and file union members would prove quite sympathetic to the idea of 'giving the unions back to the members', as the Tory propaganda had it. However, in order not to provoke accusations of direct political interference, the new Act did not substitute a straight contracting-in system for the existing system, but prescribed periodic secret ballots over the retention of the political funds. This proved to be an essential concession, leading to the first important defeat for the Thatcher government in a confrontation with the unions. The campaign by union activists to retain the political funds was not only very successful, it was successful thanks to an organizational innovation that could prove to show a way out of the paralysis in which the British trade union movement has found itself trapped since the onset of crisis: the establishment of a *centralized* Trade Union Co-ordinating Committee which organized the campaign from a *national* headquarters. This high level of union co-operation was possible 'because the political funds issue turned out to be the one area of Mrs Thatcher's industrial relations strategy that united all activists at every level and across the political spectrum in an almost unprecedented fashion' (Grant, 1987, pp. 64–5). The results of the ballots so far unambiguously show the defeat of Mrs Thatcher: the 'yes' vote has varied from a low of 75.5 per cent to a high of 91.5 per cent (Grant, 1987, p. 72).

Stephen McBride has suggested that an economic upturn might well lead to renewed union militancy (McBride, 1986, p. 338). There are indeed good reasons to doubt the lasting character of Thatcher's achievements in this area. For one thing, notwithstanding the propaganda value of the EETPU's willingness to sign no-strike and one-union deals (the first one with Toshiba in Plymouth), these deals only cover around 0.5 per cent of the labour force (Clutterbuck and Crainer, 1988, p. 43), which is surely not enough to make a lasting impact: these changes in Britain's industrial relations have not become irreversible yet.

Secondly, there are indeed signs of an upturn in union activity: 'A recent worrying sign: as the threat of unemployment has receded, the unions have seemed ready to flex their muscles again' (*Economist*, 3 December 1988). The rapidly widening rift between the privileged full-time workers in the core sectors of the economy and the increasingly marginalized workers in the peripheral sectors may develop into another source of labour unrest (Clutterbuck and Crainer, 1988, p. 63). This split in post-Fordism between the core (with its emerging company unionism and rising living standards) and the periphery (with its high turnover and low pay) poses enormous strategic problems for the trade union movement. A sustained economic upturn will certainly not reverse the trends towards 'flexibilization' and automation, and therefore the unions will have to devise a totally new strategy, which will not 'automatically' present itself (cf. van Tulder, 1987).

A post-Fordist accumulation strategy

The transition to Fordist industrial production in Britain, incomplete as it may have been, was heralded by the introduction of continuous wide-strip mills in the steel industry just before and immediately after the war. The crisis of Fordist industry could therefore not have been portrayed more aptly than by the run-down of the steel industry in the early 1980s, and the closure of the famous steel mills at Ebbw Vale and Corby. To be sure, British Steel is now the most productive steel corporation in Europe. But this has been achieved in the 'post-steel era'. The central growth industries of the post-Fordist age will not be the steel and automobile industries, but such new industries as microelectronics and biotechnology.

The neo-liberal accumulation strategy developed by the Thatcher government, intended to overcome the structural crisis of British capitalism and to direct the transition to post-Fordism, does *not* consist in an effective reindustrialization programme. On the contrary, the lack of a well-considered industrial strategy is reflected in the continued destruction of the industrial base of the British economy. Notwithstanding the gains in productivity, remarkable in the light of postwar history, the level of output per man hour in British manufacturing is still 30 per cent lower than in Japan, 40 per cent lower than in the USA, and even 50 per cent lower than in West Germany (*Economist*, 3 December 1988, p. 78). It is quite understandable, in this light, that many industrial executives argue, according to a recent survey, that 'the process of manufacturing disinvestment has gone too far and too fast in Britain' (*Financial Times*, 28 November 1988). The future for British manufacturing industry is still to be viewed with apprehension.

This state of affairs is reflected in the continued operation of another of the anti-industrial mechanisms inherent to the British class structure – the brain drain from manufacturing. On the one hand, the enormous differential between the USA and Britain in salaries for technologists (3:1) leads to a steady migration of the best and brightest British engineers to the USA (Clutterbuck and Crainer, 1988, pp. 180–1). On the other hand, British students are still very reluctant to enter science courses in the first place. And even those who do finish an engineering education go into business and commerce in increasing numbers, as a survey by the

University Grants Committee has shown (*Economist*, 24 September 1988, p. 43). The UGC foresees a growing shortage of engineers in the coming decade.

According to the Thatcher government, this state of affairs in British manufacturing is a reflection of the changes taking place in the international division of labour, and represents no cause for any great alarm.[3] Manufacturing, in the eyes of Thatcher, is being replaced by 'high-tech' production on the one hand and by services on the other. But is it?

A recent study shows that Britain's high-tech future might in fact well be a 'no-tech future', as Michael Prowse wrote in the *Financial Times* (30 March 1987). High-tech in Britain has become a net importing sector in the past ten years, with an import penetration of the domestic market of over 50 per cent. The only major 'high-tech' manufacturing sector still showing a positive trade balance (though also declining relatively) in 1985 was (defence-related!) aerospace equipment (£1 billion) (*Midland Bank Review*, Autumn 1986, p. 11). These developments have led the Association of British Chambers of Commerce (ABCC) to warn against unwarranted optimism regarding the 'high-tech' strategy: it pointed out in 1985 that even in electronics Britain had a trade deficit of 2.3 billion, and that the high-tech firms such as GEC, Plessey, STC, Racal, Thorn-EMI and BT had shed 50,000 jobs in three years (*Economist*, 28 September 1985). The recent battles between GEC and Plessey, for the time being decided in favour of GEC, are proof that the British high-tech sector is in for major upheavals in the coming years. The question is whether a single leading British electronics firm capable of competing on the world market will emerge, or whether the British electronics sector will fall prey to foreign (American or Japanese) capital. Considering the Thatcher government's record, the second possibility may well prevail. As much as Thatcherism strives to keep Britain free from foreign invasions when it comes to refugees from the Third World, it has been more than welcoming to foreign economic interests, from the USA but especially from Japan. By pursuing such a world-market oriented strategy, the structure of Britain's industrial specialization has come to resemble that of semi-peripheral countries, with its specialization in sectors that are not research-intensive (*Midland Bank Review*, Autumn 1986, p.13). Ironically, much of the progress and innovation in high-tech and R and D activities has come about in the past few years through European programmes and initiatives such as EUREKA, RACE, and ESPRIT (Clutterbuck and Crainer, 1988, p. 195).

The one area in which Mrs Thatcher has until now resisted

participation in European co-operation has been the area of financial and monetary policy. Britain refused to join the EMS and pursued a policy of specialization in international services (to be facilitated *inter alia* by Big Bang). However, the future for the service sector of the British economy hardly looks brighter than that of the economy at large. Britain's share in world invisible trade is falling, while the shares of the USA, France and Japan are rising. According to the ABCC the reason is that there is a certain (if indeterminate) relation between manufacturing exports and service exports: if one falls steadily, the other is bound to suffer as well (*Economist*, 28 September 1985). As Michael Prowse concludes, 'the notion that a shift towards services is a sign of a particularly advanced "post-industrial" economy has gone out of fashion' (*Financial Times*, 30 March 1987).

The consequences of the City's Big Bang for the structure of the British financial world are far-reaching (cf. Goodhart, 1987). Medium-sized merchant banks are very likely to become the victims of the invasion of foreign investment banks on the London Stock Exchange, which only the bigger ones (such as Mercury/Warburg) can counter by expanding their business in the USA and, more importantly, in Japan. Secondly, because of the globalization of financial markets, national autonomy in the fields of interest rate and fiscal policy will all but disappear.

The liberalization of exchanges and of the London Stock Exchange has led to a 'gigantic nova of money capital floating over London', not merely disconnected but 'estranged from any original linkage with the national economy at all' (Anderson, 1987, p. 69). Anderson is perhaps overly pessimistic: the separation between finance and industry in Britain has become less pronounced as a consequence of the liberalization of the City, argues Dimitri Vittas (1986). However, it is very doubtful that these developments will lead to better capital allocation mechanisms for non-financial companies, which is what the stock exchange business should be about (Goodhart, 1987).

The final verdict cannot yet be pronounced. But on the surface, it would seem that nine years of neo-liberal radicalism have not succeeded in definitively turning the scales. The six months from April to September 1988 have produced a £9 billion external deficit, or 4 per cent of GDP, which is one-third higher than the enormous deficit of the USA (*Economist*, 3 December 1988). The balance of payments constraint is back in full force, and can only get worse now that the North Sea oil proceeds will gradually diminish.

And yet, the future may prove the neo-liberals right after all. It is quite conceivable that precisely the failure of Fordism has put British capital in a position from which it can profit from a possible post-Fordist upturn in the world economy. The parochial structure of labour relations with weak central organizations may in the post-Thatcher era be particularly suitable for the dual structures of post-Fordism: company unions in the core industries, and probably no unions in the peripheral industries.

As it seems now, such a development would not guarantee the working class in Britain (and indeed in most other West European countries) a restoration of full employment and preservation of the basic structures of the welfare state. But why should it? The denationalization of British capital (which has progressed further than elsewhere but is not qualitatively different) has detached dominant sections of the British bourgeoisie from any direct relationship with the British working class (just as in the past the City was detached in this sense from the domestic economy). The problem here is not of an economic but of a political nature.

The final element in Thatcher's accumulation strategy which we considered in Chapter 7 was the policy of privatization. It could certainly be argued that privatization (along with the assault on the unions) has been a crucial element in the strategy of neo-liberalism, and in the short term a fairly successful one. For, it seems certain that a possible future Labour government will hardly contemplate any renationalizations: the sale of over £10 billion of state assets is irreversible. By the end of 1988, privatization had created an enormous number of small shareholders (almost 20 per cent of Britain's population) who will not be pleased with any Labour plans for restoring state ownership.

In the long run, however, it is unlikely that the laws of the market – the tendency toward concentration and centralization of capital – will allow this broadening of share ownership to become a widespread and lasting phenomenon. Thus, the number of shareholders in British Aerospace after privatization decreased within ten months from 158,000 to 27,000 because people were tempted to cash in on the profits the government had offered them by selling cheaply (*Economist*, 23 February 1985).[4] Thatcher's 'small capitalists' do not yet constitute a powerful new fraction of the British bourgeoisie, and probably never will. The *votes* of the new capitalists are welcome, but real power lies elsewhere. And this is a point to be elaborated in the context of a Left alternative.

Restructuring the landscape of British politics

Opposition to Thatcherism within the Tory Party has been all but annihilated.

216

One important nucleus of Tory resistance to Thatcherism after 1975 was the Tory Reform Group around which most of the 'wets' successively dumped by Thatcher rallied. The President of the Tory Reform Group, the only remaining wet in the second Thatcher Cabinet (where he was responsible for handling the miners' strike) was Peter Walker. In the Cabinet reshuffle after the June 1987 elections Walker was demoted to the insignificant post of Secretary of State for Wales, and it does not seem likely that he will return to the political spotlight in the near future. As a matter of fact, it is doubtful that *any* prominent wet should emerge as the new party leader. The wets are committed to a return to the social consensus of the 1950s and 1960s, and to the maintenance or rather rebuilding of the corporatist welfare state. Under the impact of the world crisis this concept has succumbed to its own internal contradictions.

The contradictions within the Thatcherite ranks between radicals and consolidators have been decided in favour of the radicals in the course of Thatcherism's 'mid-life crisis' (cf. Jessop, 1986). In its third term, the Thatcher government is faced with the necessity to map out a more reconstructive course than before. The choice dividing opinions now is the one between the market and the state as the major catalyst of change. The true *laissez-faire* liberal will of course opt for the market. But there are forces inside the Cabinet and on the Tory backbenches who would like to see the state play a more active role in the process. The most articulate programme of this kind has been put forward by Michael Heseltine. Since his resignation Heseltine has been actively building a platform to serve as an alternative for Thatcherism.[5] In this new programme there is no room for monetarism with its obsessive fears of state intervention. On the contrary, Heseltine proposes an active and interventionist industrial policy directed primarily at high technology sectors. In the area of labour relations Heseltine also proposes important innovations, including the introduction of 'Japanese-style' corporatism within firms, whereas such corporatist institutions as had been created in Britain had been limited to the central (national) level. Finally, of course, one important element of Heseltine's programme is the need for further European integration, and for a more active part for Great Britain in that process.

There are some areas where the Thatcher government has indeed complemented its deconstructive activities by constructing new state structures. This is particularly clear in the case of local and inner city politics. The government abolished the metropolitan councils, including the Greater London Council

(GLC); it abolished the rates system giving local authorities a source of income independent from central government; it has taken control over local services (such as schools) away from the local authorities. But it has not, in most cases, replaced local state control by decentralized 'market' control: instead, there has been an enormous degree of centralization of control. The rates were replaced by a regressive poll tax, the inner cities are now reconstructed in what the government believes is a twenty-first-century image by the centrally controlled urban development corporations (the oldest being the London Docklands Corporation),[6] and – notwithstanding the ideological rhetoric about parents' control – schools are also increasingly brought under centralized control.

These policies together amount to a deliberate and far-reaching shift from public to private provision of welfare, and hence to a decisive weakening of the integrative functions of the welfare state and a correspondingly stronger emphasis on law and order (cf. Jessop *et al.*, 1987, p. 113). The trial and error methods of the government not only encourage flexibility and competition, but they also disorient opposition to these policies.

Nevertheless, Thatcherism has been unable to develop an alternative overall view of the state, let alone act upon it, nor has the opposition against the demolition of the welfare state been defini tively overcome. In fact, Thatcher's third term may well be characterized by far-reaching confrontations between the government and public service trade unions over the trimming of the welfare state. In other areas, too, the problems which can be associated with the specific history and structure of the British state are unresolved. Sudden events (mini-crises in the sphere of eventual history) may reactivate crisis tendencies in the medium- and long-term historical processes of class formation and capitalist development. And indeed, the underlying deep-rooted crisis of the British social formation can very easily be kindled by an acute conjunctural crisis.

Recently – foretelling such a crisis? – the structure of the British state returned to the political agenda. One expression is the campaign by a group calling itself Charter 88 (a reference to nineteenth-century British as well as postwar Czech history) for a Bill of Rights. Proof that the issue of Scottish nationalism might again come alive can be found in the result of the Govan by-election. William Rees-Mogg sees in it a sign of a growing threat to the union, caused by Labour's inability to 'deliver the defeat of Mrs Thatcher' who is not well-liked in Scotland (*Independent*, 15 November 1988). Finally there is the debate (which has grown in intensity after Thatcher's third electoral victory) over the British electoral system. There is of course a noticeable element of opportunism in the Left's increased willingness to consider systems of proportional representation. An electoral system in which it can happen in two consecutive elections that a political formation attracts a quarter of all votes cast, yet only wins around 5 per cent of parliamentary seats, can rightfully be called undemocratic (Scargill, 1986). There is also truth to the thesis that the electoral system was a factor in the perpetuation of decline (Gamble and Walkland, 1984). But proportional representation is *not* a socialist concept, as Scargill claims, and cannot prevent neo-liberalism from building a stable electoral majority. The solution for the failure of the Left is to be found in the Left, not in this or that electoral system.

Conclusion

This is not the place to go extensively into the predicament of the British Left. But a few conclusions can be drawn from the analysis of Britain's decline and the rise of Thatcherism presented in this book. Perhaps the essence of the Left's predicament is the fact that opinion polls show a consistent non-Thatcherite majority, which Labour is unable to translate into a plurality of voters (cf. Kavanagh, 1987, pp. 292–7). Why is this so, and what might Labour do about it?

The first point to make is that Labour (and social democracy internationally) have been slow to recognize the crisis of the 1970s as a structural crisis, a crisis of the postwar settlement which was being shattered. When it was recognized that there was a crisis, furthermore, social democracy believed that it might be possible to resolve it by extending the postwar settlement to the international level. That was the meaning of international Keynesian programmes such as the Brandt Report. By the time the illusions of a social democratic New International Economic Order fell through in the 1980 Cancún Conference, Thatcher and Reagan were already in power. The neo-liberals had a fundamental advantage: they had recognized the structural character of the crisis from an early date, they made a serious analysis of its implications, and they devised a concept of control which couched their special solution to the crisis in terms of a 'general interest'. The final ingredient of their success was the fact that their views largely coincided with the interests of the class forces emerging as the core of the post-Fordist accumulation regime.

The neo-liberals have also very effectively expanded their advantage through their socio-economic, political and ideological policies. In Britain, the Thatcher government has consistently eroded the electoral basis of Labour by its anti-industrial policies[7] leading to a decline in the manufacturing workforce, by its rundown of local authorities and the public sector, and by the large-scale sale of council houses to tenants (Kavanagh, 1987, p. 299). The developing gap between the core and the periphery of post-Fordism threatens to fixate Labour in a peripheral position.

The Left, Jessop concludes, lacks 'an alternative strategy of reconstruction – one that could unify and defend the second nation while appealing to the industrial core in both its worker and consumer status' (Jessop *et al.*, 1987, p. 119). Jessop *et al.* mention four necessary elements of such an alternative strategy (p. 122):

- it must offer an alternative to the neo-liberal path to flexibilization, an alternative which is based on an industrial strategy and which protects the level of employment;
- it must contain an enhancement of the role of the state and publicly owned economic forms subjected to democratic and decentralized decision-making;
- such a strategy will have to construct a social base which reaches into the privileged core of wage-earners;
- the policies advocated must go beyond the boundaries of Thatcherism.

The fourth point is particularly relevant. Until now social democracy has only reluctantly admitted that a new age is arriving demanding new policies. Its political practice has been to let the neo-liberals dictate the political agenda, and to argue that, yes, something must be done about the public sector (or the level of taxation, or abuse of power by unions), but a bit less than the government proposes. A 'yes, but' approach is inherently weak, and is almost a guarantee for another lost election. It is indeed time that the Left started dictating the political agenda again (as it did the last time in the campaign against the Cruise missiles).

However, it is sad to see that Jessop and his co-authors themselves fall prey to another of the structural weaknesses of the British Left, namely its insularity. Surely, a strategy of the Left must comprise a coherent view of Britain's place in the world. In two areas of foreign policy the need for new constructive policies is clearly there.

'Europe 1992' requires that the Left develop a vision of what Europe should become, not in the distant future when there might be a 'socialist Europe', but in the coming decade. Will Labour leave Europe to the representatives of European transnational capital, or will it join with the European Left in the struggle for a democratic Europe?

And finally, what answer does the Left have to the new opportunities that are being offered by the rise of Mikhail Gorbachev in the Soviet Union? Here is a chance for Labour to stand firmly for peace and disarmament and yet ditch its unpopular policy of unilateralism. But so far, it has been the Thatchers and Reagans who have set the tone for the West's response. To the outsider it would seem that these issues are not politicized at all.[8]

The political arena is squarely controlled by neo-liberalism, because the Left fails to influence, let alone dictate, the selection of issues. It reacts, it does not act constructively from a position of strength on the basis of an autonomous analysis of the current situation. And it is only on the basis of such a new constructive programme, informed by a convincing analysis of the development of the world political economy, that the Left can hope to rebuild a popular basis.

Notes

Chapter 1

1 It is uncertain how far the need for such great naval capabilities has been diminished in the last decades by the enormous advances in aerospace technology. So far air power has not *replaced* naval power, but some functions which naval power fulfilled can be (and are) transferred to air or space ventures (communications, reconnaissance, and so on).

2 The implications for the notion of 'class' are spelled out by Wallerstein himself: 'Classes are usefully defined as groups that have a common relationship to the economy. But if the effective 'economy' ... is in fact a world economy ... then it follows that classes – classes *an sich* – are classes of the world economy and not of states' (Wallerstein, 1984, p. 8).

3 In his sometimes overzealously critical review, Aristide Zolberg also accuses Wallerstein of geographical determinism.

4 'The so-called reciprocal nexus we identify with feudalism, the exchange of protection for labor services, constitutes a feudal mode of production only when it *is determinative of other social relations*. But once such a "nexus" is contained *within* a capitalist world economy, its autonomous reality disappears. It becomes rather one of the many *forms* of bourgeois employment of proletarian labor to be found in a *capitalist* mode of production' (Wallerstein, 1979, p. 147).

5 Robert Miles argues the same point: he notes that capitalism must have recourse to 'unfree labour', but adds that this necessity does not transform a system based on unfree labour into a capitalist system (Miles, 1987).

6 An incorrect understanding of these relations lies at the heart of the controversy over the nature of Britain's political economy in the nineteenth and twentieth centuries. Cain and Hopkins (1986) and Ingham (1985) argue that Britain's hegemony was essentially commercial and financial, while Barratt Brown (1988) argues the 'orthodox' view of (British) imperialism being founded upon industrial capitalism. As I shall argue in more detail in Chapter 2, it was both.

7 Louis Althusser in effect discarded this notion when he claimed that all 'levels' and 'instances' have their 'own' historical time, just as they are are all (relatively) autonomous (Althusser, 1967). Edward

222

Thompson severely criticized this view. For him these different 'histories' are part of 'the same unitary experience ... eventuating in the same historical time, and moving to the same rhythm ... This integral process is the ultimate object of historical knowledge' (Thompson, 1978, p. 289).

8 Braudel goes no further than the statement that 'we must visualize a series of overlapping histories developing simultaneously' (Braudel, 1973, p. 892). Thus we are no nearer to an understanding of the inter-relationship between these different histories.

9 In his famous book *Ten Days that Shook the World* (1922), John Reed describes the Bolshevik Revolution from a short-term perspective; the writings of Trotsky ([1929] 1978) and Lenin ([1898] 1970a, [1917] 1970b, for example) place the October Revolution in the context of the development of capitalism in Russia, itself occurring in a specific phase of the development of world capitalism; Wallerstein finally sees the Russian Revolution as the first instance of the transition of the world system from capitalism to socialism. Three different temporal horizons thus dominate these works, although they are all concerned with the same historical 'event'.

10 There is actually a fourth level, which Braudel calls the *longue durée*, which considers the history of geographical and climatological processes and of such very long-term processes as the historical succession of different modes of production, seen in the transition from feudalism to capitalism in Western Europe.

11 With respect to the debate over the succession of social formations and modes of production the position of Umberto Melotti (1977), who argues for a 'multilinear' instead of the more common unilinear model, seems the most convincing. For elaboration see Overbeek and Silva, 1986.

12 On the basis of several empirical indicators Kleinknecht also concludes 'that the concept of long waves might be less relevant for the early phase of capitalism' (Kleinknecht, 1986). In so far as long waves can be taken to have existed in the history of capitalism, they are clearly linked to industrial capitalism.

13 The thesis that production itself has an inherent political dimension is persuasively argued in the work of Michael Burawoy (1985).

14 According to Gordon, capital accumulation requires a specific combination of social, political, economic and monetary institutions to proceed 'smoothly' (Gordon, 1980, p. 17). This unified structure is designated by Gordon as a 'social structure of accumulation'.

15 These functional divisions are in our view more important than the distinction between 'practical' and 'philosophical' men which Michael Barratt Brown deems so important (Brown, 1988, p. 41).

16 The *compradores* were the class of merchants in nineteenth-century Latin America who dominated the import and export trades and were thus the main protagonists of their countries' integration into the world market on the basis of exports of agricultural products and raw materials and the imports of luxury items for the small domestic

upper class. Their victory in the civil wars following decolonization from Spain condemned Latin American industry to a century of stagnation.

17 Barrington Moore Jr alludes to the same idea when he states: 'Perhaps the larger situation of which it was a part could occur only once in human history: the English bourgeoisie from the seventeenth through much of the nineteenth century had a maximum material stake in human freedom [particularly in 'economic freedom'] because it was the first bourgeoisie and had not yet brought its foreign and domestic rivals to their full powers' (Moore, 1984, p. 424).

Chapter 2

1 The notion of 'denationalization' was used with respect to the British ruling class by Bob Rowthorn (1975, p. 175).

2 Cain and Hopkins are right when they accuse Anderson and Nairn of doing exactly that (Cain and Hopkins, 1986, p. 503).

3 Throughout this book, billion is used in its US meaning of a thousand million, not in its UK meaning of a million million.

4 The repeal of the Corn Laws also demarcated the definitive succession of the landed by the moneyed interest as the hegemonic fraction of the ruling class (cf. Cain and Hopkins, 1986, pp. 516–17).

5 In the years 1832–67, 53 per cent of the Tory MPs were landowners, as against 39 per cent of Liberal MPs. Whereas 23 per cent of the Tories came from industry, commerce or finance, the comparable percentage for the Liberals was 38 per cent (Setzer, 1973, pp. 115, 136).

6 'Of the 103 men holding Cabinet offices in the years 1830–68, 68 were major landowners, 21 were merchant bankers and 14 were drawn from the legal and medical professions.' It was only after 1868 that there was a gradual decline in the proportion of landowners in political offices (Scott, 1982, pp. 100ff.).

7 The 'aristocratization' of the bourgeoisie is considered by Wallerstein to be 'a constant historical process of translating market achievement into social status' (Wallerstein, 1980, p. 119).

8 Some of the most prominent British capitalists in the postwar period have also been immigrants of one sort or another, and include Sigmund Warburg (the banker), 'Tiny' Rowland (of Lonrho), and the media tycoons Rupert Murdoch and Robert Maxwell. It should also be remembered that Lord Beaverbrook (the press magnate and close friend of Churchill) was a Canadian.

9 This exchange also laid the foundations for one of the structural features of the twentieth-century British ruling class: its transnational character. In a very real sense the British ruling class gradually became an Anglo-Saxon Commonwealth ruling class.

10 The first such instance was that of the National Electrical Manufacturers' Association in 1910 (Ingham, 1984, p. 168).

11 Through this mechanism of migration, the business cycles in the USA and in Britain became closely and inversely interconnected (cf. Thomas, 1973, pp. 99–102, 108ff.; also Kenwood and Lougheed, 1983, pp. 57–72).

12 In 1920 nine clearing banks were joined by thirteen connections to seven railway companies. Three railway companies were linked to several banks and other companies: Great Western (five links), Midland (seven links), and London South Western (six links) (Stanworth and Giddens, 1975, p. 12).

13 The Round Table group formed the core of this fraction. Such people as Amery, Smuts, Milner and Lothian were involved in the making of plans both for the further development of the Commonwealth and for Anglo-American co-operation *vis-à-vis* the problem of Germany (its debts and its general rehabilitation). See Hall (1971, p. 145) and Schmidt (1986, pp. 59–60).

Chapter 3

1 Between 1929 and 1932 the income from foreign investments had fallen by 40 per cent (from £250 million to £150 million), and other invisible income (from services) in the same period fell from £233 million to only £86 million (Hobsbawm, 1969, p. 211).

2 The TUC's Economic Committee had put forward 'proto-Keynesian suggestions in March about increasing working-class purchasing power as an antidote to the depression', but was ignored by the Labour government, and was even denied the 'benefit of consultation' (Middlemas, 1979, p. 212).

3 Nevertheless, the pound continued to fall against the dollar: from $4.86 in September 1931 its value dropped to $3.40 in December.

4 Britain's relations with countries belonging to the Sterling bloc (such as the Nordic countries) also intensified during these years, foreshadowing Britain's postwar involvement with the European Free Trade Association (EFTA).

5 He was followed by only a handful of his erstwhile Labour supporters (among whom had been Aneurin Bevan) of whom John Strachey was best known. The Labour Party expelled Mosley, who then turned to other quarters to find help. Sir William Morris, the motor manufacturer, came to his rescue and invested £50,000 in the New Party, no doubt hoping to strengthen the protectionist lobby. Earlier on, Morris had already founded the National Chamber of Commerce and Industry (NCCI) out of frustration with the FBI's continued free-trade stance (Ingham, 1984, pp. 191, 280n).

6 The Macmillan Commission was named after its chairman Lord Hugh Macmillan, a Scottish lawyer with a long non-partisan career in public service; Harold Macmillan, though at the time propagating similar policies, was not a member of the commission.

7 The share of imports in total consumption in 1937 for certain important foodstuffs was: wheat 79 per cent, sugar 73 per cent, butter 91 per cent, cheese 81 per cent, fruits 74 per cent, ham 68 per cent, beef/lamb 33 per cent, vegetables 36 per cent, eggs 33 per cent (Brady, 1950, p. 447). When considering the fact that Britain is now actually self-sufficient in many of these products, one realizes what enormous productivity gains British agriculture has made.

8 Other influential people such as Sir Samuel Hoare and Lord Londonderry also regularly took part in the Cliveden Set. The Anglo-German Fellowship counted among its corporate members such firms as the merchant banks Lazard Bros, Guinness Mahon, and J. Henry Schröder; the steel firm Firth Vickers Stainless Steel; and the internationalist firms Unilever, Thomas Cook, and Dunlop (Haxey, 1939, p. 230). The most prominent individual members were Sir Robert Kindersley (Bank of England, Lazard), Walter Runciman (Lloyds Bank, Consett Iron, P&O), W. W. Astor, Viscount Nuffield (who had financially backed Mosley's fascist party), Lord Londonderry (coal owner), Sir Geoffrey Clarke (P&O, President of the Associated Chambers of Commerce), and F. d'Arcy Cooper and Paul Rijkens of Unilever. Viscount Halifax (Foreign Secretary from 1938 on) was an occasional guest of honour of the fellowship (Haxey, 1939; Mowat [1955] 1971, pp. 589–657).

9 In 1943 Lord McGowan of Imperial Chemical Industries complained that coal was too expensive for the energy-intensive new industries (Heinemann, 1944, pp. 93–5). In 1944, a special committee chaired by Sir Charles Reid found that during the previous years productivity increases in Britain (14 per cent) were far surpassed by those in France (c. 25 per cent), Belgium (50 per cent), the Ruhr (80 per cent), and the Netherlands (117 per cent) (Burn, 1958).

10 In 1938 the BISF even paid bonuses to the German steel industry under the provisions of the international steel cartel: the German steel barons failed to realize the export quotas they were allowed because of the massive requirements of German armaments production (Aaronovitch, 1955, p. 91).

11 These were named after Reginald McKenna, Liberal Chancellor of the Exchequer during the First World War, and later Chairman of Midland Bank with its strong base in the Midlands industrial centres, the heart of the new car industry.

12 In 1927 Reginald McKenna, Chairman of the Midland Bank, invited Gerald Swope of General Electric Company (USA) to come to Britain to negotiate the takeover of Metropolitan-Vickers Electrical Co. Swope went much further, however, and attempted to acquire all major British electrical firms. In 1929 Metropolitan-Vickers (now a GE subsidiary) merged with British Thomson-Houston and two smaller firms to form Associated Electrical Industries (AEI). In the meantime General Electric Ltd, originally an independent British firm, had also become a subsidiary (60 per cent) of General Electric (USA) (Lewis, 1948, p. 150; Wilkins, 1974, pp. 65–9).

13　Harris has described this process quite well: 'Of course, for the largest producers in the older industries, there was no question of their elimination. Their interests became slowly disentangled from the mass of their fellow producers, and absorbed into those of new industry. Some, technically, became actually integrated in new industry, as cotton manufacture became increasingly linked to chemicals. Others depended for their consumers upon the now predominant newer industries' (Harris, 1972, p. 47).

Chapter 4

1　The major vehicle of growth in the extensive mode of accumulation is that of physical expansion of production on a stable technical basis. The change to the intensive mode of accumulation entailed growth through the reduction of necessary labour time, or, in the words of another author, 'the transition from the dominance of despotic factory regimes to hegemonic factory regimes' (cf. Burawoy, 1985). Wladimir Andreff has refined this analysis by pointing out that the notion of 'mode of accumulation', like the notion of 'mode of production', is an abstraction which in reality always appears in a particular combination of several modes of accumulation. On this basis Andreff distinguishes a third major mode of accumulation, the *progressive* one, which combines elements of the *extensive* and the *intensive* modes, but constitutes itself on the *international* level (Andreff, 1982, pp. 107–8). For our purposes we do not need to go into the finer distinctions between the different definitions; we shall retain Andreff's emphasis on the *international* character of the postwar mode of accumulation, which accords fully with our own point of departure.

2　These phenomena are also analysed under the heading of 'corporatism', for instance by the contributors to the volume edited by Schmitter and Lehmbruch (1979).

3　In Chapter 5, the domestic side of the coin is analysed, both as regards the development of the productive forces and the relations of production, and as regards the development of the mode of regulation by the state.

4　The British also handed over to the Americans all knowledge about nuclear energy for use in developing the atomic bomb, on condition (accepted by Roosevelt in their encounters in Quebec in 1943 and in Hyde Park in 1944) that after the war Britain would be given access to American nuclear capabilities (Taylor, 1975, pp. 654–5; also Calvocoressi, 1979, p. 209).

5　In December 1945 Britain secured an American loan of just over £930 million, followed by a Canadian loan in March 1946 of almost £300 million. In the years 1947–50 the UK secured loans from South Africa, the ECA, Belgium, Portugal, and the EPU, totalling £468 million (Boyd, 1975, p. 49).

6 Counterpart funds were the funds which recipient countries were obliged to furnish in their own currency and which were used at the discretion of the Americans to cover local costs such as wages and building materials.

7 Brett mentions a third consequence often quoted: the negative effect on the innovativeness of British industry of the maintenance of protected markets. He agrees that fuller competition would have eliminated inefficient firms, but is unsure whether 'anything better' would have been put in their place. In the light of recent experience this reservation is quite plausible.

8 This meant that 'the tendency for the economy, so pronounced in the 1930s, to become inward-looking and to grow within itself was thus reversed' (Youngson, 1976, p. 156). In other words, the spread of Fordism in Britain was thwarted by external commitments.

9 This 'Foreign Office option' had its prewar origins in the activities of the Economic Section of the Foreign Office in devising plans for the economic appeasement of Germany (cf. Schmidt, 1986).

10 Britain started to temper the dismantling of German industry as early as May 1946: only those factories which had already been designated by name were dismantled after that date. Britain also took a leading part in the drive to unify the western occupation zones (Feis, 1970, pp. 120, 159–60).

11 In consequence of this changed orientation, the TUC left the 'communist-dominated' World Federation of Trade Unions in 1948 (Epstein, 1954, p. 133).

12 When during the Berlin crisis in June 1948 the USA requested permission to use airbases in Britain for the airlift to Berlin, Bevin was very pleased, so pleased in fact that the British government gave the Americans *carte blanche*, only realizing afterwards the need to establish certain guarantees as to ultimate British sovereignty (Baylis, 1986). Eventually the matter was resolved in a rather vague agreement in October 1951, in which the Americans admitted that Britain retained 'ultimate control' over the use of the bases. The British government curiously enough promised not to divulge this information to the British public unless absolutely forced to do so (Baylis, 1986, p. 157). In 1986 the matter again received attention when American bombers started their raids on Libya from airbases in Britain.

13 The final arousal of old imperialist sentiment occurred in 1965. The occasion was the Unilateral Declaration of Independence (UDI) by the Rhodesian settler regime of Ian Smith (Gamble, 1974, p. 179).

14 It is against this background that the foundation of the European Movement in October 1948 must be seen: its diverse membership (including Clement Attlee, Winston Churchill, Julian Amery, Edward Heath, Harold Wilson, Robert Boothby, Anthony Eden, and Jeremy Thorpe) suggests that perhaps the only common denominator for these people was their anti-communism. The Special Finance Committee of the movement, which included Lord

McGowan (ICI), Lord Balfour (Lloyds Bank) and Sir Andrew Duncan (BISF), could raise little more than £20,000 (in 1947), and was eventually disbanded in 1951 (cf. Rebattet, 1962, pp. 24–7).

15 In view of his expressed wish for Britain to become part of a united Europe and his purposeful action in that direction later, the most likely explanation is that his political instinct told him that the balance of forces in the government would make it impossible to carry the day, and that it was therefore wiser to remain in the background. According to Robert Blake, it was Eden who was the primary opponent behind the scenes of accepting the invitation to Messina, and Macmillan's position was too weak to withstand him (Blake, 1985, p. 285).

16 It has since then become clear that British Intelligence fostered a 'well-established plot to murder President Nasser' at the time (Campbell, Forbes and Jenkins, 1986).

17 Between 1958 and 1965 British overseas exports increased by 30 per cent, but exports to EFTA countries increased by 109 per cent and to EEC countries by 116 per cent (cf. Mandel, 1968, p. 60).

18 In 1957 the Economist Intelligence Unit published a report, commissioned by a long list of British firms (among them Austin, Barclays Bank, Boots, BEA, BISF, Courtaulds, Delta Metal, General Electric Company, GKN, Lazards, Lloyds Bank, Midland Bank, National Provincial Bank, Plessey, Vickers and Westminster Bank) and American interests in Britain (the 'American Committee on United Europe', Esso, Ford, and General Motors), as well as most important trade unions, all united in the Britain and Europe Fund. On the basis of a detailed analysis of changing trade patterns, the report concluded that the formation of a free trade area including Britain and the Common Market was essential for the future of Britain (EIU, 1957).

19 For more detailed information on all these campaigns and committees, see Pfaltzgraff, 1964.

20 For a more extensive treatment of this episode I refer the reader to the next chapter.

21 According to Murray, 'hedging' (in this case undervaluation of exports and overvaluation of imports in anticipation of a Sterling crisis) by multinationals led to the actual crisis in November. He quotes Fortune of 15 September 1968 as claiming 'that most firms with European subsidiaries asked them to defer payment for goods from the UK for 6–7 months prior to devaluation'. Among these firms were International Harvester, Texas Instruments, ITT, Singer, BP, ICI, Dunlop, Bowater, and IBM (Murray, 1975, pp. 35–6).

22 The British banking system, as opposed to the German system, has traditionally maintained a legally enforced separation of different banking functions. The clearing banks, the large commercial deposit banks, were largely barred from holding significant numbers

of shares in industrial companies until the deregulation of the City in the 1980s. The merchant banks, comparable to the American investment banks, were allowed to own shares, but since they lacked a sufficient capital basis their most important role was that of managing the investment portfolios of the large institutional investors, such as insurance companies. The move towards co-operation (even merger) between clearing banks and merchant banks tended to overcome the limitations of both.

Chapter 5

1 The stagnation in the basic industries is also borne out by the fact that investment in the nationalized industries was lower than in the prewar years, and the overall investment share (including both the private and the public sectors) in real terms of gross domestic product fell by 3 per cent (Armstrong, Glyn and Harrison, 1984, pp. 100–2).

2 This line is taken by Smith (cf. Aaronovitch and Smith, 1981), and more recently by Fine and Harris, 1985. In both instances the positive effects of retaining wartime controls and of planning are held to be responsible for the successful rationalization of basic industries, even though in other places these authors acknowledge the defects of Labour's plans. Very little 'credit' for the recovery is given to the positive external influences outside the control of the Labour government.

3 What was interesting in the successful campaign against these new nationalizations was not so much the role of Lord Lyle, for instance, but rather the support the campaign received from the trade unions, both from the TUC and the NUGMW, the National Union of General and Municipal Workers (Pelling, 1985, pp. 212–18).

4 The different activities of the steel industry had differential rates of profit, with the profits in the production of heavy steel products being 20–30 per cent lower than in the manufacturing sectors (Burn, 1961, p. 47).

5 The relations of the Westminster Bank with the steel industry date back to the early 1920s when many firms ran into serious financial problems in consequence of the recession following the postwar boom of 1919–20. Two ministers of the Conservative Cabinet which denationalized the steel industry after 1951, Sir Anthony Eden and Lord Salisbury, were directors of the Westminster Bank (Aaronovitch, 1955, p. 85).

6 In fact, there was not even an analysis of what would be required for a conscious restructuring of a capitalist economy, and the strategy was actually limited to administrative measures. This state of affairs was common in West European social democracy (Therborn, 1980, p. 217).

7   Beveridge had been preoccupied with the problem of unemploy-
     ment as early as 1909, when he wrote *Unemployment: A Problem of
     Industry*. This study still contained a classical liberal view of unem-
     ployment, and specifically rejected Hobson's (proto-Keynesian)
     ideas on underconsumption (see Winch, 1972, pp. 58–63).

8   The second important result of postwar planning for better social
     conditions was the 1944 Education Act, drafted by R. A. Butler,
     the former pupil of Appeaser Sir Samuel Hoare (Beer, 1969, p.
     312).

9   This is confirmed by recent surveys of migration developments (see
     United Nations, 1982; OECD, 1987).

10   The position of foreign and black workers in Britain was *not*
     particularly strengthened by the attitude of the trade unions. These
     remained at best silent during the anti-immigration campaigns,
     and often admitted black workers only reluctantly (cf. Miles and
     Phizacklea, 1984, pp. 73–5).

11   Nuclear energy was organized in a public authority upon the advice
     of a committee in which prominent corporate liberals set the
     tone: Lord Waverley (formerly Sir John Anderson, Vickers, ICI),
     Sir Wallace Akers (ICI) and Sir John Woods (English Electric).
     The Atomic Energy Authority was presided over by Sir Edwin
     Plowden (of British Aluminum), and counted among its members I.
     Stedeford (Tube Investments) and K. L. Stretch (ICI) (Aaronovitch,
     1955, pp. 103–4).

12   These Labour leaders shared with Harold Macmillan and Edward
     Heath the 'blessed' heritage of having attended Balliol College
     Oxford (see Sampson, 1965, pp. 226–7).

13   That not everybody was convinced of Labour's basic trustworthi-
     ness for the established order became clear when in 1968 MI5
     uncovered a plot in the armed forces for a *coup d'état*, which
     they reported to the Home Secretary. The reality of this plot
     was confirmed by Mrs Thatcher's Cabinet Secretary Sir Robert
     Armstrong, when appearing in an Australian courtroom to attempt
     to prohibit publication of the revealing book about the intelligence
     services by the former agent Peter Wright.

14   The data for the following statements have been taken from the
     July 1986 issue of *European Economy*, which gives a detailed survey
     of economic indicators for most OECD countries for the period
     1960–80.

Chapter 6

1   Recent studies of the crisis of US capitalism which employ a
     framework comparable to that of the 'regulation approach'
     are those by Bowles, Gordon and Weisskopf, 1984, and Piore
     and Sabel, 1984. It is remarkable that these studies do not
     contain a single reference to this extensive European literature.

2 This cannot be read from the declining shares in world production and world exports without several qualifications, since American firms had strongly internationalized during the 1950s and 1960s.

3 A survey held by the Confederation of British Industry in 1982 sheds some light on this question (albeit probably conjuncturally determined, and therefore not conclusive). When firms were asked to indicate which factors were responsible for limiting capital expenditure in manufacturing, 52 per cent answered that uncertainty about demand played a role, and a further 36 per cent answered that inadequate expected returns were a major problem. Twenty-six per cent of respondents mentioned a shortage of internal finance, and only 4 per cent mentioned the cost of (external) finance as a factor (NEDC, 1983).

4 Among this diverse company we also find Mancur Olson who explains Britain's slow rate of growth by reference to its longstanding democratic order: 'it suffers from institutional sclerosis' (Olson, 1982, p. 77).

5 The following is based on Glyn and Harrison, 1980, pp. 57–90.

6 This victory for the miners brought national fame to Arthur Scargill, and put him in a strong position in the NUM National Executive (Crick, 1985, pp. 52–66).

7 'The preservation and expansion of freedom are today threatened from two directions. The one threat is ... coming from the evil men in the Kremlin who promise to bury us. The other ... is the internal threat coming from men of good intentions and good will who wish to reform us ... If they gained the power, they would ... produce a collective state from which they would recoil in horror and of which they would be among the first victims' (Friedman, 1962, p. 201). These ideas formed the basis for the popular TV series 'Free to Choose' and for the book with the same name (Friedman and Friedman, 1980).

8 The Chicago boys were Chilean economists who had been trained either in Chicago or by Chicago economists teaching at the Catholic University of Santiago (cf. Silva, 1987, pp. 122–32).

9 This name was taken from the title of *The Constitution of Liberty*, written by Hayek in 1960.

10 Most of the funds put at the disposal of the NEB (£1 billion for four years) eventually went to two 'lame ducks': Rolls Royce and British Leyland (Coates, 1980, pp. 114–31).

11 Colin Leys argues that this episode expresses the power accumulated by the unions in the era of corporatism. This is only partly true, however. An important part of the concessions won in 1974–5 can be explained only by reference to the conjuncture of the crisis in 1974, and must be considered (as indeed they proved to be) as temporary concessions to be withdrawn once the immediate threat to the social order was averted (cf. Leys, 1985, p. 17).

12 These doubts were reinforced by the affair caused by Peter Wright's book *Spycatcher*. Wilson was twice (in 1968 and again in 1975) faced

with plots from military or intelligence circles. The 1975 affair (which developed within MI5) was dealt with, *after* Wilson's resignation, by internal disciplinary action. The Home Secretary (Roy Jenkins) was not informed (*Observer*, 14 December 1986).

13 The 1977 plenary session of the Trilateral Commission held in Bonn discussed Eurocommunism, which was seen by those present (among them Zbigniew Brzezinski) as a serious threat to 'the very cohesion of the West' (Gill, 1987, pp. 362ff.)

14 The year 1976 was also the year in which the phenomenon of cash limits was introduced in the nationalized industries, which were thus directly subjected to the operation of the law of value (Fine and Harris, 1985, p. 159).

15 This of course was also the period during which the government became dependent upon parliamentary support from the Scottish National Party (SNP) and the Liberal Party. Eventually, the deflationary policies pursued by Callaghan and Healey facilitated the conclusion of the 'Lib–Lab Pact' in March 1977 (Coates, 1980, pp. 152–4; Leys, 1986, pp. 86–8).

16 A concise account of the development of the British economy and of British economic policy during the 'decade of discontent' is provided by Nick Gardner (1987).

17 Of course, this was a trend common to all developed capitalist countries; however, the trend was stronger in Britain than in most other countries, precisely because Fordist modernization of industry had lagged behind for so long.

Chapter 7

1 That the operation of the market has led to the very problems the market is now expected to resolve is not seen so clearly by the neo-liberals: this fatal flaw in the liberal creed is mercilessly exposed by Polanyi (1957).

2 To say that Thatcherism is coherent is not meant to imply that there are no internal inconsistencies. But 'given the lack of logical coherence required by commonsense ideologies, contradictions may be a strength rather than a weakness' (Levitas, 1986, p. 11), as long as these contradictions in the ideology do not produce actual political conflicts among Thatcherites.

3 This brand of neo-liberalism is quite akin to some currents within the British SDP.

4 In this sense the conflicts surrounding the rescue of the helicopter firm Westland plc have been very revealing since this affair clearly brought the strategic difference of opinion out into the open (cf. Overbeek, 1986; Freedman, 1987).

5 The parallel between British policy at the time of the Suez crisis (still, of course, the logical continuation of Churchill's line) and British policy with respect to Argentina and the Falkland islands

is too obvious to ignore (cf. Hobsbawm, 1983; Nairn, 1983; Garton Ash, 1986),

6 'The backing from influential people with Pentagon links like Mr Tower [the Republican Senator from Texas] turned out to be critical, since the British victory over Argentina depended to a large extent on American help' ('There is life in the special relationship yet') (*Economist*, 22 December 1984, pp. 29–30).

7 'Wet' was the word used by Thatcher to depict the qualities of those Tories who disagreed with the harsh socio-economic policies of the new government.

8 The *Financial Times* for instance, with the City's extensive interests in Argentina and the rest of South America in mind: see Barnett, 1982, p. 11.

9 I have analysed the Westland Affair in the context of these underlying contradictions more fully in an article in *Capital and Class* (1986).

10 This view was expounded by RIIA prominents Admiral Sir James Eberle, John Roper, William Wallace and Phil Williams, (Eberle *et al.*, 1984). The position of these prominent spokesmen of the Royal Institute of International Affairs was fully in line with the position developed by Heseltine in the context of the IEPG.

11 As early as May 1973, Heseltine (then Aerospace Minister in the Heath Cabinet) called for European co-operation in the aerospace industry (*Financial Times*, 17 May 1973).

12 Mrs Thatcher may also have played a role in the Irangate Affair. The report by the US Senate committee chaired by John Tower shows that Thatcher was involved in talks with White House officials intimately involved in the delivery of weapons to Iran and of money to the Contras in Nicaragua. A Foreign Office spokesman declared that 'permission was never granted for arms deliveries to the Contras', thus not ruling out that they might in fact have occurred (*NRC Handelsblad*, 25 March 1987).

13 Richardson and Moon (1984) have argued that Britain has proved to be a 'mature democracy' because 'hyperunemployment' has not led to 'fundamental political change'. A strong argument could be made to underline exactly the opposite: if hyperunemployment does not lead to fundamental political changes, this might point to sclerosis, not maturity, of the political process.

14 Even such a staunch supporter of Thatcher as Samuel Brittan recognizes that the gains in productivity do not constitute a real improvement in production conditions in British manufacturing, and is worried about the consequences (*Financial Times*, 23 March 1987).

15 In a sense, the income from the exploitation of North Sea oil has financed this build-up of foreign assets: according to the Bank of England, the value of oil rents up to the end of 1985 can be estimated at 73 billion pounds, which is within 10 billion pounds of the increase in net assets abroad (*Economist*, 13 December 1986). From another perspective, the oil rents have enabled the Thatcher

government to pursue its policy of consciously letting unemployment rise to unprecedented levels: the oil rents have approximately equalled total unemployment benefits (Anderson, 1987, p. 71).

16 'Privatization' has become one more 'invisible export': many neo-liberal regimes, varying from Western European governments to the People's Republic of China, have called in British experts to advise them on their own privatization programmes (*Financial Times*, 29 July 1985).

17 According to one estimate, these costs amount to 3 per cent of total proceeds, which would be £300 million (*Le Monde*, 23 September 1987).

18 The data on which these statements regarding the distribution of taxes and surplus value among different fractions of capital are based can be found in my PhD dissertation (Overbeek, 1988). They were calculated from the *OECD National Accounts Statistics*.

19 Recent information has shown that developments in Japan have lagged behind those in the other major capitalist countries, but Japanese corporations have in the past few years also been turning away from production and have diverted into finance, real estate, and so on. See the *Economist*, 22 August 1987.

20 See Note 16 on page p. 223

21 The new law led many companies to channel their donations through one or another of the anti-socialist, pro-free-enterprise organizations that are active in gathering funds for the Tory Party or in anti-Labour election campaigns of their own (Pinto-Duschinsky, 1981, pp. 228–9). The best known of these organizations are:
- the Economic League, which was established in 1919. This organization's main activity is keeping up-to-date blacklists of trade union activists;
- Aims of Industry, established in 1942 to protect the interests of 'free enterprise'. During the 1983 elections its anti-Labour campaign cost over £250,000 (Pinto-Duschinsky, 1985, p. 339);
- British United Industrialists, established in 1948, which has only a single employee (one Colonel Juan Hobbs), whose main job it is to transfer the donations from BUI's accounts to those of the Conservative Party;
- the Centre for Policy Studies, established by the Thatcher wing of the Tories in 1975, which also receives regular company donations.

Chapter 8

1 Protectionism can also be used as a weapon to enforce liberalization, as the case of Reagan's measures against Japan showed (Gill, 1986b, p. 334).

2 The indignant reactions among most West European politicians were in many instances quite hypocritical: Mrs Thatcher expressed

doubts and reservations about 'Europe 1992' which are widely shared but for ideological reasons cannot publicly be uttered.

3 Such alarm was ventilated in the report by the Select Committee on Overseas Trade of the House of Lords, succinctly summarized by Lord Aldington (1986).

4 Black Monday, 19 October 1987, with its worldwide crash of stockmarkets, certainly did not induce small savers to entrust their money in the future to the risky business of stockholding. Subsequent developments have shown another unexpected complication: the interest of foreign raiders in British public enterprises which are to be privatized.

5 Heseltine has spelled out his programme in his book *Where There's a Will* (1987).

6 It should be remembered that it was Michael Heseltine who pioneered the Tories' urban strategy when he was at the Department of the Environment.

7 Notwithstanding the recovery since 1982–3, industrial production in 1988 was still lower than in 1973!

8 Again, I must emphasize that most of the other European social democratic parties do not perform any better.

References

Aaronovitch, S. (1955), *Monopoly, a Study of British Monopoly Capitalism* (London: Lawrence & Wishart).

Aaronovitch, S. (1981), *The Road from Thatcherism* (London: Lawrence & Wishart).

Aaronovitch, S., and Sawyer, M. (1975), *Big Business. Theoretical and Empirical Aspects of Concentration and Mergers in the United Kingdom* (London: Macmillan).

Aaronovitch, S., and Smith, R. (1981), *The Political Economy of British Capitalism* (London: McGraw Hill).

Abromeit, H. (1986), 'Veränderung ohne Reform. Die britische Privatisierungspolitik (1979–1985)', *Politisches Vierteljahresschrift*, vol. 27, no. 3, pp. 271–89.

Aglietta, M. (1979), *A Theory of Capitalist Regulation. The US Experience* (London: New Left Books) (orig. pub. 1976).

Aglietta, M. (1982), 'World capitalism in the eighties', *New Left Review*, no. 136, pp. 5–41.

Aglietta, M., and Sautter, C. (eds.) (1978), *Quatre économies dominantes sur longue période* (Paris: Institut National de la Statistique et des Etudes Economiques (INSEE)).

Aldington, Lord (1986), 'Britain's manufacturing industry', *Royal Bank of Scotland Review*, no. 151, pp. 3–13.

Allen, V. L. (1960), *Trade Unions and the Government* (London: Longman).

Allen, V. L. (1972), *Militant Trade Unionism* (London: Merlin) (orig. pub. 1966).

Althusser, L. (1967), *Pour Marx* (Paris: Maspéro).

Amin, S. (1976), *Unequal Development. An Essay on the Social Formations of Peripheral Capitalism* (Hassocks: Harvester).

Anderson, P. (1964), 'Origins of the present crisis', *New Left Review* (ed.), *Towards Socialism* (London: Fontana), pp. 11–52.

Anderson, P. (1966), 'Socialism and pseudo-empiricism', *New Left Review*, no. 35, pp. 2–42.

Anderson, P. (1980), *Arguments Within English Marxism* (London: Verso).

Anderson, P. (1987), 'The figures of descent', *New Left Review*, no. 161, pp. 20–77.

Andreff, W. (1982), 'Régimes d'accumulation et insertion des nations dans l'économie mondiale', in Reiffers, op. cit., pp. 104–30.

Andreff, W. (1984), 'The international centralization of capital and the re-ordering of world capitalism', *Capital and Class*, no. 22, pp. 58–80.

Anouil, G. (1960), 'La Grande Bretagne et la Communautée Européenne du Charbon et de l'Acier', PhD thesis, University of Bordeaux.

Armstrong, P., Glyn, A., and Harrison, J. (1984), *Capitalism since World War II. The Making and Break-up of the Great Boom* (London: Fontana).

Atkins, F. (1986), 'Thatcherism, populist authoritarianism and the search for a new left political strategy', *Capital and Class*, no. 28, pp. 25–48.

Bach, R. (1982), 'On the holism of a world-systems perspective', in Hopkins and Wallerstein, op. cit., pp. 159–91.

Bacon, R., and Eltis, W. (1978), *Britain's Economic Problem: Too Few Producers* (London: Macmillan).

Barker, E. (1971), *Britain in a Divided Europe 1945–1970* (London: Weidenfeld & Nicholson).

Barnett, A. (1973), 'Class struggle and the Heath government', *New Left Review*, no. 77, pp. 3–41.

Barnett, A. (1982), 'Iron Britannia. War over the Falklands', *New Left Review*, no. 134, pp. 5–96.

Barou, Y. (1978), 'Salariat Britannique et développement économique', in Aglietta and Sautter, op. cit., pp. 91–123.

Barraclough, G. (1967), *An Introduction to Contemporary History* (Harmondsworth: Penguin).

Barry, E. Eldon (1965), *Nationalisation in British Politics. The Historical Background* (London: Cape).

Baudet, H., and Fennema, M. (1983), *Het Nederlands belang bij Indië* (Utrecht and Antwerp: Aula).

Baylis, J. (1986), 'American bases in Britain: the "Truman–Attlee understandings" ', *The World Today*, August–September, pp. 155–9.

Beer, Samuel H. (1969), *British Politics in the Collectivist Age* (New York: Vintage Books) (orig. pub. 1965).

Beloff, M. (1963), *The United States and the Unity of Europe* (Washington: Brookings Institution).

Belsey, A. (1986), 'The New Right, social order and civil liberties', in Levitas, op. cit., pp. 167–97.

Bergesen, A. (1982), 'Economic crisis and merger movements. 1880s Britain and 1980s United States', in Friedman, op. cit., pp. 27–39.

Bergesen, A. (1983), 'The class structure of the world-system', in Thompson, op. cit., pp. 43–54.

Beveridge, W. H. (1944), *Full Employment in a Free Society* (London: Allen & Unwin).

Beynon, H. (1983), 'False hopes and real dilemmas. The politics of collapse in British manufacturing', *Critique*, no. 16, pp. 1–22.

Blackburn, P., Coombes, R., and Green, K. (1985), *Technology, Economic Growth and the Labour Process* (London: Macmillan).

Blake, R. (1985), *The Conservative Party from Peel to Thatcher* (London: Fontana).

Bode, R. (1975), 'De Lotgevallen van een sektor', unpublished research paper, University of Amsterdam.

Bode, R. (1979), 'De Nederlandse bourgeoisie tussen de twee wereldoorlogen', *Cahiers voor de politieke en sociale wetenschappen*, vol. 2, no. 4, pp. 9–50.

REFERENCES

Bousquet, N. (1980), 'From hegemony to core competition: cycles of the core', in Hopkins and Wallerstein, op. cit., 46–83.

Bowles, S., Gordon, D. M., and Weisskopf, T. E. (1984), *Beyond the Waste Land. A Democratic Alternative to Economic Decline* (Garden City, NY: Doubleday).

Boyd, L. V. (1975), *Britain's Search for a Role* (Farnborough: Saxon House).

Brady, R. A. (1945), *Business as a System of Power* (New York: Columbia University Press).

Brady, R. A. (1950), *Crisis in Britain. Plans and Achievements of the Labour Government* (London: Cambridge University Press).

Braudel, F. (1972–3), *The Mediterranean and the Mediterranean World in the Age of Philip II*, 2 vols (New York: Harper & Row) (French edition published 1949–66).

Brenner, R. (1977), 'The origins of capitalist development. A critique of Neo-Smithian Marxism', *New Left Review*, no. 104, pp. 25–93.

Brett, E. A. (1985), *The World Economy since the War. The Politics of Uneven Development* (Basingstoke and London: Macmillan).

Brittan, S. (1977), 'Can democracy manage an economy?', in Skidelsky, op. cit., pp. 41–9.

Brown, M. Barratt (1970), *After Imperialism* (London: Heinemann) (orig. pub. 1963).

Brown, M. Barratt (1973), 'The controllers of British industry', in Urry and Wakeford, op. cit., pp. 73–116.

Brown, M. Barratt (1988), 'Away with all the great arches: Anderson's history of British capitalism', *New Left Review*, no. 167, pp. 22–51.

Brown, W. A., and Opie, R (1954), *American Foreign Assistance* (Washington, DC: Brookings Institution).

Brunhoff, S. de (1976), 'Crise capitaliste et politique économique', in Poulantzas, op. cit., pp. 133–51.

Bukharin, N. (1972), *Imperialism and World Economy* (London: Merlin) (orig. pub. 1917).

Burawoy, M. (1985), *The Politics of Production. Factory Regimes Under Capitalism and Socialism* (London: Verso).

Burn, D. L. (1940), *The Economic History of Steelmaking 1867–1939* (London: Cambridge University Press).

Burn, D. L. (1958), *The Structure of British Industry*, National Institute for Economic and Social Research (NIESR), 2 vols (Cambridge: Cambridge University Press).

Burn, D. L. (1961), *The Steel Industry 1939–1959. A Study in Competition and Planning* (Cambridge: Cambridge University Press).

Butler, D., and Kitzinger, U. (1976), *The 1975 Referendum* (London: Macmillan).

Butler, E., (1983), *Hayek. His Contribution to the Political and Economic Thought of Our Time* (London: Temple Smith/Adam Smith Institute).

Cain, P. J., and Hopkins, A. G. (1986), 'Gentlemanly capitalism and British expansion overseas I. the old colonial system, 1688–1850', *Economic History Review*, 2nd series, vol. 39, no. 4, pp. 501–25.

239

Cain, P. J., and Hopkins, A. G. (1987), 'Gentlemanly capitalism and British expansion overseas II: new imperialism, 1850–1945', *Economic History Review*, 2nd series, vol. 40, no. 1, pp. 1–26.

Callaghan, J. (1987), *Time and Chance* (London: Collins).

Calvocoressi, P. (1979), *The British Experience 1945–75* (Harmondsworth: Penguin).

Campbell, D., Forbes, P. and Jenkins, F. (1986), 'The MI5 affair: can the spooks be trusted?', *New Statesman*, 5 December, p. 14.

Camps, M. (1964), *Britain and the European Community 1955–1963* (Princeton and London: Princeton University Press and Oxford University Press).

Carchedi, G. (1979), 'Authority and foreign labour: some notes on a late capitalist form of capital accumulation and state intervention', *Studies in Political Economy*, vol. 2, pp. 37–74.

Carr, E. H. (1939), *The Twenty Years' Crisis 1919–1939. An Introduction to the Study of International Relations* (New York: Harper & Row) (late- editions 1946, 1964, 1977).

Carr, E. H. (1945), *Nationalism and After* (London: Macmillan).

Castells, M. (1975), 'Immigrant workers and class struggles in advanced capitalism: the Western European experience', *Politics and Society*, vol. 5, no. 1, pp. 33–66.

Castle, B. (1980), *The Castle Diaries 1974–1976* (London: Weidenfeld & Nicholson).

Chalfont, Lord (1986), 'Britain 30 years after Suez', *Defence and Foreign Affairs*, October, pp. 8–11.

Chase-Dunn, C. (1983), 'The kernel of the capitalist world-economy: three approaches', in Thompson, op. cit., pp. 55–78.

Childs, D. (1979), *Britain Since 1945. A Political History* (London: Benn).

Cipolla, C. M. (ed.) (1976), *The Fontana Economic History of Europe: Contemporary Economies 1* (Glasgow: Fontana/Collins).

CIS Report (1984), *Assault on the Unions*, report no. 34 (London: Counter Information Services).

Clarke, S. (1983), 'State, class struggle, and the reproduction of capital', *Kapitalistate*, no. 11–12, pp. 113–30.

Clarke, S. (1988), *Keynesianism, Monetarism, and the Crisis of the State* (Aldershot: Edward Elgar).

Clutterbuck, D., and Crainer, S. (1988), *The Decline and Rise of British Industry* (London: W. H. Allen).

Coakley, J. (1984), 'The internationalization of bank capital', *Capital and Class*, no. 23, pp. 107–20.

Coates, D. (1980), *Labour in Power? A Study of the Labour Government 1974–1979* (London and New York: Longman).

Coates, D. (1982), 'Britain in the 1970s: economic crisis and the resurgence of radicalism', in Cox, op. cit., pp. 141–66.

Coates, D. and Hillard, J. (eds.) (1986), *The Economic Decline of Modern Britain: The Debate between Left and Right* (Brighton: Wheatsheaf).

Coates, D. and Johnston, G. (eds.) (1983), *Socialist Arguments* (Oxford: Martin Robertson).

REFERENCES

Cox, A. (ed.) (1982), *Politics, Policy and the European Recession* (London: Macmillan).

Cox, R. W. (1983), 'Gramsci, hegemony and international relations. An essay in method', *Millennium: Journal of International Studies*, vol. 12, no. 2, pp. 162–75.

Crick, M. (1985), *Scargill and the Miners* (Harmondsworth: Penguin).

Crosland, A. (1957), *The Future of Socialism* (London: Cape).

Davis, M. (1984), 'The political economy of late-imperial America', *New Left Review*, no. 143, pp. 6–38.

Davis, M. (1985), 'Reaganomics' magical mystery tour', *New Left Review*, no. 149, pp. 45–66.

Deppe, F. (ed.) (1975), *Europäische Wirtschaftsgemeinschaft (EWG): Zur politischen Oekonomie der westeuropäischen Integration* (Reinbek bei Hamburg: Rowohlt).

Dobb, M. (1973), *Studies in the Development of Capitalism* (New York: International).

Douglas, J. (1983), 'The Conservative Party: from pragmatism to ideology – and back?', *West European Politics*, vol. 6, no. 4, pp. 56–74.

Dunford, M., and Perrons, D. (1983), *The Arena of Capital* (London: Macmillan).

Dunning, J. H. (1958), *American Investment in British Manufacturing Industry* (London: Allen & Unwin).

Eberle, J., Roper, J., Wallace, W., and Williams, P. (1984), 'European security cooperation and British interests', *International Affairs*, no. 4, pp. 545–60.

Economist Intelligence Unit (1957), *Britain and Europe. A Study of the Effects on British Manufacturing Industry of a Free Trade Area and the Common Market* (London: The Economist Intelligence Unit).

Epstein, L. D. (1954), *Britain – Uneasy Ally* (Chicago: University of Chicago Press).

Fallick, J. L., and Elliott, R. F. (eds.) (1981), *Incomes Policies, Inflation and Relative Pay* (London: Allen & Unwin).

Feis, H. (1970), *From Trust to Terror. The Onset of the Cold War 1945–1950* (New York: Norton).

Fennema, M., and Van der Pijl, K. (1986), 'International bank capital and the New Liberalism', in M. Schwartz and M. Mizruchi (eds.), *Structural Analysis of Business* (New York: Cambridge University Press), pp. 298–319.

Ferris, P. (1970), *Men and Money. Financial Europe Today* (Harmondsworth: Penguin).

Fine, B. (1984), 'The future of British coal', *Capital and Class*, no. 23, Summer, pp. 67–82.

Fine, B., and Harris, L. (1985), *The Peculiarities of the British Economy* (London: Lawrence & Wishart).

Flanagan, R. J., Soskice, D. W., and Ulman, L., (1983), *Unionism, Economic Stabilization, and Incomes Policies. European Experience* (Washington, DC: Brookings Institution).

241

Frank, A. G. (1963), *On Capitalist Underdevelopment* (Bombay: Oxford University Press).
Frank, A. G. (1980), *Crisis in the World Economy* (London: Heinemann).
Franko, L. G. (1976), *The European Multinationals. A Renewed Challenge to American and British Big Business* (Stanford, Calif: Greylock).
Freedman, L. (1987), 'The case of Westland and the bias to Europe', *International Affairs*, no. 1, pp. 1–19.
Freeman, C. (ed.) (1983), *Long Waves in the World Economy* (London: Butterworths).
Frieden, J. (1977), 'The Trilateral Commission: economics and politics in the 1970s', *Monthly Review*, vol. 29, no. 7, pp. 1–18.
Frieden, J. (1981), 'Third World indebted industrialization: international finance and state capitalism in Mexico, Brazil, Algeria, and South Korea', *International Organization*, vol. 35, no. 3, pp. 407–31.
Friedman, E. (ed.) (1982), *Ascent and Decline in the World-System* (Beverly Hills and London: Sage), pp. 41–68.
Friedman, M. (1962), *Capitalism and Freedom* (Chicago: University of Chicago Press).
Friedman, M. and R. (1980), *Free to Choose* (Harmondsworth: Penguin).
Furtado, C. (1987), 'Transnationalization and monetarism', in S. Raw (ed.), *The Debt Crisis in Latin America, International Journal of Political Economy*, vol. 17, no. 1, pp. 15–44.

Gallagher, J. (1982), *The Decline, Revival and Fall of the British Empire. The Ford Lectures and other Essays* ed. Anil Seal (Cambridge: Cambridge University Press).
Gallagher, J. and Robinson, R. (1982), 'The imperialism of free trade', in Gallagher, op. cit., pp. 1–18.
Gamble, A. (1974), *The Conservative Nation* (London: Routledge & Kegan Paul).
Gamble, A. (1981), *Britain in Decline. Economic Policy, Political Strategy, and the British State* (London: Macmillan).
Gamble, A. (1983), 'Monetarism and the social market economy', in Coates and Johnston, op. cit., pp. 7–32.
Gamble, A. (1988), *The Free Economy and the Strong State* (Basingstoke: Macmillan).
Gamble, A., and Walkland, S. A. (1984), *The British Party System and Economic Policy 1945–1983* (Oxford: Clarendon Press).
Gamble, A., and Walton, P. (1976), *Capitalism in Crisis. Inflation and the State* (London: Macmillan).
Gardiner, J. (1980), 'The development of the British working class', in Aaronovitch and Smith, op. cit., pp. 316–33.
Gardner, N. (1987), *Decade of Discontent. The Changing British Economy Since 1973* (Oxford: Blackwell).
Garton Ash, T. (1986), 'The trouble with Trident', *Spectator*, 12 April, pp. 8–15.
Gerstenberger, H. (1973), 'Zur Theorie der historischen Konstitution des bürgerlichen Staates', *Prokla*, no. 8–9, pp. 207–26.

242

REFERENCES

Giddens, A. (1981), *A Contemporary Critique of Historical Materialism* (London: Macmillan).

Gill, S. (1986a), 'Hegemony, consensus and trilateralism', *Review of International Studies*, vol. 12, no. 3, pp. 205–22.

Gill, S. (1986b), 'American hegemony: its limits and prospects in the Reagan era', *Millennium Journal of International Studies*, vol. 15, no. 3, pp. 311–66.

Gill, S. (1987), 'American hegemony and the Trilateral Commission', PhD thesis, University of Birmingham.

Gillman, J. M. (1969), *Das Gesetz des tendenziellen Falls der Profitrate* (Frankfurt: Europäische Verlagsanstalt).

Glyn, A. (1986), 'Capital flight and exchange controls', *New Left Review*, no. 155, pp. 37–49.

Glyn, A., and Harrison, J. (1980), *The British Economic Disaster* (London: Pluto).

Glyn, A., and Sutcliffe, B. (1972), *British Capitalism, Workers and the Profits Squeeze* (Harmondsworth: Penguin).

Goodhart, C. A. E. (1987), 'The economics of "Big Bang" ', *Midland Bank Review*, Summer, pp. 6–15.

Goralczyk, D. (1975), 'Die Marxsche Theorie der Weltmarktbewegung des Kapitals und die Rekonstruktion des Weltmarkts nach 1945', in Deppe, op. cit., pp. 14–52.

Gordon, D. M. (1980), 'Stages of accumulation and long economic cycles', in Hopkins and Wallerstein, op. cit., pp. 9–45.

Gourevitch, P. (1986), *Politics in Hard Times. Comparative Responses to International Economic Crises* (Ithaca, NY, and London:Cornell University Press).

Gramsci, A. (1971), *Selections from the Prison Notebooks* (New York: International).

Grant, D. (1987), 'Mrs Thatcher's own goal: unions and the political funds ballots', *Parliamentary Affairs*, vol. 40, no. 1, pp. 57–72.

Grant, W. (1980), 'Business interests and the British Conservative Party', *Government and Opposition*, vol. 15, no. 2, pp. 143–61.

Grant, W. (1983), 'The business lobby: political attitudes and strategies', *West European Politics*, vol. 6, no. 4, pp. 163–82.

Grant, W., and Marsh, D. (1977), *The CBI* (London: Hodder and Stoughton).

Gray, R. (1983), 'The Falklands factor', in Hall and Jacques, op. cit., pp. 271–80.

Gregory, R. (1985), 'Industrial relations, the law and government strategy', *Political Quarterly*, vol. 56, no. 1, pp. 23–32.

Hain, P. (1986), *Political Strikes. The State and Trade Unionism in Britain* (Harmondsworth: Penguin).

Hall, H. Duncan (1971), *Commonwealth. A History of the British Commonwealth of Nations* (London: Van Nostrand Reinhold).

Hall, S. (1983), 'The Great Moving Right Show', in Hall and Jacques, op. cit., pp. 19–39.

Hall, S. (1985), 'Authoritarian populism: a reply to Jessop et al.', New Left Review, no. 151, pp. 115–24.
Hall, S., and Jacques, M. (eds.) (1983), The Politics of Thatcherism (London: Lawrence & Wishart).
Harris, N. (1972), Competition and the Corporate Society. British Conservatives, the State and Industry 1945–1964 (London: Methuen).
Haxey, S. (1939), Tory MP (London: Gollancz).
Hayek, F. (1960), The Constitution of Liberty (London: Routledge & Kegan Paul).
Hayek, F. (1986), '1980s unemployment and the unions', in Coates and Hillard, op. cit., pp. 106–14 (orig. pub. 1984).
Heinemann, M. (1944), Britain's Coal (London: Labour Research Department and Gollancz).
Heseltine, M. (1984), 'The Atlantic Alliance: an agenda for 1984', NATO Review, vol. 32, no. 1, pp. 1–3.
Heseltine, M. (1987), Where There's A Will (London: Hutchinson).
Hickel, R. (1975), 'Kapitalfraktionen; Thesen zur Analyse der herrschende Klasse', Kursbuch no. 42, pp. 141–52.
Hilferding, R. (1973), Das Finanzkapital (Frankfurt: EVA) (orig. pub. 1910).
Hobsbawm, E. (1969), Industry and Empire (Harmondsworth: Penguin).
Hobsbawm, E. (1983), 'Falklands fallout', in Hall and Jacques, op. cit., pp. 257–70.
Hobson, J. A. (1968), Imperialism. A Study (London: Allen & Unwin) (orig. pub. 1902).
Hodgson, G. (1981), Labour at the Crossroads. The Political and Economic Challenge to the Labour Party in the 1980s (Oxford: Martin Robertson).
Hodgson, G. (1984), 'Thatcherism: the miracle that never happened', in Nell, op. cit., pp. 184–208.
Holloway, J., and Picciotto, S. (eds.) (1978), State and Capital. A Marxist Debate (London: Edward Arnold).
Hopkins, T. K., and Wallerstein, I. (eds.) (1980), Processes of the World System (Beverly Hills and London: Sage).
House of Lords (1985), Report from the Select Committee on Overseas Trade, vol. 1 (London: HMSO).
Iersel, J. P. van (1976), 'Europese fusiecontrole nog niet in zicht', Nieuw Europa, vol. 29, no. 3, pp. 138–50.
Ingham, G. (1984), Capitalism Divided? The City and Industry in British Social Development (London: Macmillan).
IPW (Institut für Internationale Politik und Wirtschaft) (1982), Die Wirtschaft Kapitalistischer Länder in Zahlen (Berlin: IPW-Forschungshefte, January).
Jacobs, D. (1988), 'Gereguleerd Staal. Nationale en internationale economische regulering in de westeuropese staalindustrie, 1750–1950', PhD thesis, University of Nijmegen.
Jacques, M. (1983), 'Thatcherism – breaking out of the impasse', in Hall and Jacques, op. cit., pp. 40–62.
Jalée, P. (1970), L'impérialisme en 1970 (Paris: Maspéro).

REFERENCES

Jessop, B. (1980), 'The transformation of the state in post-war Britain', in Scase, op. cit., pp. 23–93.

Jessop, B. (1983a), 'Accumulation strategies, state forms, and hegemonic projects', *Kapitalistate*, no. 10–11, pp. 89–111.

Jessop, B. (1983b), 'The capitalist state and the rule of capital: problems in the analysis of business associations', *West European Politics*, vol. 6, no. 2, pp. 139–62.

Jessop, B. (1986), 'The mid-life crisis of Thatcherism and the birth-pangs of post-Fordism', *New Socialist*, no. 36.

Jessop, B., Bonnett, K., Bromley, S., and Ling, T. (1984), 'Authoritarian populism, two nations and Thatcherism', *New Left Review*, no. 147, pp. 32–60.

Jessop, B., Bonnett, K., Bromley, S., and Ling, T. (1985), 'Thatcherism and the politics of hegemony: a reply to Stuart Hall', *New Left Review*, no. 153, pp. 87–101.

Jessop, B., Bonnett, K., Bromley, S., and Ling, T. (1987), 'Popular capitalism, flexible accumulation and Left strategy', *New Left Review*, no. 165, pp. 104–22.

Joseph, Sir Keith (1986), 'Solving the union problem is the way to Britain's recovery', in Coates and Hillard, op. cit., pp. 98–105.

Junne, G. (1982), 'Internationale arbeidsdeling en politiek proces', inaugural address, University of Amsterdam.

Kahn, P., Lewis, N., Livock, R. and Wiles, P. (1983), *Picketing. Industrial Disputes, Tactics and the Law* (London: Routledge & Kegan Paul).

Kaldor, M., Sharp, M., and Walker, W. (1986), 'Industrial competitiveness and Britain's defence', *Lloyds Bank Review*, October, pp. 31–49.

Kavanagh, D. (1987), *Thatcherism and British Politics. The End of Consensus?* (Oxford: Oxford University Press).

Keegan, W. (1985), *Mrs Thatcher's Economic Experiment* (Harmondsworth: Penguin).

Keegan, W. (1986), 'Towards a New Bretton Woods?', *Royal Bank of Scotland Review*, no. 149, pp. 3–10.

Keegan, W., and Pennant-Rea, R. (1979), *Who Runs the Economy? Control and Influence in British Economic Policy* (London: Maurice Temple Smith).

Kegley Jr, C. W., and McGowan, P. (eds.) (1983), *Foreign Policy and the Modern World System* (Beverly Hills and London: Sage).

Kennedy, P. (1988), *The Rise and Fall of the Great Powers. Economic Change and Military Conflict from 1500 to 2000* (London, Sydney and Wellington: Unwin Hyman).

Kenwood, A. G., and Lougheed, A. L. (1983), *The Growth of the International Economy 1820–1980* (London: Allen & Unwin).

Kilpatrick, A., and Lawson, T. (1980), 'On the nature of industrial decline in the UK', *Cambridge Journal of Economics*, no. 4, pp. 85–102.

Kleinknecht, A. (1986), 'Long Waves, depression, and innovation', *De Economist*, vol. 134, no. 1, pp. 84–108.

Kolko, J. (1974), *America and the Crisis of World Capitalism* (Boston: Beacon).

Kolko, J., and Kolko, G. (1972), *The Limits of Power. The World and United States Foreign Policy, 1945–1954* (New York: Harper & Row).
Kölling, M. (1984), *Führungsmacht in Westeuropa? Grossbritanniens Anspruch und Scheitern 1944–1950* (Berlin: Akademie der Wissenschaften der DDR).
Krasner, S. D. (ed.) (1983), *International Regimes* (Ithaca, NY, and London: Cornell University Press).
Krasner, S. D. (1985), *Structural Conflict. The Third World Against Global Liberalism* (Berkeley: University of California Press).

Lenin, W. I. (1970a), *Die Entwicklung des Kapitalismus in Russland, Lenin Werke* (Berlin/DDR: Dietz Verlag) (orig. pub. 1898).
Lenin, W. I. (1970b), 'Ein Vortrag über die Revolution von 1905', in *Lenin Ausgewählte Werke* (Berlin/DDR: Dietz Verlag) vol. 1, pp. 884–900 (orig. pub. 1917).
Lenin, W. I., (1978), *Imperialism, the Highest Stage of Capitalism* (Moscow: Progress) (orig. pub. 1917).
Leruez, J., (1972) *Planification et politique en Grande-Bretagne 1945–1971* (Paris: Colin) 2 vols.
Leruez, J. (ed.) (1984), *Le Thatchérisme: doctrine et action* (Paris: Documentation Française).
Lever-Tracy, C. (1983), 'Immigrant workers and post-war capitalism: in reserve or core troops in the front line?', *Politics and Society*, vol. 12, no. 2, pp. 127–58.
Levitas, R. (ed.) (1986), *The Ideology of the New Right* (Cambridge: Polity).
Lewis, C. (1948), *The United States and Foreign Investment Problems* (Washington, DC: Brookings Institution).
Leys, C. (1985), 'Thatcherism and British manufacturing: a question of hegemony', *New Left Review*, no. 151, pp. 5–25.
Leys, C. (1986), *Politics in Britain. An Introduction* (London: Verso) (orig. pub. 1983).
Liberal Industrial Inquiry Report (1928), *Britain's Industrial Future* (London: Benn).
Lieber, R. J. (1970), *British Politics and European Unity. Parties, Elites and Pressure Groups* (Berkeley and Los Angeles: University of California Press).
Lipietz, A. (1982), 'Towards global Fordism?', *New Left Review*, no. 133, pp. 33–47.
Lipietz, A. (1985), *The Enchanted World. Inflation, Credit, and the World Crisis* (London: Verso).
Lipset, S. M. (1960), *Political Man* (London: Heinemann).
Livingstone, K. (1983), 'Monetarism in London', *New Left Review*, no. 137, pp. 68–77.
Luxemburg, R. (1970), *Die Akkumulation des Kapitals. Ein Beitrag zur ökonomischen Erklärung des Imperialismus* (Frankfurt: Verlag Neue Kritik) (orig. pub. 1912).

McBride, S. (1986), 'Mrs Thatcher and the post-war consensus: the case of trade union policy', *Parliamentary Affairs*, vol. 39, no. 3, pp. 330–40.

REFERENCES

McEachern, D. (1979), 'Party government and the class interest of capital. Conflict over the steel industry 1945–1970', *Capital and Class*, no. 8, Summer, pp. 125–43.

McGeehan, R. (1985), 'European defence cooperation: a political perspective', *The World Today*, vol. 4, no. 6, pp. 116–19.

Macleod, I., and Maude, A. (eds.) (1950), *One Nation. A Tory Approach to Social Problems* (London: Conservative Political Centre).

Macmillan, H. (1939), *The Middle Way. A Study of the Problem of Economic and Social Progress in a Free and Democratic Society* (London: Macmillan).

Mandel, E. (1968), *De EEG en de rivaliteit Europa-Amerika* (Amsterdam: Van Gennep).

Mandel, E. (1974), *Decline of the Dollar. A Marxist View of the Monetary Crisis* (New York: Monthly Review Press).

Mandel, E. (1975), *Late Capitalism* (London: Verso and New Left Books).

Mandel, E. (1980), *Long Waves of Capitalist Development. The Marxist Interpretation* (Cambridge: Cambridge University Press).

Marx, K. [1867, 1885, 1894] (1979), *Capital*, 3 vols (Harmondsworth: Penguin).

Melissen, J., and Zeeman, B. (1987), 'Britain and Western Europe 1945–1951: opportunities lost?', *International Affairs*, no. 1, pp. 81–95.

Melotti, U. (1977), *Marx and the Third World* (London: Macmillan).

Middlemas, K. (1979), *Politics in Industrial Society. The Experience of the British System since 1911* (London: Deutsch).

Mikesell, R. (ed.) (1962), *US Private Investment*, Eugene, Oregon.

Miles, R. (1982), *Racism and Migrant Labour* (London: Routledge & Kegan Paul).

Miles, R. (1987), *Capitalism and Unfree Labour. Anomaly or Necessity* (London and New York: Tavistock).

Miles, R., and Phizacklea, A. (1984), *White Man's Country. Racism in British Politics* (London: Pluto).

Miliband, R. (1972), *Parliamentary Socialism*, 2nd edn (London: Merlin).

Miliband, R. (1973), *The State in Capitalist Society* (London: Quartet) (orig. pub. 1969).

Mills, C. W. (1970), *The Sociological Imagination* (Harmondsworth: Penguin) (orig. pub. 1959).

Mistral, J. (1985), 'Assainissement ou déclin de l'économie britannique?', *Critiques de l'économie politique*, no. 3, pp. 25–62.

Mitchell, B. R. (1978), *European Historical Statistics 1750–1970* (London: Macmillan).

Mitchell, N. J. (1987), 'Where traditional Tories fear to tread: Mrs Thatcher's trade union policy', *West European Politics*, vol. 10, no. 1, pp. 33–45.

Modelski, G. (1981), 'Long cycles, Kondratieffs, and alternating innovations: implications for U.S. foreign policy', in Kegley and McGowan, op. cit., pp. 63–83.

Modelski, G. (1983), 'Long cycles of world leadership', in Thompson, op. cit., pp. 115–39.

Moock, R. van (1977), 'US Investeringen en US Hulp in het Verenigd Koninkrijk', unpublished research paper, University of Amsterdam.

Moore Jr, Barrington (1984), *Social Origins of Dictatorship and Democracy. Lord and Peasant in the Making of the Modern World* (Harmondsworth: Penguin) (orig. pub. 1966).

Moore, R. (1982), 'Free market economics, trade union law and the labour market', *Cambridge Journal of Economics*, no. 6, pp. 297–315.

Morgan, K. O. (1985), *Labour in Power 1945–1951* (Oxford and New York: Oxford University Press).

Morus, (1956), *Achter de schermen. De groten der wereldeconomie* (Amsterdam: Duwaer).

Mowat, C. L. (1971), *Britain Between the Wars 1918–1940* (Boston: Beacon) (orig. pub. 1955).

Murray, R. (1975), *Multinational Companies and Nation States* (Nottingham: Spokesman).

Nairn, T. (1973), *The Left Against Europe?* (Harmondsworth: Penguin) (orig. ed. *New Left Review*, no. 75, 1972).

Nairn, T. (1977), 'The twilight of the British state', *New Left Review*, no. 101–2, pp. 3–61.

Nairn, T. (1979), 'The future of Britain's crisis', *New Left Review*, no. 113–14, pp. 43–70.

Nairn, T. (1983), 'Britain's living legacy', in Hall and Jacques, op. cit., pp. 281–8.

NEDC (1982), 'Productivity and investment trends', memorandum by the Director-General, National Economic Development Council, London.

NEDC (1983), *Company Profitability and Finance* (London: National Economic Development Council).

Nell, E. (ed.) (1984), *Free Market Conservatism. A Critique of Theory and Practice* (London: Allen & Unwin).

Newton, S. (1985), 'The 1949 sterling crisis and British policy towards European integration', *Review of International Studies*, no. 11, pp. 169–82.

O'Brien, P., and Roddick, J. (1983), *Chile: The Pinochet Decade. The Rise and Fall of the Chicago Boys* (London: Latin America Bureau).

O'Connor, J. (1973), *The Fiscal Crisis of the State* (New York: St. Martin's Press).

O'Donnell, K. (1985), 'Brought to account: the NCB and the case for coal', *Capital and Class*, no. 26, pp. 105–23.

OECD (1987), *The Future of Migration* (Paris: OECD).

Olson, M. (1982), *The Rise and Decline of Nations. Economic Growth, Stagflation and Social Rigidities* (New Haven and London: Yale University Press).

Overbeek, H. W. (1980), 'Finance capital and the crisis in Britain', *Capital and Class*, no. 11, pp. 99–120.

Overbeek, H. W. (1984), 'Over het einde der Amerikaanse hegemonie', *Tijdschrift voor Politieke Ekonomie*, vol. 7, no. 3, pp. 42–67.

Overbeek, H. W. (1986), 'The Westland Affair: collision over the future of British capitalism', *Capital and Class*, no. 29, pp. 12–26.

Overbeek, H. W. (1988), 'Global capitalism and Britain's decline', PhD thesis, University of Amsterdam.

Overbeek, H. W., and Silva, P. (1986), 'Historic mission of capital. Three cases of Marxist reduction', *Marxist Review*, vol. 19, no. 3, pp. 202–19.

Palloix, C. (1982), 'Crise et nouvelles formes de l'impérialisme. Economie de crédit international et extension internationale du salariat', in Reiffers, op. cit., pp. 131–57.

Panitch, L. (1979), 'The development of corporatism in liberal democracies', in Schmitter and Lehmbruch, op. cit., pp. 119–46.

Parboni, R. (1981), *The Dollar and its Rivals: Recession, Inflation and International Finance* (Verso: London).

Parboni, R. (1986), 'The dollar weapon: from Nixon to Reagan', *New Left Review*, no. 158, pp. 5–18.

Pelling, H. (1985), *The Labour Governments 1945–1951* (London and Basingstoke: Macmillan).

Petras, J., and Rhodes, R. (1976), 'The reconsolidation of US hegemony', *New Left Review*, no. 97, pp. 37–53.

Pfaltzgraff Jr, R. L. (1964), 'Great Britain and the European Economic Community: a study of the development of British support for Common Market membership between 1956 and 1961', PhD thesis, University of Pennsylvania.

Pijl, K. Van der (1978), *Een Amerikaans Plan voor Europa* (Amsterdam: SUA).

Pijl, K. Van der (1984), *The Making of an Atlantic Ruling Class* (London: Verso).

Pijl, K. Van der (1988), 'Class struggle in the state system and the transition to socialism', *After the Crisis: Current Research on Capital and Strategy*, no. 4 (Amsterdam: University of Amsterdam).

Pinto-Duschinsky, M. (1981), *British Political Finance 1830–1980* (Washington and London: American Enterprise Institute for Public Policy Research).

Pinto-Duschinsky, M. (1985), 'Trends in British political funding 1979–1983', *Parliamentary Affairs*, vol. 38, no. 3, pp. 328–47.

Piore, M. J., and Sabel, C. F. (1984), *The Second Industrial Divide, Possibilities for Prosperity* (New York: Basic Books).

Plender, J. (1987), 'London's Big Bang in international context', *International Affairs*, vol. 63, no. 1, pp. 39–48.

Plowden, W. (1973), *The Motor Car and Politics in Britain* (Harmondsworth: Penguin).

Polanyi, K. (1957), *The Great Transformation. The Political and Economic Origins of Our Time* (Boston: Beacon) (orig. pub. 1944).

Pollard, S. (1982), *The Wasting of the British Economy. British Economic Policy 1945 to the Present* (London: Croom Helm).

Pollard, S. (1985), 'Capital exports 1870–1914: Harmful or beneficial?', *Economic History Review*, second series, vol. 38, no. 4, pp. 489–514.

Portes, A. (1978), 'Migration and underdevelopment', *Politics and Society*, vol. 8, no. 1, pp. 1–48.

Poulantzas, N. (1975), *Classes in Contemporary Capitalism* (London: New Left Books).

Poulantzas, N. (ed) (1976a), *La Crise d'Etat* (Paris: Presses Universitaires de France).

Poulantzas, N. (1976b), 'Les transformations actuelles de l'Etat, la crise politique et la crise de l'Etat', in Poulantzas, op. cit., pp. 19–58.

Powell, E. (1983), 'Bad days for British foreign policy', *Guardian Weekly*, 25 September.

Radice, H. (ed.) (1975), *International Firms and Modern Imperialism* (Harmondsworth: Penguin).

Radice, H. (1984), 'The national economy: a Keynesian myth?', *Capital and Class*, no. 22, pp. 111–40.

Ravier, J.-P. (1984), 'Mme Thatcher et les syndicats', in Lerueź, op. cit., pp. 57–68.

Rebattet, F. X. (1962), 'The European Movement 1945–1953', PhD dissertation, University of Oxford.

Reddaway, W. B., et al. (1967), *The Effects of U.K. Direct Investment Overseas, Interim and Final Reports* (Cambridge: Cambridge University Press).

Reed, J. (1961), *Ten Days That Shook The World* (New York: Vintage) (orig. pub. 1922).

Reiffers, J. L. (ed.) (1982), *Economie et Finance Internationales* (Paris: Dunod).

Richardson, J. J., and Moon, J. (1984), 'The politics of unemployment in Britain', *Political Quarterly*, vol. 55, no. 1, pp. 29–37.

Riddell, P. (1983), *The Thatcher Government* (Oxford: Martin Robertson).

Rogow, A., and Shore, P. (1955), *The Labour Government and British Industry 1945–1951* (Oxford: Blackwell).

Roobeek, A. J. M. (1987), 'The crisis in Fordism and the rise of a new technological paradigm', *Futures*, vol. 19, no. 2, pp. 129–54.

Ross, J. (1983), *Thatcher and Friends. The Anatomy of the Tory Party* (London: Pluto).

Rothenberg, R. (1984), *The Neo-Liberals. Creating the New American Politics* (New York: Simon and Schuster).

Rowthorn, B. 1975, 'Imperialism in the 1970s – unity or rivalry', in Radice, op. cit., pp. 158–80 (orig. pub. 1971).

Ruggie, J. G. (1983), 'International regimes, transactions, and change: embedded liberalism in the postwar economic order', in Krasner, op. cit., pp. 195–231.

Rustin, M. (1986), 'Restructuring the state', *New Left Review*, no. 158, pp. 43–58.

Rybczynski, T. M. (1985), 'Financial systems, risk and public policy', *Royal Bank of Scotland Review*, no. 148, pp. 35–45.

Sampson, A. (1965), *Anatomy of Britain Today* (London: Hodder and Stoughton).

REFERENCES

Sampson, A. (1983), *The Changing Anatomy of Britain* (Sevenoaks: Coronet).

Sargent, J. A. (1983), 'British finance and industrial capital and the European communities', *West European Politics*, vol. 6, no. 2, pp. 14–35.

Sassen-Koob, S. (1981), 'Notes toward a conceptualization of immigrant labour', *Social Problems*, no. 29, pp. 65–85.

Scargill, A. (1986), 'Proportional representation: a socialist concept', *New Left Review*, no. 158, pp. 76–80.

Scase, R. (ed.) (1980), *The State in Western Europe* (London: Croom Helm).

Schmidt, G. (1986), *The Politics and Economics of Appeasement. British Foreign Policy in the 1930s* (Leamington Spa: Berg).

Schmitter, P. C., and Lehmbruch, G. (eds.) (1979), *Trends Toward Corporatist Intermediation* (Beverly Hills and London: Sage).

Schneider, H. (1968), *Großbritanniens Weg nach Europa. Eine Untersuchung über das Verhalten und die Rolle des britischen Handel und Industrieverbände, Gewerkschaften und Farmerorganisationen zwischen 1955/56 (Spaakkomitee) und 1961 (EWG-Beitrittsverhandlungen)* (Freiburg: Rombach Verlag).

Schumpeter, J. A. (1975), *Capitalism, Socialism and Democracy* (New York: Harper & Row)(orig. pub. 1942).

Scott, J. (1982), *The Upper Classes. Property and Privilege in Britain* (London: Macmillan).

Setzer, H. (1973), *Wahlsystem und Parteienentwicklung in England. Wege zur Demokratisierung der Institutionen 1832 bis 1948* (Frankfurt: Suhrkamp).

Shanks, M. (1977), *Planning and Politics. The British Experience 1960–1976* (London: Allen & Unwin).

Shortall, F. C. (1986), 'Fixed and circulating capital', *Capital and Class*, no. 28, pp. 160–85.

Silva, P. (1987), *Estado, neoliberalismo y la politica agraria en Chile 1973–1981* (Dordrecht and Providence: Foris and CEDLA).

Singer, J. D. (1961), 'The level-of-analysis problem in international relations', *World Politics*, vol. 14, no. 1, pp. 77–92.

Skidelsky, R. (ed.) (1977a), *The End of the Keynesian Era. Essays on the Disintegration of the Keynesian Political Economy* (London: Macmillan).

Skidelsky, R. (1977b), 'The political meaning of the Keynesian revolution', in Skidelsky, op. cit., pp. 33–40.

Skocpol, T. (1977), 'Wallerstein's world capitalist system: a theoretical and historical critique', *American Journal of Sociology*, vol. 82, no. 5, pp. 1075–90.

Skocpol, T. (1979), *States and Social Revolutions* (Cambridge: Cambridge University Press).

Smith, K. (1984), *The British Economic Crisis* (Harmondsworth: Penguin).

Spiegelberg, R. (1973) *'The City'. Power Without Accountability* (London: Quartet).

Stanworth, P., and Giddens, A. (1975), 'The modern corporate economy. Interlocking directorships in Britain, 1906–1970', *Sociological Review*, vol. 23, no. 1, February, pp. 5–28.

Sweezy, P. M. (1968), *The Theory of Capitalist Development. Principles of Marxian Political Economy* (New York: Monthly Review Press) (orig. pub. 1942).

Taylor, A. J. (1985), 'The politics of coal: some aspects of the miners' strike', *Politics*, vol. 5, no. 1, pp. 3–9.

Taylor, A. J. P. (1975), *English History 1914–1945* (Harmondsworth: Penguin) (orig. pub. 1965).

Taylor, G. (1985), 'The splits within the NUM: the productivity deal, its origins and consequences', *Politics*, vol. 5, no. 1, pp. 10–17.

Taylor, T. (1986), 'Britain's response to the Strategic Defense Initiative', *International Affairs*, no. 2, pp. 217–30.

Therborn, G. (1980), *What does the Ruling Class Do When it Rules?* (London: Verso).

Therborn, G. (1984), 'The prospects of labour and the transformation of advanced capitalism', *New Left Review*, no. 145, pp. 5–38.

Thomas, B. (1973), *Migration and Economic Growth: A Study of Great Britain and the Atlantic economy*, 2nd edn (Cambridge: Cambridge University Press) (orig. pub. 1954).

Thompson, E. P. (1965), 'The peculiarities of the English', *Socialist Register*, pp. 311–62.

Thompson, E. P. (1978), *The Poverty of Theory and Other Essays* (London: Merlin).

Thompson, W. R. (1983a), 'The world-economy, the long cycle, and the question of world-system time', in Kegley and McGowan, op. cit., pp. 35–62.

Thompson, W. R. (ed.) (1983b), *Contending Approaches to World System Analysis* (Beverly Hills, London and New Delhi: Sage).

Ticktin, H. (1983), 'The transitional epoch, finance capital and Britain', *Critique*, no. 16, pp. 23–42.

Trotsky, L. D. (1978), *Geschiedenis van de Russische Revolutie*, 3 vols (Amsterdam: Van Gennep) (orig. pub. 1929).

Tulder, R. van (1987), *Work, Productivity and Income: A Scenario for Metalworkers* (Geneva: International Metalworkers Federation).

Tylecote, A. B. (1982), 'German ascent and British decline 1870–1980: the role of upper-class structure and values', in Friedman, op. cit., pp. 41–67.

United Nations (1982), *International Migration Policies and Programmes: A World Survey* (New York: United Nations).

Urry, J., and Wakeford, J. (eds.) (1973), *Power in Britain* (London: Heinemann).

Vincent, J. (1972), *The Formation of the British Liberal Party 1857–1868* (Harmondsworth: Penguin).

Vittas, D. (1986), 'Banks' relations with industry: an international survey', *National Westminster Bank Quarterly Review*, February, pp. 2–14.

REFERENCES

Vroey, M. De (1984), 'A regulation approach interpretation of the con- temporary crisis', *Capital and Class*, no. 23, pp. 45–66.

Wallerstein, I. (1974), *The Modern World-System*, vol. 1, *Capitalist Agriculture and the Origins of the European World-Economy in the Sixteenth Century* (New York: Academic).

Wallerstein, I. (1979), *The Capitalist World-Economy* (Cambridge: Cambridge University Press).

Wallerstein, I. (1980), *The Modern World-System*, vol. 2, *Mercantilism and the Consolidation of the European World-Economy 1600–1750* (New York: Academic).

Wallerstein, I. (1983), *Historical Capitalism* (London: Verso).

Wallerstein, I. (1984), *The Politics of the World-Economy. The States, the Movements and the Civilizations* (Cambridge: Cambridge University Press).

Westergaard, J., and Resler, H. (1974), *Class in Capitalist Society: A Study of Contemporary Britain* (London: Heinemann).

White, B., and Vittas, D. (1986), 'Barriers in international banking', *Lloyds Bank Review*, no. 161, pp. 19–31.

Wiener, M. J. (1981), *English Culture and the Decline of the Industrial Spirit 1850–1980* (Cambridge: Cambridge University Press).

Wilkins, M. (1974), *The Maturing of Multinational Enterprise: American Business Abroad from 1914 to 1974* (Cambridge, Mass.: Harvard University Press).

Williams, E. (1983), *Capitalism and Slavery* (London: Deutsch) (orig. pub. 1944).

Willoughby, J. A. (1979), 'The Lenin–Kautsky unity–rivalry debate', *Review of Radical Political Economics*, vol. 11, no. 4, pp. 91–101.

Wilson, H. (1979), *Final Term. The Labour Government 1974–1976* (London: Weidenfeld & Nicholson).

Wilson, T. (1966), *The Downfall of the Liberal Party 1914–1935* (London: Collins).

Winch, D. (1972), *Economics and Policy. A Historical Survey* (London: Collins/Fontana) (orig. pub. 1969).

Winkler, J. T. (1977), 'The coming corporatism', in Skidelsky, op. cit., pp. 78–87.

Wolf, E. (1982), *Europe and the People without History* (Berkeley, Calif.: University of California Press).

Woolf, L. (1919), *Empire and Commerce in Africa. A Study in Economic Imperialism* (London: Labour Research Department and Allen & Unwin).

Wright, A. (1987), 'British decline: political or economic?', *Parliamentary Affairs*, vol. 40, no. 1, January, pp. 41–56.

Yaffe, D. (1973), 'The crisis of profitability: a critique of the Glyn–Sutcliffe thesis', *New Left Review*, no. 80, pp. 45–62.

Young, S. (1986), 'The nature of privatisation in Britain 1979–1985', *West European Politics*, vol. 9, no. 2, pp. 235–52.

Young, S. (1987), 'Privatisation and the fiscal crisis of the state: Thatcher contra Offe and O'Connor', *Politics*, vol. 7, no. 1, pp. 29–34.

Youngson, A. J. (1960), *The British Economy 1920–1957* (London: Allen & Unwin).

Youngson, A. J. (1976), 'Great Britain 1920–1970', in Cipolla, op. cit., pp. 128–79.

Zeeman, B. (1986), 'Britain and the Cold War: an alternative approach. The Treaty of Dunkirk example', *European History Quarterly*, vol. 16, no. 3, July, pp. 343–67.

Zolberg, A. R. (1981), 'Origins of the modern world system: a missing link?', *World Politics*, vol. 33, no. 2, pp. 253–81.

Subject Index

accumulation
  modes of 227
  regimes 23, 86–7
accumulation strategy
  of Heath government 156
  neoliberal 193–4
  post-Fordist 213–16
Adam Smith Institute 164, 197
Amalgamated Engineering Union (AEU) 66
American hegemony 33, 87, 88
  decline of 145–6
American investment in UK 78–80, 105
American loan 90–1, 96
Anderson/Nairn thesis 35
Anglo-American defence cooperation 99, 101
Anglo-American rivalry 55, 78–9, 88–93, 97–9
Anglo-German Fellowship 69
Atlantic Charter 89, 129
Atlantic Partnership 181–2
authoritarian populism 176–7

Baghdad pact 98
Bank of England 93
  and 1929 Labour government 65
  and cotton industry 74
  and steel industry 76
  and City 108–9
  controls monetary policy 132
  pressures Labour government 169
  criticizes Dalton 121
  re-establishes monetary restrictions 159
Barclays Bank 229
Beveridge Report 119–20
bourgeoisie 14
  generations of 29–34
  internationalism of British 31–2, 38
  early fractionation of British 36–7
  aristocratization of 44–5
  de-nationalization of 152, 216

British Aerospace
  role in Westland affair 185
  participates in SDI 186
  privatized 199, 216
British Coal (see also National Coal Board) 190
British Iron and Steel Federation 70, 74–6, 117–18
British Leyland 135, 168, 174, 232
British Petroleum 98, 172, 229
British Steel 158, 189, 213
Brussels Treaty 95, 97

Campaign for a European Political Community (Campaign for Europe) 103
capital costs 149
capital exports (see also foreign investment)
  in 19th century 40, 49–51
  resumption after World War Two 92, 106
capital fractions 23–5, 93
  changing balance between 107
  in CBI 134
  under Thatcherism 200–2
capitalist mode of production 14–15
cartellization 71–6
Centre for Policy Studies 164, 235
Churchillism 93–5, 182–4
circulating capital 25, 27
City of London 33, 46, 60
  global orientation 49, 50–1
  and return to Gold Standard 55
  weakened by Depression 61, 63, 80
  involved in Morgan loan 62
  unwilling to invest in coalmining 72–3
  thwarts modernization of steel industry 75
  renewed postwar dominance 93, 106–11, 152
  relations with Bank of England 108–9
  and Eurodollar market 109–10, 156–7
  not in NEDC 134
  opposes devaluation 136

City of London (*continued*)
  as off-shore centre 151
  and rise of monetarism 162–3
  liberalization (Big Bang) 196–7, 215
  conflicts with Thatcher government 203
class formation 16–20, 45
class structure 35–6, 39–41
clearing banks
  as centres of finance capital 157
  profit from Big Bang 196–7, 215
Coal Mines Act 72–3
Coal Mines Reorganization Commission 73
coal mining 72
  nationalization 115, 118
Common Agricultural Policy 184
Commonwealth 33, 98, 102
  capital exports to 49, 63
  and Anglo-American rivalry 55
  Ottawa Conference 62
  US penetration 78
  postwar position 90, 93, 96
  nuisance to Thatcher 182–3
concentration of capital
  after World War One 54
  in Interbellum 77
  after World War Two 123–5
concepts of control
  four hegemonic concepts 4
  definition 25–6, 27–8, 178, 181
  conflicting concepts 54–5, 56–7, 138, 154
  and theories of crisis 142
  Thatcherism as concept of control 176–81
Confederation of British Industry 134–5, 158–9, 160–1, 169, 184, 202–3
Conservative Party
  shifts to Thatcherism 8
  mouthpiece of landed interests 42
  remains as main ruling class party 56
  and protectionism 60–1
  and industrial policy 64
  dominates War Cabinet 70
  supports Bevin's foreign policy 95
  and coal nationalization 115
  opposes Beveridge Report 119–20
  accepts state intervention 128
  rise of neoliberals 161–5
  supports continued EEC membership 168
  company donations 204–6
  opposition to Thatcher in 217
Conservative Research Department 164
convertibility of Sterling 90–1

corporate liberal bourgeoisie 60
  growth in 1930s 71
  views on American loan 91
  dominates Conservative Party 128–32
corporate liberalism 4, 33
  rise in 1930s 63–8
  predominance in 1950s 114, 129
  not hegemonic 120
  expounded by Heath 155, 161
  and Trilateralism 170
corporatism 26, 81, 133, 135–7, 203
Council of Europe 96–7
crisis 5, 19–20
  structural crisis in capitalism 23
  1929 crisis as historical rupture 82–3
  classical view 141
  Keynesian view 142
  Marxist views 142–3
  structural nature 143–4, 166, 180
  'conjuncture' of crises 5, 166, 176
  in world economy 144–7
  in Britain 147–54
  political crisis of 1974 165–8

decline of Britain 122–3
  interpretations of 2, 151, 173–4
  long-term perspective 35–58
  necessity of 82–3
  Milton Friedman's view 170
  and Falklands war 183
  reversed by Thatcher? 207–8
defence
  defence expenditure as cause of crisis 149–50
  defence industry prospers 195
de-industrialization 173
  under Thatcher 195–6, 215
devaluation 109–10, 121, 136, 158, 169–70

economic liberalism 4
  laissez faire liberalism 30–1, 48–9
  demise in Depression 80
  views on crisis 141–2
  element of neoliberalism 162, 179–80, 193–4
electoral system 218–19
Electrical, Electronic, Telecommunications and Plumbing Union (EETPU) 192, 212
Empire Economic Union 61
Empire Industries Association 60–1
energy
  need for comprehensive policy 191

Engineering Employers' Federation (EEF) 131
criticizes Keynesian compromise 155
Euro (dollar) markets 109–10, 156–7
European Coal and Steel Community (ECSC) 96–7, 114, 116, 118–19
European Defence Community (EDC) 97
European defence cooperation 185–6, 210
European Economic Community (EEC) 97
and Britain 100–2, 104, 156–7, 167
American view on UK membership 102–3
effects on UK capital exports 106
mergers in 124
strained relations with USA 146
Referendum on 168
Thatcher and 183–4, 210–11
European Free Trade Association (EFTA) 100–1, 225
European League for Economic Co-operation (ELEC) 95
European Monetary System (EMS) 184, 215

Falklands war 183
Federal Union 103
Federation of British Industry (FBI) 53
and Gold Standard 55
favours protection 61, 68
favours rationalization of mines 71–2
views on EEC 100–1
calls for industrial policy 128
urges establishment of NEDC 132
merged in CBI 134
Morris leaves 225
finance capital 32
relative absence in Britain 51
restructuring 110
early centrality of merchant banks 124–5
clearing banks' role increases 157
as organizer of production 201
less tightly knit 203
financial/commercial aristocracy 59
Ford Motor Company 77, 79, 229
and steel nationalization 117
largest car importer 174
Fordism 23
failure 6–7, 137–40
international spread 33
introduction in UK 64, 71
fordist industries prosper 76–81

role of American investment 78–80
global Fordism 84–8
Gramsci's view 85
social dimension 85–7
Aglietta's view 86
strict definition 138
empirical indicators 139–40
foreign investment 90, 151
(see also capital exports)
in Europe 101, 106
under Thatcher 196
foreign policy
Bevin's view 93–4
towards Europe 93–7, 100–4
French Revolution 39
effect on UK 39–40

General Agreement on Tariffs and Trade (GATT) 91, 96, 102, 197
General Electric Company (GEC) 79, 135, 226, 228, 229, 231
success in Europe 168
participates in SDI 186–7
battle with Plessey 214
General and Municipal Workers Union (GMWU) 66
General Strike 58, 143, 166, 211
Great Depression 60–1, 82–3
Greater London Council (GLC) 217

hegemonic projects 177–8
hegemony
in the world system 11, 13, 17
of bourgeoisie 23
Gramsci's view 28–9
of aristocracy 44–5
hegemonic crisis 143–4, 166, 174
Heritage Foundation 164
high tech sector 214

Imperial Chemical Industries (ICI) 45, 61, 64, 70, 74, 79, 117, 226, 228, 229, 231
bulwark of state-monopoly bourgeoisie 68–9
invests in Europe 101, 168
takes part in SDI 186
Imperial Preference 62
effect on modernization of basic industries 72
Import Duties Act 62
Import Duties Advisory Committee (IDAC) 62, 74

Independent European Programme Group (IEPG) 185
industrial capital
rise in UK 41–4
subordination to City 49–51
Industrial Policy Committee 128
Industrial Relations Act 156, 159–61, 188
Industrial Reorganization Corporation (IRC) 134–5, 158
Industrial Reorganization League 64
Institute of Directors (IoD) 188, 202–3
Institute of Economic Affairs (IAE) 162
interest rates
as cause of crisis 148–9
international economic position of Britain 90, 100
International Monetary Fund (IMF) 99, 109
worried over UK payments deficit 158
imposes monetary targets 163
loan to Britain 170–2
internationalization
of British capital 151
of British economy 196
of capital 30, 32–3
investment
low investment as cause of crisis 148
iron and steel industry
in 1930s 74–6
nationalization 116–19
denationalization 123

Japanese capital in Britain 196, 214

Labour Committee for Europe 103
Labour Common Market Committee 103
Labour government 57, 65, 103–4
plans for modernization 108–9
turns to IMF 109–10
nationalization policy 114–19
in 'sixties 132–7
in 'seventies 166–75
pacifies unions 166–7
surrenders to IMF 171
introduces monetarism 172
labour movement
reformism 80–1
Labour Party 7
integration into bourgeois state 53
replaces Liberal Party 56
in power before war 57, 65

economic orthodoxy 66–7
and Schuman Plan 96
critical of Suez-policy 98
views on Europe 103
committed to nationalization 119
debate between traditionalists and reformists 133
executes demise of Keynesianism 172
elements of new strategy 220–1
labour relations
character of early British 51–3
postwar 125–8
Lend Lease Act 88
Lend Lease Agreement 89
Lend Lease aid stopped 96
levels of analysis
debate in international relations theory 2–3
debate in Marxism 181
liberal bourgeoisie 59, 71, 76
Liberal Party
social composition in 19th century 42–3
downfall 55–6
position on industrial policy 64
Depression deals blow to 80, 83
supports continued EEC membership 168
in 'Lib-Lab' Pact 233
logic of priority 32, 38–9, 46, 140
long waves controversy 21–2
long waves theory and crisis 142–3

Marshall Plan 91, 95, 105, 114
execution in UK 92
and nationalization of steel industry 117
Midland Bank 68, 226, 229
migrant labour 127
capital's need for 127–8
legal position in UK 128
military coup
possibility of 166
miners' strikes 57, 160–1, 165, 188–91, 193
Mond-Turner talks 67
monetarism 162
popularization of 163
conversion of Keith Joseph 164
increasing influence 170–1
replaces Keynesianism 172
as element of neoliberal concept of control 174–5

SUBJECT INDEX

money capital
  central role in restructuring 146–7
  international resurgence 200
  rising share of surplus value 200
money-capital concept
  hegemonic in Britain 51, 93
  institutionally embedded 134–5
Mont Pelerin Society 28
  international activities 162, 164
motor car industry 77–8

National Board for Prices and Incomes 133
National Coal Board (NCB) 189–90
  (see also British Coal)
National Economic Development Council
  (NEDC) 121, 132, 134
  Thatcher's demise of 197, 203
National Enterprise Board (NEB) 167
National Health Service (NHS) 120, 122
National Provincial Bank 229
National Union of Mineworkers (NUM) 9
  strikes against Heath government
  160–1, 165
  target of Thatcher government 188–93
nationalization
  of class relations 32, 37–8
  by Labour government 114–19
  class character 118–19
neo-conservatism 179–80
neo-liberalism
  rise 7–9, 28, 34
  view of trade unions 153
  becomes dominant in Conservative
  Party 161–5
  definition 178–9
  transatlantic context 181–7
  analogy with 19th century liberalism
  193–4
  rise related to resurgence of money
  capital 202
  strength 219–20
New International Economic Order
  (NIEO) 146, 168–9, 219
North Atlantic Treaty Organization
  (NATO) 95, 96–7

Organization for European Economic
  Cooperation (OEEC) 96
Ottawa Conference 62

people's capitalism 198–9
Plessey 214, 229
  participation in SDI 186

donations to Conservative Party 205
battle with GEC 214
post-Fordism 180–1, 212–16
privatization 158, 197
  aims 198–9
productive capital 25–7
  productive capital concept 113
  Labour's adherence 118
  monetization 200–2
productivity
  growth stagnates 145
  in international comparison 173, 191
  growth under Thatcher 195, 213
  in coalmining 226
profitability
  in coal 72
  in steel 74, 116, 230
  falling worldwide 144
  erosion in Britain 147
  in manufacturing 167
  and capital fractions 200–4
  restored by monetarism 207
proletariat
  rise of 52
protectionism 60
  rise after 1929 60–3
  in motor car industry 77–8

Quakers 39, 45

research and development
  as cause of crisis 150

Safeguarding of Industries Act 79
Schuman Plan 96, 118
Scottish National Party (SNP) 233
social democracy 27, 63
  and incorporation of labour movement
  51–5
  in 'thirties 66–7
  failure 177, 219, 230, 239
  need for new direction 220–1
social imperialism 47–8, 53
stages of capitalist development 22–3
  (see also Fordism)
state
  multinational character of British 31, 38
  role in Fordism 86
  role increases under Thatcher 217–18
state intervention
  capitalists' experience with 70
  state expenditure 131–2
  and crisis 142, 149

259

state-monopoly bourgeoisie 60, 68–70
state-monopoly tendency 4, 33, 114, 129
Steel Company of Wales (SCOW) 75, 117
steel industry: *see* iron and steel industry
stop-go cycle 108, 132–3, 152
Strategic Defense Initiative (SDI) 186–7
strikes 125, 136, 140, 160
Suez-crisis 98–9, 131

Thatcherism 9, 176–81
    expresses outlook of transnational
        capital 180
    coincides with resurgence of money
        capital 202
    social basis 203
    defined as concept of control 206
Tory Reform Group 217
Trade Union Act 192, 211–12
trade unions 57–8
    and Schuman Plan 96
    participation in nationalization 114–15,
        117
    organizational structure 125–7, 211–12
    membership figures 54, 66–8, 140, 161
    their strength as cause of crisis 152–4
    clash with Tory government 165
    accept IMF-recipe 172–3
    and Thatcher government 187–93
    political funds ballots 211–12
Trades Union Congress (TUC) 52–4, 66–8
    and General Strike 58
    favours protection 61, 68
    and nationalized industries 120–1
    weakness of central structure 134
    boycotts Industrial Relations Act 160
    calls for expansion 225
    leaves World Federation of Trade
        Unions (WFTU) 228
Transport and General Workers Union
    (TGWU) 66
Treasury 108, 121, 132
    Treasury-City-Bank axis 134–5

relation with Department of Industry
    169
ensures return to orthodoxy 169
Trilateral Commission (TC) 169–70
trilateralism 169–70

unemployment 57, 67, 173
unilateralism
    in Reagan's foreign policy 182, 208–9
    in Thatcher's foreign policy 186
    in Labour's foreign policy 220–1
Union of Democratic Mineworkers
    (UDM) 190
United States of America
    rise as world power 40

Vickers 70, 77, 229, 231
    and steel nationalization 117

wages
    high wages as cause of crisis 149
    increases in 1973–5 167
Warburg, S. G. & Co. 103, 135, 215
    first in Eurodollars 109
welfare state
    origins 53
    postwar 113, 119–22
    Conservative views on 128–9
    development stagnates 130
West European Union (WEU) 97, 210
West European unity
    contending views 93–4
    Thatcher's views 210–11
Westland affair 185–6, 208, 210
Westminster Bank 229
    central position in steel industry
        117–18
working class strength 106
world system approach 11–13
    geographical determinism 14
    and long cycles 20–1

Name Index

Acheson, Dean 94
Adamson, Campbell 160–1
Akers, Sir Wallace 231
Amery, Leo 56, 61, 225
Amery, Julian 96, 228
Anderson, Sir John 70, 117, 231
d'Arcy Cooper, F. 226
Armstrong, Sir Robert 231
Armstrong, Sir William 166
Aron, Raymond 133
Astor, W. W. 226
Attlee, Clement 65, 121, 228

Bacon, Robert 162
Baldwin, Stanley 56–8, 66
Balfour, Lord 229
Barber, Anthony 158, 163
Beaverbrook, Lord 68, 129, 224
Beckett, Sir Terence 202
Bell, Daniel 133
Benn, Tony 8, 168–9, 171
Bennett, Sir Peter 128
Beveridge, Sir William 103, 119–20, 231
Bevin, Ernest 66–8, 70, 93–5
Bevan, Aneurin 122
Bidault, Georges 95
Birch, Nigel 131
Birkenhead, Lord 56
Boothby, Robert 67, 91, 98, 228
Brandt, Willy 159, 170
Brittan, Leon 185
Brittan, Samuel 162–3, 175, 234
Broackes, Sir Nigel 206
Brown, George 134–5
Brzezinski, Zbigniew 233
Buchanan, James 162
Burns, Arthur 171
Bush, George 209
Butler, Sir Harold 95
Butler, R. A. 128, 130–1, 133, 231

Callaghan, James 9–10, 154, 169–71, 173–4, 233

Carter, Jimmy 146, 170
Cayzer, Lord 205
Chamberlain, Joseph 48, 60
Chamberlain, Neville 61–2, 68–9
Chambers, Paul 101
Chirac, Jacques 9
Churchill, Winston 55, 58, 61, 88–9, 93–4, 113, 129–30, 182–4, 187, 224, 228, 233
Clarke, Sir Geoffrey 226
Craven, Sir Charles 117
Cripps, Stafford 121
Crosland, Anthony 133
Crossman, Richard 133
Cunliffe-Lister, Sir P. 62

Dalton, Hugh 92, 121
Disraeli, Benjamin 48, 128
Douglas-Home, Sir Alec 132
Duncan, Sir Andrew 70, 76, 229

Eccles, David 95, 128
Eden, Anthony 88, 95, 97, 99, 129–31, 182, 228–30
Eisenhower, Dwight 99, 101
Eltis, Walter 162

Farouk, King of Egypt 98
Firth, Sir William 75
Ford, Henry 85
Ford, Gerald 146, 171
Forte, Lord 206
Friedman, Milton 28, 162–4, 170, 193–4, 232
Fyfe, David Maxwell 128

Gaitskell, Hugh 133
de Gaulle, Charles 102, 104, 132
Giscard d'Estaing, Valérie 104, 156, 170
Gladwyn, Lord 103
Goldsmith, Walter 202
Gorbachev, Mikhail 210, 220
Grierson, Ronald 135

Halifax, Viscount 226
Hanson, Lord 205
Harberger, Arnold 164
Harrison, Sir Ernest 205
Harrod, Sir Roy 95
Hayek, Friedrich 28, 133, 153, 162–4, 193, 232
Healey, Denis 103, 109, 133, 168, 170–3, 233
Heath, Edward 8, 96, 102–4, 129, 131, 154–61, 163–6, 174, 188, 193, 228, 231
Heathcoat Amory, Derick 128
Heffer, Eric 169
Heseltine, Michael 185–6, 210, 217, 234, 236
Hoare, Sir Samuel 226, 231
Hobbs, Juan 235
Hoffman, Paul 117
Hoskyns, Sir John 203
van Houwelingen, Jan 185
Howe, Sir Geoffrey 197
Hutchison, J. R. H. 128

Jay, Peter 162–3, 170–1
Jenkin, Patrick 203
Jenkins, Roy 103, 109, 133, 163, 168, 233
Johnson, Harry 163
Joseph, Sir Keith 98, 153, 161, 163–4, 171, 189, 203
de Jouvenel, Bertrand 133

Kennedy, John F. 7, 102, 104, 179, 181
Keynes, John Maynard 33, 64, 67, 73, 83, 90, 92, 120–1, 146
Kindersley, Sir Robert 226
Kissinger, Henry 146, 168, 171
Kohl, Helmut 9

Laidler, David 163
Lawson, Nigel 171, 203
Layton, Lord 95
Lipset, Seymour 133
Lloyd, Selwyn 131–2
Lloyd George, David 53, 57
Londonderry, Lord 226
Lothian, Lord 225
Loveday, Alexander 95
Lubbers, Ruud 9
Lygo, Sir Raymond 185
Lyle, Lord 230
Lyttelton, Oliver 69–70, 128

MacDonald, Ramsay 61–2, 65–6
MacGregor, Ian 189
Macleod, Iain 131, 155
Macmillan, Harold 7, 64, 67, 91, 95, 97–9, 101–2, 110, 128, 130–2, 156, 225, 228, 231
Macmillan, Lord Hugh 225
Marshall, George C. 91, 95
Martens, W. 9
Matthews, Lord 206
Maudling, Reginald 101, 131–3
Maxwell, Robert 224
McAlpine of Newarthill, Lord 205–6
McAlpine, Alastair 205
McFadzean, William 101
McGahey, Mick 166
McGowan, Sir (Lord) Harry 68, 74, 79, 226, 228
McKenna, Reginald 226
Meade, James E. 162
Meaney, Sir Patrick 206
Milner, Lord 225
Molotov, V. 95
Mond, Alfred (later Lord Melchett) 45, 61, 64, 67–8, 70
Morgan, J. P. 40, 62, 65
Morris, Sir William (later Viscount Nuffield) 225, 226
Morrison, Herbert 66, 118
Mosley, Sir Oswald 63, 65, 166, 225–6
Mossadeq, M. 98
Mountbatten, Lord 98
Murdoch, Rupert 190, 224

Naguib, M. 98
Nasser, Gamal Abdel 98, 229
Nixon, Richard M. 146, 159
Norman, Lord Montagu 76

Owen, David 170, 185, 187

Parkin, Michael 163
Parkinson, Cecil 203
Pinochet, General Augusto 164
Plowden, Sir Edwin 231
Pompidou, Georges 104, 170
Powell, Enoch 103–4, 129, 131, 162–3, 184
Prior, James 187
Profumo, John 132
Pym, Francis 183

Reagan, Ronald 9, 34, 182, 186–7, 208–10, 219, 221, 235

Rees-Mogg, William 162, 218
Reid, Sir Charles 226
Ricardo, David 193
Ridley, Nicholas 158, 188
Rijkens, Paul 226
Roosevelt, F. D. 89, 227
Rowland, 'Tiny' 224
Runciman, Walter 226
Rylands, Sir Peter 71–2

Samuel, Sir Herbert 65
Salisbury, Lord 230
Sandys, Duncan 95, 101–2
Scargill, Arthur 189–90, 219, 232
Schmidt, Helmut 170–1
Schumann, Maurice 96
Sherman, Alfred 164
Shinwell, Emanuel 118
Simon, Sir John 69
Simon, William 171
Smith, Ian 228
Smuts, Jan 225
Snowden, Philip 62, 65–6
Soames, Christopher 102, 131
Spaak, Paul-Henri 97
Stanley, Oliver 128
Strachey, John 225
Stretch, K. L. 231
Swope, Gerald 226

Taylor, Frederick 85
Taylor, Lord 206
Tebbit, Norman 203, 211
Terry, Belaúnde 183
Thatcher, Margaret 2, 8, 9, 34, 127, 161,
    165, 172, 178, 181–4, 186–9, 191–2,
    194–7, 199, 202–3, 205–8, 210–14,
    216–19, 221, 231, 234–5
Thorneycroft, Peter 129, 131
Thorpe, Jeremy 228
Tower, John 234
Truman, Harry S. 89, 187

Villiers, Charles 135

Walker, Patrick Gordon 103
Walker, Peter 155, 217
Wallace, H. 89
Walters, Alan 163
Warburg, Sigmund 224
Weeks, Sir Ronald 117
Williams, Shirley 103
Wilson, Harold 7, 8, 103, 122, 126, 132–4,
    136, 154, 156, 167, 169–70, 174, 205,
    228, 231–3
Woods, Sir John 231
Wright, Peter 231–2
Wyldebore-Smith, Sir Brian 205

Author Index

(*Explanatory note:* only those instances are included where authors are directly quoted or where their views are discussed in the text. Simple references are not included.)

Aaronovitch, S. 70, 77, 152
Aaronovitch, S., and R. Smith 230
Aglietta, M. 6, 23, 86
Althusser, L. 222
Anderson, P. 19, 30, 35, 44, 48, 215, 224
Andreff, W. 227
Atkins, F. 177

Barnett, A. 183
Barou, Y. 126–7, 137
Barraclough, G. 55
Beer, S. 108
Belsey, A. 179
Bergesen, A. 14, 47
Beveridge, W. 119–20, 231
Bode, R. 23, 26
Bousquet, N. 21
Bowles, S., D. Gordon, T. Weisskopf 231
Boyd, L. V. 100
Brady, R. A. 75
Braudel, F. 17, 223
Brenner, R. 15
Brett, E. A. 90, 92, 108, 228
Brown, M. B. 30, 40, 45, 51, 222, 223
Burawoy, M. 223, 227
Burn, D. 77

Cain, P. J., and A. G. Hopkins 35, 222, 224
Campbell, D., P. Forbes, F. Jenkins 229
Camps, M. 102
Carr, E. H. 32
Chalfont, Lord 98–9
Childs, D. 91
Coates, D. 161
Cox, R. 13, 17
Crosland, A. 133

Dunford, M., and D. Perrons 73, 78

Epstein, L. D. 94

Ferris, P. 109
Fine, B., and L. Harris 153–4, 230
Flanagan, R. J., D. W. Soskice, and L. Ulman 126, 133–4
Frank, A. G. 13
Frieden, J. 33
Friedman, M. 232

Gamble, A. 26, 95, 99, 152, 161
Gerstenberger, H. 37
Gill, S. 209
Glyn, A., and J. Harrison 152, 153
Glyn, A., and B. Sutcliffe 136, 149
Goralczyk, D. 112
Gordon, D. 223
Gramsci, A. 13, 23, 28–9, 85, 178, 179
Grant, W. 212

Hall, S. 177, 180
Hall, S., and M. Jacques 177, 179
Harris, N. 129, 227
Hayek, F. 153
Heinemann, M. 73
Heseltine, M. 186
Hobson, J. A. 47
Hodgson, G. 147

Ingham, G. 35, 108, 134

Jessop, B. 6, 26, 106, 108, 137, 177, 179, 199, 217, 220
Joseph, K. 153

Kaldor, M., M. Sharp, W. Walker 150, 195–6
Keegan, W. 155, 164
Kennedy, P. 1
Kilpatrick, A., and T. Lawson 153

Kleinknecht, A. 223
Kondratieff, N. 21

Labrousse, E. 18
Lenin, V. I. 22, 33
Leruez, J. 120
Levitas, R. 233
Leys, C. 199
Lipietz, A. 86, 138

Mandel, E. 22, 113
Marx, K. 15–16, 24
McBride, S. 192
McEachern, D. 118
Melotti, U. 223
Middlemas, K. 67, 71–2, 119, 155, 167, 172, 225
Miles, R. 127, 222
Miliband, R. 118
Mills, C. W. 20
Modelski, G. 12–13
Moore, B. 37, 43, 224
Moore, R. 188
Morgan, K. 87, 121
Murray, R. 109, 229

Nairn, T. 19, 35, 39, 46, 156, 157, 163, 224
Newton, S. 95

Olson, M. 232

Panitch, L. 136, 137
Petras, F., and R. Rhodes 146

Pijl, K. van der 28
Piore, M. J., and C. F. Sabel 231
Polanyi, K. 49, 57, 194, 233
Poulantzas, N. 26, 27
Powell, E. 184

Radice, H. 90
Richardson, J. J., and J. Moon 234
Riddell, P. 172, 202
Ross, J. 199
Rowthorn, R. 152, 224
Ruggie, J. 91

Sampson, A. 189, 203
Scott, J. 36, 40, 224
Shortall, F. C. 26
Smith, K. 150
Spiegelberg, R. 124

Taylor, A. J. 191
Taylor, T. 186, 187
Thompson, E. P. 222–3
Thompson, W. R. 19
Tylecote, A. B. 45, 47

Vincent, J. 42
Vittas, D. 215

Wallerstein, I. 11–16, 18, 222, 223, 224

Yaffe, D. 156
Youngson, A. J. 228

Zolberg, A. R. 222